Purnell's Pictorial Encyclopedia of
Trains and Railways

829
Amtrak

Purnell's
Pictorial Encyclopedia of

Trains and Railways

Edited by Alan Williams

Executive Editor: Campbell L Goldsmid
Editor: Alan Williams
Picture Research: Anne-Marie Ehrlich
Contributors: Alan Williams
                      Basil Cooper
                      Christopher Heaps
                      Geoffrey Kichenside
                      David Percival

SBN 361 04201 9
© Purnell and Sons Limited 1978

Designed and produced for Purnell Books
by Autumn Publishing Ltd, 44/45 West Street,
Chichester, Sussex.

Published by Purnell Books, Berkshire House,
Queen Street, Maidenhead, Berkshire.

Printed in Great Britain by Purnell & Sons Ltd.,
Paulton (Bristol) and London.

Contents

The First Railways

The first railways were developed in mines and collieries in the Middle Ages, long before mechanical traction was considered. The earliest recorded use of a railway was in the mines of Leberthal in Alsace in 1550; by the end of the 16th century mine railways were in general use throughout central Europe. At first the 'rails' were simply parallel timbers, sometimes faced with metal plates, on which the wheels of the colliery wagons ran, while the horses or pit ponies which pulled them walked between. But the major problem was keeping the wheels of the wagons on the narrow rails, especially if it was wet and muddy, or the horses less than well behaved. So the next development was to fit wooden guides to the timbers, or flanges to the metal plates, to form 'flangeways' which restricted the lateral movement of the wagons.

In County Durham, England, besides the various pit railways, several quite lengthy lines were built from the pit heads to nearby rivers and canals, passing through the intermediate countryside by means of way-leaves. A notable example was the Tanfield wagonway, built in 1671 and considerably extended about 1726; one section involved the construction of the famous Tanfield (or Causey) arch of 31.4m (103ft) span, completed in 1727. Cast-iron rails were first used in Cumberland in 1738, at Coalbrookdale in 1767 and in Sheffield in 1776, and on June 9, 1758, the first railway to be authorized by the British Parliament, from Middleton to Leeds, was sanctioned.

By this time the ordinary wagon wheel running on a flanged rail had given way to the 'edge' railway which we know today, in which a flanged wheel runs on a raised, bar-like rail. In 1789 William Jessop used this method for his line from Nanpantan to the Loughborough Canal; the wagons ran on rails cast in 5ft lengths, with 'feet' at each end for support, and with joints shaped in such a way that the rails slotted into one another to form a continuous running surface. But despite the spread of railways of both the 'plate' and 'edge' variety, they all remained in private use for the specific carriage of minerals, mainly coal, and it was not until May 21, 1801, that Parliament sanctioned construction of the first public railway, the Surrey Iron Railway (SIR), from Wandsworth to Croydon. Even the SIR did not carry passengers—indeed it had no rolling stock of its own at all—and the concept was truly one of a 'public' railway upon which, by payment of a toll, any person could haul his wagons. The rails were cast-iron

The first practical use of steam engines for rail traction was in the collieries of north-east England; developed from the stationary steam engines used for winding and pumping in the pits, these 'Puffing Billies' as can be seen in the early view of Hetton Colliery (above) were used to haul the wagon of coal from the pit head to the riverside wharves.

The increasing need to move freight over the unmade and often almost unpassable roads of 18th-century Europe encouraged the construction of both canals and private wagonways. But traction was either manual or at best horse-drawn, as on the wagonway built by Ralph Alten in 1752 in the grounds of Prior Park (right). The early lines remained short and unconnected. Even the first public railway, the Surrey Iron Railway, opened in 1803, relied entirely on teams of horses and donkeys to power the wagons which ran on cast-iron flanged plates spiked to wooden or stone blocks (above).

plates a yard long spiked to stone blocks or wooden sleepers, and motive power was provided by teams of horses and donkeys. The line was opened to Croydon on July 26, 1803, and extended to Godstone via the sand and chalk quarries of Merstham on July 24, 1805. The very openness of the line proved its undoing in that there was no signalling or timetable, and delays and congestion were inevitable. It remained in use until about 1845, when part of the course was used by the then new London, Brighton and South Coast Railway, and the remainder became derelict. But, despite its disadvantages, the SIR proved conclusively that impressive loads could be moved by rail, even with horse-power, and that, whilst it would need to be controlled, there was a demand for a public railway.

Like all the early railways, the Surrey Iron Railway (above) was built exclusively for the conveyance of freight. With the arrival of steam, people expected speed and efficiency from the new iron horse, and right across Europe crowds turned out every time a new line opened or was extended; this was the scene (left) at the opening of the Berlin-Potsdam line on September 22, 1838.

Railway Mania

Throughout the 1830s railway development and construction progressed slowly, although lines were being projected in all directions, often in direct competition with each other. Some of the early lines were surveyed under great difficulty; many landowners were bitterly opposed to railways crossing their land, fearing both that their land would lose its value and that crops and trees would be damaged by smoke, steam and sparks. There were many reported instances of surveyors working for railway companies being arrested for trespass, or becoming involved in violent altercations with gamekeepers and estate employees.

Many writers of the period were opposed to railways; John Bull in 1835 denounced them as 'destructive of the country in a thousand particulars'. 'Railroads,' he proclaimed, 'will in their efforts to gain ground do incalculable mischief.' Others were less condemnatory, but there was a general fear of 'being dragged through the air at the rate of twenty miles an hour', of the consequences of a derailment and, particularly, of the 'detriment to health' of tunnels.

Eminent doctors and chemists were called upon to assure the timid that their fears of horrific asphyxiation were groundless!

Gradually, public opinion throughout Europe swung in favour of railways, as the advantages in terms of speed and reliability over the road transport of the day became obvious. By 1841 railways in England radiated from London to Brighton, Southampton, Bristol, Birmingham, Manchester, Liverpool, and York, and the various individual lines began to link up to form a system, although the Great Western Railway from London to Bristol was laid to Brunel's 2.13m (7ft) 'broad' gauge, whereas all other lines were laid to the 'standard' gauge of 1.44m (4ft 8½in).

Many of the large property owners who had opposed the railways in Parliament and forced them to adopt alternative, more expensive or circuitous routes began to regret their opposition, for they saw the price of land in close proximity to railways, far from falling as they had feared, actually increasing as demand grew, both domestic and industrial, to be near the new railways. Many local authorities, too, had successfully protested against the early railways coming into their towns, only to find a few years later that they had to petition for a branch line to connect them to the very main line which, but for their disdain, could

The rapid spread of railways in the 1840s spelt the final demise of many canals; few canal companies competed in price and none in speed with the faster, more direct railways, some of whom actually bought the ailing canal companies and starved them of traffic to ensure a lack of competition! This engraving (below), dating from 1845, shows the newly-opened Manchester-Leeds line striding across both road and canal on the Whiteley viaduct above Charleston curves.

have been built through their town. This indeed is the reason why, even today, many main railway routes throughout Europe appear to avoid places of importance, and why main stations in those towns that are on the original main lines are often located a mile or more from the old town centre and surrounded instead by a 'new town' which has grown up in the one-time green fields surrounding the station.

But perhaps the greatest single boost to the expansion of the railways, and what finally made rail travel respectable, was the decision by Queen Victoria to travel by rail for the first

build railways to almost every quarter of Europe that the public were persuaded to invest far beyond their means, often in schemes of very dubious potential. Some people made fortunes, but hundreds lost money, and some were ruined by the craze for speculation.

One aspect of the growth of railways which is worth remark is the resultant standardization of time. Prior to the coming of the railways there was no such thing as standard time throughout any of the countries of Europe. Almost every town had public buildings and churches with clocks, but they all

Mid-nineteenth century railway architecture reflected the confident, expansive mood of the times, and many elegant, if sometimes extravagant, examples were built by the major railway companies. Certainly among the former was the engine house at Swindon (below).

time—from Windsor to London by the Great Western Railway—on June 13, 1842. Suddenly railways were the accepted means of transport, whether for passengers or for freight, and every town of any size began to clamour for a railway, and to promote or back all manner of schemes. So many were projected—far more than could ever pay, and some often in direct competition with each other —that the period 1843-46 is often known as the 'Railway Mania'. Such was the desire to

showed 'local time', which often varied quite considerably from centre to centre for geographical and other reasons. Such discrepancies were clearly of no use to any railway trying to run to timetabled schedules, and in the early days many companies broadcast a system-wide time check each day by telegraph to ensure that signal-box and station clocks were all correct to 'railway time' as opposed to local time, and this practice continued until the advent of telephones and radio.

The First Steam Engines

The first steam engine to work on a railway was designed and built by a wrestler and inventor named Richard Trevithick who came from Cornwall in England. After experimenting with models, he built an engine with road wheels which was put to work on a 'flange' railway at Merthyr Tydfil in Wales in 1804. Although steam engines had been in use for pumping and winding for some years, Trevithick was the first man to prove the ability of the steam engine to haul heavy loads on a railway of ordinary gradient simply by adhesion. Following this success, Trevithick designed a second locomotive, built by John Whinfield of Gateshead-on-Tyne. This 'Newcastle' locomotive was the first to have flanged wheels but was driven not by rods but by a huge cogwheel, mounted centrally on one side of the boiler and in turn driving smaller cogs built onto the rail wheels. But still these engines worked on industrial railways, tucked

Richard Trevithick (left) a fiery professional wrestler and inventor from Cornwall, was the first to use the adhesion of a steam locomotive to haul heavy loads. Anxious to prove the versatility of steam engines, and their ability to move passengers as well as freight, Trevithick demonstrated his 'Catch-me-who-can' on a small circular track in Euston Square in 1808 (right).

Perhaps the most famous of all old steam engines, George Stephenson's 'Locomotion No 1' (below) preserved at Darlington, enjoys the unique reputation of being the very first steam locomotive to run on the first ever steam worked public railway. Some engineers were not convinced that mere adhesion was sufficient, and various systems were suggested using cog-and-tooth methods. Blenkinsop's patented rack system employed cogwheels on the locomotives which engaged in teeth cast on rails (above).

away in the corners of Britain. Yet Trevithick was anxious to demonstrate that his locomotives could haul passengers as well as freight. So he built a third locomotive, the 'Catch-me-who-can', which he put to work in 1808 on a small circular demonstration track near London's Tottenham Court Road. It was quite deliberately a show line, and a charge of one shilling per trip was made, the first recorded instance of passengers paying to travel behind a steam locomotive.

Other engineers were not idle: in 1811 John Blenkinsop patented a rack system which took Trevithick's cogwheel drive a stage further, the cogged driving wheels actually engaging with teeth cast on the rails. Lines using this system were laid from Middleton to Leeds in 1812, and from the Kenton and Coxlodge collieries to the River Tyne in 1813. It was claimed that loads five times the weight of those possible with adhesion locomotives could be moved with ease, but the system did not catch on. About the same time, William

"

'Puffing Billy' is a general term of endearment nowadays applied to almost any veteran steam engine; the original locomotive of this name, built by William Hedley in 1813 with vertical cylinders and cog-driven driving wheels, survived in regular use at Wylam Colliery on Tyneside until 1865 (right) and is now preserved in the London Science Museum, the oldest surviving steam engine in the world.

Hedley, the viewer at Wylam Colliery, constructed and patented his 'Puffing Billy' design, which worked between the colliery and Lemington-on-Tyne until 1865, when it was transferred to South Kensington in London, where, as the oldest surviving steam engine in the world, it is on display in the Science Museum.

Also at work on his first design in 1814 was George Stephenson, perhaps the most famous and successful of all the early British locomotive engineers. Working first on the engines at Killingworth pit, Stephenson soon became fascinated by steam engines; his first locomotive, built in the engine shops of West-Moor, was tried out on July 25, 1814, and successfully drew a load of 29.5 tonne at 6.4km/h (4mph).

As a result of this and other work, Stephenson was appointed engineer of the proposed Stockton and Darlington Railway in 1821. In 1823 he started his own engine works at Newcastle, and began work on designs for the 32.9km (20 miles) long Stockton and Darlington, which was to be the first public railway on which steam locomotives were used. For the opening on September 27, 1825, Stephenson designed and built his now famous 'Locomotion No 1'. On the opening day the new engine pulled six wagons of coal, the passenger carriage 'Experiment' containing the committee and other proprietors, 21 wagons, some fitted with seats, and six more loaded coal wagons, from Shildon to Darlington at speeds up to 24km/h (15mph). Although on the opening day 'Locomotion No 1' was said to have hauled between 600 and 700 passengers, including a band, it was not generally used for passenger traffic, the line having been built as a coal and freight railway. The sole passenger carriage 'Experiment'—in reality little more than a road stage-coach with flanged wheels —was generally hauled between Stockton and Darlington, once each way daily, by horse. Nevertheless, Stephenson had successfully paired the steam adhesion locomotive with the public railway. The age of steam railways had begun!

Steam driven colliery engines were also George Stephenson's first introduction to steam traction, and his first steam locomotive, built in 1814, was for use on the colliery railway at Killingworth pit. Stephenson, with his son Robert, is seen here (below) in a rare family group.

Rocket and the Rainhill Trials

The Liverpool and Manchester Railway, engineered by George Stephenson and the first to be projected specifically for the conveyance of steam-hauled trains for fare-paying passengers as well as freight, was nearing completion in 1829, and the directors had to decide whether to employ locomotives or stationary winding engines. In April it was decided to offer a prize of £500 for the best locomotive constructed in accordance with certain 'Stipulations and Conditions', the most important of which were that 'the engine must effectually consume its own smoke', be within definite limits of weight, and haul continuously a given load at 16km/h (10mph).

Five engines appeared before the judges at the trials, which commenced on October 6 on a completed level section of the line at Rainhill, just outside Liverpool. They were the 'Rocket', entered by George and Robert Stephenson; the 'Novelty', built by John Braithwaite and John Ericsson; Timothy Hackworth's 'Sans Pareil'; the 'Perseverance', built by Timothy Burstall; and 'Cycloped', a strange horse-driven machine entered by T. S. Brandreth.

After some initial trials 'Rocket', which was the only entry to have a tubed boiler and forced draught from the exhaust, was put through its paces first, on October 8, and drawing a load three times its own weight completed the entire trip at an average speed of 20km/h (12.5mph). The maximum speed was 38.6km/h (24mph) and, running light, a speed of 46.7km/h (29mph) was attained. Costs for fuel were said to average 'three half pence per mile'.

'Novelty', the apparent favourite, was tried on October 10 and again on October 14, but on both occasions failed to complete its trip because of mechanical failures. Its maximum speed with the test train was 33.4km/h (20.75mph), but running light it attained the astonishing speed, for the period, of 51.5km/h (32mph). Fuel costs were said to be cheaper, at only one halfpenny per mile, but the machine was clearly less reliable.

Meanwhile, Hackworth's 'Sans Pareil' appeared before the judges on October 13, but it was soon found to weigh 4.69 tonne, and the Rules quite clearly required that any locomotive over 4.4 tonne should be carried on six wheels. It was therefore disqualified from the competition but allowed to demonstrate its abilities, which it proceeded to do in fine style, running for no less than 43.4km (27 miles) at an average speed of 20km/h (12.5mph), and attaining a maximum of 28km/h (17.5mph). Neither 'Perseverance' nor 'Cycloped' could achieve speeds in excess of 9.6km/h (6mph) and were withdrawn from the competition, which was won by the 'Rocket' as the only entry to complete the journeys and fulfil all the conditions. Enlarged versions of the 'Rocket' were built for the opening of the Liverpool and Manchester Railway on September 15, 1830; no less than eight trains of guests, dignitaries and officials, each hauled by a Stephenson engine, were run from Liverpool to Manchester to inaugurate the service, and it was during a stop for water at Parkside that Mr Huskisson, local Member of Parliament, was run down and fatally injured by a following train, thus becoming the first person in the world to be killed in a railway accident.

Just as the opening of the Stockton and Darlington five years earlier had marked the beginning of the steam railway age with its cheap freight costs, so the inauguration of services on the Liverpool and Manchester marked the beginning of passenger-carrying railways in which speed, rather than convenience or cheapness, was the attraction.

The railway age was now under way; Stephenson, Hackworth and others were busy refining their locomotive designs, and experimenting with forced draughting and fixed, horizontal cylinders, while new railways were

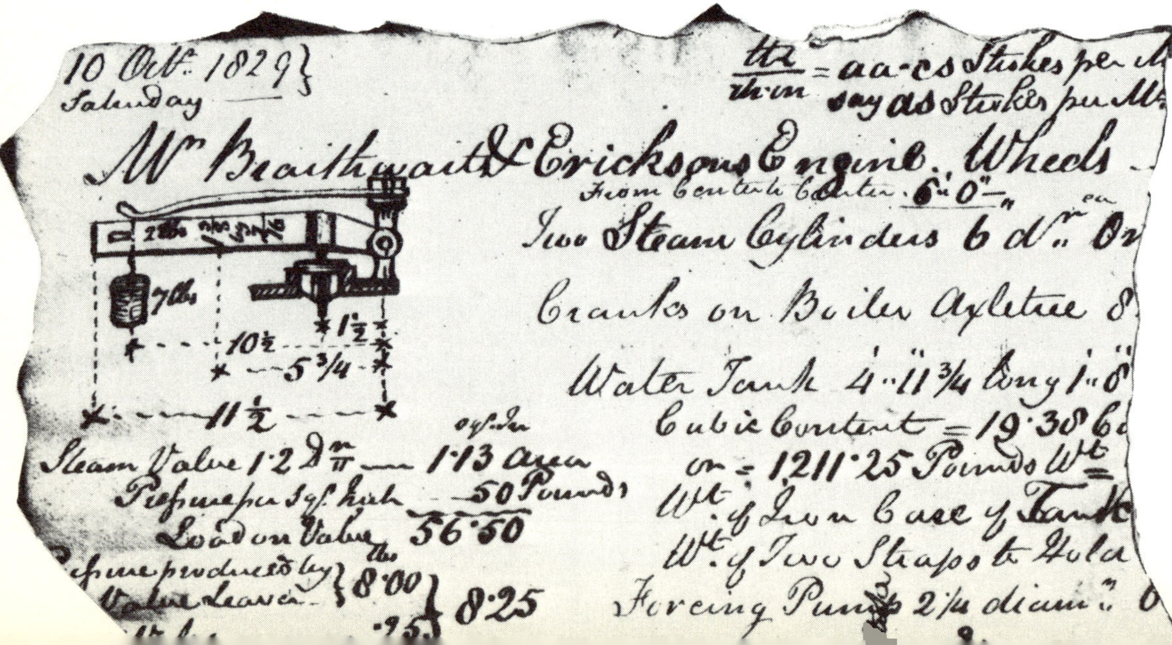

The Directors of the Liverpool and Manchester Railway took the Rainhill trials very seriously; this is a page from Rastrick's highly-detailed notebook (left) of the events of October 10, 1829, when Braithwaite and Ericsson's 'Novelty', the favourite, was first tried out.

Timothy Hackworth's 'Sans Pareil' (above) looking at first sight not unlike 'Rocket' put up a fine performance at Rainhill.

With the success of the Stockton and Darlington and Liverpool and Manchester lines, Britain became the railway centre of the world. One of the first steam engines in the United States was 'Stourbridge Lion' (above), a vertical-cylindered 0-4-0 built in Britain in 1827 for the opening of the Delaware and Hudson Railroad in the following year.

Along with 'Locomotion No 1' Stephenson's 'Rocket' (above) must surely be the world's most famous steam engine; its success at Rainhill greatly enhanced Stephenson's reputation, and proved to be the prototype for the whole first generation of steam engines across the world.

beginning to appear elsewhere, both in Britain and overseas.

In the United States construction of railways with horse-drawn vehicles in the mid 1820s was followed by the use of 'Stourbridge Lion', a locomotive purchased in England in 1827 for the opening of the Delaware and Hudson Railroad in 1828. In Europe the first public railways appeared in France and Austria in 1828 (although not at first with steam locomotives); in Belgium and Germany in 1835; Russia in 1838, Italy in 1838 and Switzerland in 1844. In Canada the first railway, the St Lawrence and Champlain, was opened on July 23, 1836, but its first trains had to be hauled by a team of horses as the engine, purchased from England, and named 'Kitten', could not at first be persuaded to work!

13

The Gauge War

The inside measurement between the heads of the two running rails on any railway track is known as the gauge. There are many gauges in use today, ranging from the mere 185mm (7¼in), between rails of miniature amusement lines, to 1.68m (5ft 6in). But over 60 per cent of the world's railways are laid to the now 'Standard' gauge of 1.44m (4ft 8½in). Just how this rather odd figure came to be adopted as 'standard' is not clear, although it seems first to have appeared on British mine 'plateways'.

There is some evidence to suggest that Roman chariots measured a similar distance between their wheels, and that in the Middle Ages the British continued to build the wheels of their carts to the same width so as to take advantage of the deep ruts cut in the road surfaces by the Roman chariots. It seems it was these carts, later fitted with flanges, which ran on the early plateways and thus established the 'standard' gauge.

Throughout the world, the 'standard' gauge of 1.44m (4ft 8½in) is now predominant, but in the early days of railways, when few envisaged just how extensive railway networks were to become, the question of standardization of gauges appeared less important and individual companies built lines to several different gauges. Even in Europe, lines were built to the wider gauges of 1.52m (5ft) in Russia and Finland, 1.6m (5ft 3in) in Ireland and 1.68m (5ft 6in) in Spain and Portugal, and these different gauges persist to the present day, presenting problems of through running and interworking of stock. However, the majority of the European railways, and those in most other countries, now employ the

Disagreement over track gauges was an acute problem for the early railways, for a break of gauge precluded through running of trains. Even in Britain, birthplace of the 'Standard' gauge, the influential Great Western Railway opted instead for Brunel's 2.13m (7ft) 'Broad' gauge. This print (below) shows gangs at work at Saltash, on the approaches to the Royal Albert Bridge, re-gauging the tracks in May 1892, when in one incredible weekend, over 420 miles of track were relaid

standard gauge, with narrower gauges for minor lines and mountain railways. Most of the early non-standard gauge lines, except in the countries listed above, were rebuilt to 1.44m (4ft 8½in) gauge.

In Britain the great majority of railway companies adopted the standard gauge of 1.44m (4ft 8½in), with rails laid on transverse sleepers, but Brunel built the Great Western railway to his 'broad gauge' of 2.13m (7ft) on longitudinal sleepers with tie-bars. Many of the lines connecting with the Great Western, and hoping to attract traffic from it, were also built to the wider gauge. As more railways were built, and the demand for through pas-

This early view of the approaches to the new Swindon Works of the Great Western Railway in 1847 amply illustrates the expansive nature of Brunel's broad gauge system. Notice the railway policemen, the early hut or 'signalman's box', and the lofty disc and crossbar signals.

senger and freight traffic grew, the shortcomings of a break of gauge between the Great Western and its associates and the remainder of the companies became apparent. Passengers could change trains without too much difficulty, provided adequate facilities were provided, although it can be imagined that they did not relish the delay and inconvenience caused simply by a change of gauge. Freight, however, presented a much greater problem, because all goods had to be transhipped from one vehicle to another en route, adding to the cost and causing much delay. The solution was clearly to have a single, unified gauge, but each faction thought its favoured gauge should prevail over the others.

At the height of the Railway Mania in 1845 there occurred in Britain the Battle of the Gauges in which both parties made strenuous efforts to convince new companies to build their lines to their preferred gauge, and in fact several lines were built to dual gauge, with three running rails, so that trains of both gauges could be run. Realizing the waste and inconvenience that would be caused if this situation persisted, Parliament set up a Royal Commission 'to consider a uniform railway gauge' and in 1846 it reported in favour of the 1.44m (4ft 8½in) gauge, with the recommendation that no more broad-gauge lines be built.

From then on, more and more broad-gauge lines were equipped with a third rail so that

Brunel's broad gauge had a scale and dignity all of its own; the additional space allowed the development of quite massive single-wheelers, while the carriages offered an unrivalled roominess in each compartment. But this May 1892 view of staff and passengers posing for the cameraman before the departure of the last broad gauge train from Paddington also co-incidentally illustrates the complexity of the trackwork necessary with dual gauge at important junctions, and explains why the Great Western eventually changed to the 'Standard' gauge adopted by all other British systems.

standard-gauge trains could also be worked, and in 1861 the Great Western, realizing that it must eventually abandon its 2.13m (7ft) gauge, began to systematically convert its lines to standard gauge, introducing its own standard-gauge locomotives and rolling stock. This process continued in Britain steadily for almost three decades until, by 1890, only those lines in Devon and Cornwall, over which a third standard-gauge rail had never been laid, remained to be converted. Rather than endure a prolonged period of inconvenience and disruption as each section was gradually converted, the astonishing decision was taken to convert the entire 676km (420 mile) stretch of line over three days during the weekend of May 20–22, 1892.

The operation required a tremendous amount of organization, for all the broad-gauge locomotives and rolling stock had to be brought east before the rails were lifted and repositioned. Special horse-drawn carriages and vans were provided for the passengers, and hundreds of permanent-way staff were brought in for the weekend from other parts of the railway. The operation was evidently a success, because the records show that on May 20, 1892, the up night mail train left Penzance behind a broad-gauge engine, followed by the engine and empty coaches of the last down train, while three days later standard-gauge engines were in charge!

The Railway Age

The 1850s and 1860s saw railways spread across the world; the first railway on the African continent was built in Egypt in 1852, and the first in South Africa, a short line built in 1860 between the centre of Durban and its harbour, was unusual in that it was built to the standard gauge of 1.44m (4ft 8½in), but later altered to the narrower 1.07m (3ft 6in) gauge which subsequently became standard throughout South Africa.

Japan's first railway, the line from Tokyo through Kyoto to Kobe, was projected in 1869. Complete with branches serving Yokohama and Tauraga, this ambitious scheme was financed and built by British engineers with such speed and proficiency that the first section opened in September 1872.

Even in China, at that time still traditionally conservative and hostile to mechanization, the British built a line from Shanghai to Woosung in 1875. Although regarded with deep suspicion, the railway was tolerated until someone was accidentally run down by a train and killed, whereupon the Government took over the railway, tore up the rails and dumped them on the island of Formosa—thus bringing the first Railway Age in China to an early and abrupt end! But not for long, according to some reports, for it appears that in 1881 C. W. Kinder, a British engineer working at the mines in Kaiping, built a home-made locomotive, named 'The Rocket of China', to work coal from the mines; history has it that when news of this illicit machine reached officialdom it was ordered to be destroyed, but when officials were sent to investigate, no trace could be found and wagons were being hauled by mules. The engineer, knowing the fate of the earlier line, had dug a pit and buried the locomotive until it was safe to use again!

In Britain and across Europe, rail became the accepted mode of transport for both passengers and freight; the early companies extended and consolidated, expanding their stations and increasing both the regularity and comfort of their services. In America, George Pullman founded the Pullman Palace Car Company in 1867, based on the belief that passengers would be prepared to pay a supplementary fare for greater comfort and privacy, and the idea was introduced to Britain in 1874 when bogie Pullman cars began working on the Midland Railway. But the advent of larger, more powerful locomotives, coupled with safer methods of working, improved trackwork and more comfortable rolling stock, introduced the most important new element to railway competition—speed.

In both America and Britain, rivalry be-

First published in 1839, George Bradshaw's 'Railway Time Tables' brought together the timetables of all the rapidly expanding railways of Britain. Just two years later, it had become 'Bradshaw's Railway Guide' (below) and claimed to give 'a correct account of the hours of arrival and departure of the trains on every railway in Great Britain', as well as a map of lines 'completed and in progress' and a list of fares. This was no mean feat in view of the disparate nature of the many highly-individualistic railway companies, and Bradshaw's Guide blossomed with the Railway Age to become the standard reference for rail services throughout the world.

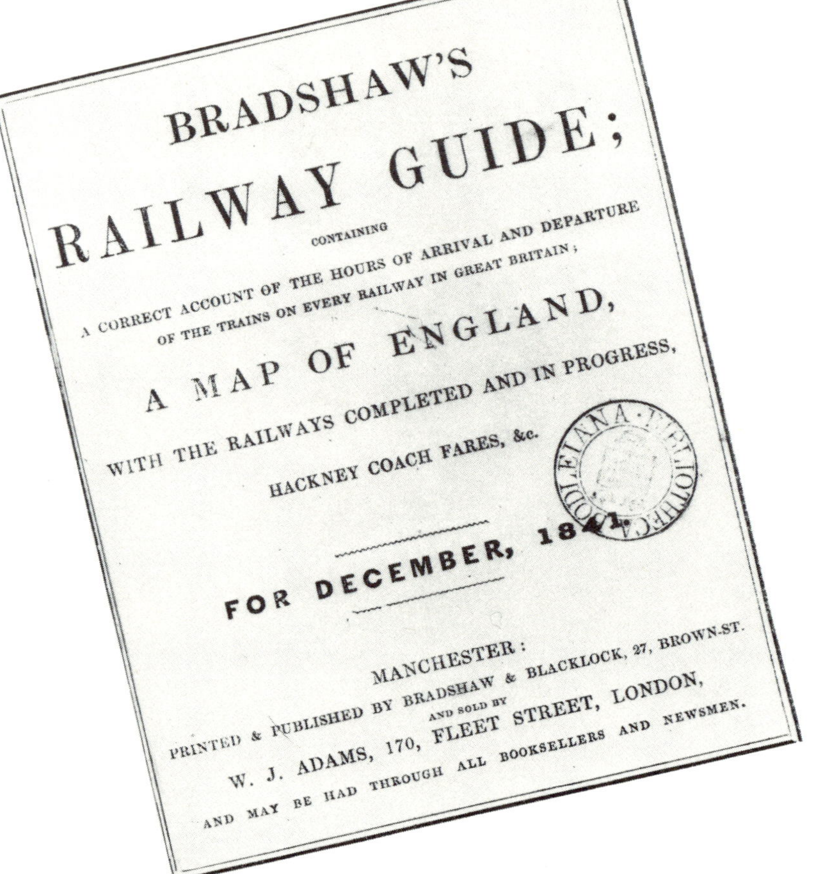

tween the major companies was intense, the staff of each company being jealously proud of their reputations, and always keen to outsmart the competition. In Britain, the rivalry between the 'East Coast' route companies—the Great Northern, North Eastern and North British—and the 'West Coast' route companies—the London and North Western and Caledonian—actually led to competitive racing, first between London and Edinburgh in the summer of 1888, and then between London and Aberdeen in 1895.

What was perhaps the Golden Age of railways ran from this time to the outbreak of World War I; railways were prospering throughout the world, their speed, comfort, reliability and safety unchallenged, for the motor car was still in its infancy and airliners still very much a thing of the future. Almost all of the British main-line companies widened their principal lines to four tracks during this period, so as to separate the increasingly fast express trains from the slower suburban and freight trains. The application of electro-pneumatic techniques to railway signalling allowed the installation of the first practical power-operated system at Bishopsgate in London in 1899, and the opening years of the 20th century saw the perfection and installation of the first track-circuit controlled signals

on both the London and South Western Railway in Britain (1902) and the North Shore Railroad in California (1903). Electrification of suburban and underground railways became a real and attractive prospect. The first electric tube line, the City and South London, was opened in 1890, and the world's first urban electric railway, the Liverpool Overhead, with automatic signals, opened in 1893.

The first decade of the 20th century brought further new innovations, heavier trains and larger locomotives to pull them. Every edition of Bradshaw's 'Railway Time Tables'—first published in Britain as early as 1839—brought news of additional lines and services across all five continents, and it seemed inconceivable when war broke out in 1914 that the total disarray in which the railways of Europe swiftly found themselves could be more than a temporary setback. But events proved otherwise: even as the railways worked to keep the front lines supplied, the internal combustion engine was being developed for use both on land and in the air with such vigour that, with the cessation of hostilities, the railways found themselves with two new competitors—the motor car and the aeroplane. After almost a century, railways were no longer the only form of fast, efficient, transport. The Railway Age was over.

With the steady improvement of both locomotives and track in Britain, Europe and America, speed became an increasingly important competitive element in the battle for traffic between rival companies. In Britain, the rival 'East Coast' and 'West Coast' routes to Scotland saw competitive racing in 1888, and again in 1895. The 'races' caught the public's imagination and they benefited by distinctly faster, if slightly hair-raising schedules. For the first time, steam engines were being driven hard for speed. The London and North Western and Caledonian Railways made up the victorious West Coast partnership; both the LNWR's 2-4-0 No. 790 'Hardwicke', pictured here (above) at Crewe shortly after its final record-breaking run on August 22, 1895, and the Caledonian's 'Single' 2-2-2 No. 123, are now preserved.

The Steam Engine Develops

By the second half of the 19th century the general form of the steam locomotive was becoming established. There were still many variations in detail design, particularly from one country to another, but the fundamentals were taking shape. A noteworthy exception was the Crampton locomotive, with its boiler mounted so low that there was no room underneath it for the driving axle, which was therefore placed to the rear of the firebox and immediately below the footplate. Thomas Russell Crampton, the English engineer who designed the arrangement, considered that a low centre of gravity was necessary for stability.

Locomotives of Crampton's design were more widely used on the mainland of Europe than in England, particularly in France and Germany. Although the first Cramptons were built as early as 1848, the type remained in production for railways in Germany up to the

middle 1860s, while the last Crampton in Denmark was not withdrawn until 1881. One of the French Cramptons, 'Le Continent', is preserved in the railway museum at Mulhouse. The drawback of the Crampton locomotive was that it could have only one driving axle, and this was insufficient for adhesion as trains became heavier.

By 1860 locomotives with two, three, and even four coupled axles were in use in different parts of the world. A limit is placed on the number of coupled axles that can be used in a conventional locomotive by the curvature of the track, because the coupled wheelbase is normally rigid. This posed problems when locomotives were required for the Sudbahn in

The early locomotive engineers soon realized that dry steam was much more efficient than wet, because less energy was lost in condensation. Early experiments included Petiet's 'drying boiler' (above) and various elaborate forms of smokebox-mounted steam dryer before the practice of superheating became established.

Austria, whose main line from Vienna to Trieste climbed over the Semmering range with long 1 in 40 gradients and continuous sharp curves. Four prototype locomotives competed in trials on the route in 1851, and the award was given to the 'Bavaria', which had four coupled axles in the main frame and two more under the tender, with a chain drive from the rear locomotive axle to the leading tender axle.

In the 1860s engineers were increasingly conscious of the low efficiency of the steam locomotive in terms of work done for the quantity of fuel burned. One reason for this was that the steam admitted to the cylinders still contained moisture, which condensed on coming into contact with the cooler cylinder walls and resulted in a loss of energy. Jules Petiet, Chief Engineer of the Northern Railway of France, in 1860 designed a locomotive with a second, smaller boiler perched on top of the main one. Hot gases from the fire flowed through tubes in the main boiler as usual, then reversed their direction to pass through similar tubes in the smaller boiler. This arrangement increased the transfer of heat to the water and steam and resulted in drier steam with consequently less condensation in the cylinders.

Other designers studied the firebox itself to

had been raised to 10.5kg/cm^2 (150lb/in^2) by the end of the decade. In the United States at this period the four-coupled locomotive with a leading bogie (4-4-0) had become so widespread that it was generally known as the 'American' type and typically had a boiler pressure of 9.8kg/cm^2 (140lb/in^2).

Improvements in valve gears helped drivers to make the most effective use of steam by cutting off admission early in the piston stroke and allowing the steam already in the cylinder to do its work by expansion. When this process was pushed to the practicable limit, however, there was still considerable energy

Anatole Mallet (above) a Geneva engineer, was one of the early exponents of compounding, but he is chiefly associated with the articulated steam locomotive, which he developed and which type now bears his name.

ensure full combustion of the fuel. A fundamental improvement which lasted throughout the life of the steam locomotive was achieved by Charles Markham of the Midland Railway in England. He placed an arch of firebrick inside the firebox in such a position that hot air from the fire could not pass directly into the boiler tubes but was deflected backwards so that it flowed across the whole of the firebed, and in close contact with it, before curving upwards and over the top of the arch to enter the tubes.

A high steam pressure was recognized as another step towards efficiency. But moves in this direction were gradual. At the beginning of the Sixties pressures were generally around 8.4kg/cm^2 (120lb/in^2) but with improved boiler materials and methods of construction they

left in the steam exhausted at the end of the stroke. In 1875 Anatole Mallet, a citizen of Geneva, designed a locomotive in which the steam first expanded in a high-pressure cylinder, and then in a low-pressure cylinder of larger diameter before being exhausted to atmosphere. The principle was already used in stationary and marine engines, but its application in the restricted space of a steam locomotive was a major engineering achievement. It is known as 'compounding' and has been the basis of some of the most successful designs in steam locomotive history. By dividing the overall fall in steam temperature and pressure into two stages, the temperature drop in each cylinder was halved.

Three tank locomotives built according to Mallet's proposals were tested in 1876 on the

Bayonne-Biarritz Railway and showed appreciable improvements in utilization of steam and fuel consumption compared with conventional simple-expansion locomotives. However, Mallet's name is chiefly associated with his development of the articulated locomotive. Other engineers were working at the same period on compound propulsion, notably August von Borries, Chief Mechanical Engineer of the Prussian State Railways, who had two small compound tank locomotives built in 1880. Although the early compounds showed improvements in efficiency, their performance at starting was poor. Since steam could not enter the low-pressure cylinder until the piston in the high-pressure cylinder had completed its stroke, the locomotive was in effect starting on one cylinder only. Various methods of overcoming the difficulty were devised, mainly based on devices for admitting steam direct from the boiler to the low-pressure cylinder. In England Francis Webb of the London and North Western Railway built three-cylinder compounds with two high-pressure cylinders and one low-pressure, so that the engines started with two cylinders in operation, but they encountered other difficulties which impaired their performance.

Some highly successful compound locomotives were to appear later, but throughout the history of the steam locomotive some designers remained faithful to the simple-expansion principle and concentrated their efforts on improving efficiency by other methods.

A development to find much more general acceptance than compounding was superheating, or raising the temperature of the steam on its passage from the boiler to the cylinders. A superheater was introduced as early as 1839, being made by the firm of R. & W. Hawthorn in England, but practical development of the principle stemmed from the superheater introduced in 1898 by the German engineer Wilhelm Schmidt. Steam collected in the boiler, where it is in contact with the water, is called 'saturated' steam because of its moisture content. In the superheater further heat is added to the steam after it has left the boiler, so that the moisture it contains is converted into steam, increasing the volume produced while removing the cause of condensation and loss of energy in the cylinders. The increase of temperature is between 315 and 400°C (600 and 750°F) above that of the steam at the point of production in the boiler. The steam enters the superheater 'header' in the smokebox and is turned back into the boiler to flow through steam pipes fitted inside large diameter flue tubes carrying hot gases from the fire. On returning to the smokebox the steam passes into the main steam pipes feeding the cylinders in the usual way.

A significant feature of the last two decades of the 19th century was the growing interest in scientific testing of locomotives. Dynamometer cars with instrumentation to show the work done by a locomotive when hauling a train had by that time been in use for many years, but the changing gradients of most railway routes meant that it was difficult to make measurements in stable conditions for

This colossal 2-10-10-2 freight locomotive was built in 1911 by the Santa Fe Railway in the USA by articulating two existing locomotive frames together on the Mallet principle. Ten of these giants were built, each with a wheelbase of 108ft and a length, without tender, of 120ft. Not surprisingly, they proved to be just too big, and were subsequently rebuilt back to orthodox 2-10-2 freight locomotives.

The Baldwin Co of Philadelphia were one of the great American locomotive builders; this is an early proposal for 'Iron City' an 0-8-0 version of the familiar 'American' 4-4-0, with cylinders mounted above the frames, and a flangeless third driving wheel to enable negotiation of sharp curves, but retaining the familiar spark-arresting chimney, round-top boiler and ornate domes.

long enough for the readings to provide useful information. This was less of a problem in Russia, with its long stretches of near-level or constantly graded track, and some pioneer experiments were made there by the engineers Borodin and Loewy. Early in the present century Professor G. V. Lomonossoff further developed the system of locomotive testing in controlled conditions on the Russian railways, where so much importance was attached to the research that his test train was accorded a priority second only to that of the Tsar's own special. On the foundations laid by Lomonossoff, and with the understanding gained from his experiments, the steam locomotive was to attain its zenith of success some 30 years later.

It has been seen already that in seeking to

improve adhesion by increasing the number of coupled axles, designers confronted the problem of negotiating curvature with locomotives having a long rigid wheelbase. One solution was the articulated locomotive, but Karl Gölsdorf, Chief Engineer of the Imperial Royal Austrian State Railways, found a more orthodox construction by allowing some of the coupled axles to have a degree of controlled sideways movement. This also involved a design of coupling rod bearing which enabled the rods to pivot slightly in the horizontal plane so that as the locomotive rounded a sharp curve the line of coupling rods 'bent' at certain points with a hingeing action.

In the United States the 'American' 4-4-0 continued to flourish into the closing years of the century, although joined by the 4-6-0 type from the mid-1860s. Another development from the 4-4-0 was the 4-4-2, the rear pair of wheels being added because the firebox was moved back behind the second pair of driving wheels so that it could occupy the full width of the frame and provide a larger grate area. This arrangement originated on the Lehigh Valley Railroad in 1888. In 1894 it was adopted by the Atlantic Coast Line for a four-cylinder compound express locomotive built on the Vauclain system with high and low-

Introduced in 1900, the Northern Railway of France de Glehn/du Bousquet compound Atlantics (top) were both handsome and efficient, remaining in front-line service for over 40 years. The Great Western Railway experimented with a de Glehn built compound, but remained unconvinced, and it was left to the North Eastern and Midland Railways to pursue compounding in Britain. Many railway companies in Britain traditionally built their own locomotives, but there were also several thriving private locomotive builders who enjoyed a reputation second to none in supplying steam locomotives to countries throughout the world. This 2-6-4T (above) built by the North British Loco Co in 1908 for the Buenos Aires West Railway, is very British in both outline and detail, and makes an interesting comparison with the American locomotives on the facing page.

pressure cylinders .one above the other on each side of the locomotive, each pair driving a common crosshead. The popularity of the 4-4-2 wheel arrangement in America earned it the name of 'Atlantic' and it was soon to be seen in many parts of the world. A curious feature of some early U.S. Atlantics was that the driver's cab was perched on top of the boiler, the fireman having a separate cab at normal footplate level in the usual position.

The year 1900 saw the first of a famous family of express Atlantic locomotives in Europe—those of the Northern Railway of France. They were four-cylinder compounds on the system introduced in 1885 for the same railway by Alfred de Glehn and Gaston du Bousquet. The first of the de Glehn-du Bousquet compounds had two driving axles independently driven, but in later locomotives the driving axles were coupled to give the 4-4-0 wheel arrangement. The compound Atlantics which followed had an active working life in fast passenger service for some 40 years. A few compound Atlantics were built in Great Britain for the North Eastern Railway, but the classic British Atlantic was the two-cylinder simple introduced by H. A. Ivatt on the Great Northern Railway in 1898, followed by a version with a larger boiler in 1900, which did not achieve its best performance until superheated and modified in later years.

The Atlantic was a step towards the 4-6-2, or Pacific, wheel arrangement. Again this was first seen on the Lehigh Valley Railroad in the United States, where it actually preceded the first Atlantic by two years, although its use on an international scale was to come much later. In 1911 G. J. Churchward built a Pacific, 'The Great Bear', for the Great Western Railway. Its range of action was limited by a high axleload and it was withdrawn in 1923. The day of the Pacific for express traffic was not to come until after the First World War.

Grouping and the Big Four

With the outbreak of the First World War in 1914, the British Government took control of the entire British railway system, which it directed through a committee formed of the General Managers of the major companies. At the end of the war in 1919, a Ministry of Transport was set up and one of its first major tasks was to plan the future form and organization of the railways. The original intention was to nationalize all the railway companies and set up a State railway system, as had been done in several other countries, but the proposal evoked such fierce opposition that a compromise was evolved, and the Railways Act of 1921 decreed that all but the smallest of

that their separate identities would be quickly lost in the large new groupings, resented the enforced merger, often with their arch rivals, to give what amounted to a monopoly service over large parts of Britain. Only on a few trunk lines, where alternative routes existed, such as from London to the West Country, and from London to Scotland, did real competition still exist; elsewhere, although accidents of history took, for example, the new Midland/North Western grouping into both Scotland and Wales, it was not so much a question of competition as senseless duplication.

Even the apparently simple task of selecting

In 1923 the four newly-formed 'Group' companies had to face an immediate requirement for faster, more powerful locomotives than they inherited from any of their constituent Railways. Continental boat train traffic increased, and in 1926 the first of 15 handsome 'Lord Nelson' Class 4-6-0s appeared; this is 'Sir Richard Grenville' (below) in full cry on a Continental boat train in 1928.

the 130 railway companies in England, Scotland and Wales should be 'grouped' into four large companies.

The groupings were based on company rather than geographical boundaries, and ignored the national boundaries of England, Scotland and Wales. An early proposal for a separate grouping of the Scottish companies was ruled out because of doubts about the financial strength of such an amalgamation.

It was little wonder that some companies, particularly the smaller ones who could see

names for the four new groups proved to be something of a problem; but eventually the companies settled on the titles Great Western Railway, Southern Railway, London, Midland and Scottish Railway, and London and North Eastern Railway.

With their formation on January 1, 1923, the four new group companies—the 'Big Four', as they soon came to be known—were among the largest organizations of their kind, and their performance was watched not only by those with interests in railways, but all intrigued by

their curious position midway between the original companies and State ownership. They did not have long to wait, for all four companies soon began to turn out new locomotives and rolling stock in an effort to improve and standardize their services. By 1927 all had produced big new passenger locomotives for their heaviest express traffic—the Great Western their four-cylinder 'King' Class 4-6-0s, the SR its 'Lord Nelson' Class 4-6-0s, the LMS its famous 'Royal Scot' 4-6-0s and the LNER the first of their immortal A3 Class Pacifics.

Soon after grouping, the Southern Railway announced its intention to electrify the extensive suburban networks in South London of all three of its major constituent companies, and this feat was achieved in the remarkably short period of seven years. From 1930 onwards the Southern, which was the most passenger-orientated of the four groups, began to electrify its main-line services, but the other three companies turned down electrification in favour of further development of the steam engine, a somewhat short-sighted if not altogether surprising decision in view of the cheapness and abundance of both coal and labour at the time.

Both the LMS and the LNER put a great deal of effort into further improving their Anglo-Scottish services, on which they were competitors; from May 1, 1928, the LNER inaugurated non-stop running between London and Edinburgh on the 'Flying Scotsman', using Gresley's new A3 Class Pacifics with special corridor tenders to allow a change of engine crew while the train was travelling at speed. Covering a distance of 632km (393 miles) in 8¼ hours, this was the world's longest non-stop run; nine years later, when the LNER, using Gresley's streamlined A4 Pacifics, introduced its 'Coronation' train, the overall time had been slashed to six hours, with an overall average speed of 105km/h (65.5mph). In the same year, the LMS, not to be outdone, introduced its own high-speed train, the 'Coronation Scot', between London and Glasgow, using the newly introduced, streamlined 'Coronation' Class Pacifics.

With the continued pressure for heavier trains to run at faster speeds, it was not surprising that many records were broken in the 1930s. To celebrate the Silver Jubilee of King George V in 1935, the LNER introduced a new high-speed train of that name using specially constructed rolling stock and the then new streamlined A4 Pacifics; it was whilst working this train on August 27 that one of the class, 'Silver Fox', attained the remarkable maximum speed of 182km/h (113mph). But the achievement was short-lived, for less than a year later, on June 29, 1937, the record was pushed to 183km/h (114mph) by the LMS during a trial run for the new 'Coronation Scot' express, and it was just a further year later, on July 3, 1938, that the LNER snatched the record back for good when the A4 Pacific 'Mallard' achieved a world record for steam traction—which still holds today—of 203 km/h (126mph) with a seven-coach train of 263 tonne on the East Coast main line.

These exploits apart, all four systems had further improved the standard and speed of their major services to such an extent that, when war was declared in 1939 and the Government again took control of the railways, it inherited a system that was by reputation second to none in the world. The experiment of the 'Big Four' had succeeded, laying useful foundations for nationalization when it became inevitable after the Second World War.

Anglo-Scottish rail services presented one of the few opportunities for the Grouping companies to enter into the spirit of true competition; both the LMS and LNER provided prestigious expresses ('The Royal Scot' and the 'Flying Scotsman') from London to Scotland, and in the 1930s the competition in speed began to hot up. This was also the era of streamlining and on the LMS Stanier developed his streamlined 'Coronation' Pacifics for the 'Coronation Scot' and other crack services, while on the LNER Gresley built a streamlined version of his highly successful A3 Pacifics—the equally successful A4. One of this class of thoroughbreds, 'Mallard' was to snatch the world speed record for steam traction in 1938, but all 35 engines spent their entire lives working crack expresses on the East Coast route. When first introduced in 1935, some of the class, like 'Silver Link' (above) were painted silver to work the similarly-finished 'Silver Jubilee' expresses.

Royal Scot

Despite their size and importance, the 'Royal Scot' Class 4-6-0s of the London Midland and Scottish Railway (LMS) were designed and built in 1927 in a shorter time than any other express locomotive. Certainly there was none of the testing of one or two prototypes, as has been done in recent years by British Railways with the new High Speed Trains and Advanced Passenger Trains, and the 'Royal Scots' went straight into production from the drawing board. Their speedy construction was forced on the LMS locomotive authorities when it was realized that the rival London and North Eastern Railway (LNER) was building larger and more powerful engines which could improve Anglo-Scottish services by hauling heavier trains at higher speeds.

Under the Grouping arrangement of 1923, the LMS took over the ex-London and North Western Railway West Coast route to Scotland from Euston to Glasgow. It included two sections of steeply graded line to climb over Shap Fell in Cumberland at over 274m (900ft) above sea level and to a summit near Beattock in the Scottish Southern Uplands at just over 305m (1,000ft) above sea level.

The new 'Royal Scot' 4-6-0s were intended to take most expresses over these sections single handed, and to avoid the need for two engines which had been necessary for most trains until then. When the LMS authorities suddenly realized that they did not have a large modern express type suitable for the job the new engines had to be designed and built quickly and the LMS workshops did not have the capacity. The LMS placed the order with the North British Locomotive Company in Glasgow for 50 engines, and within nine months the first locomotive came off the production line.

The new locomotives carried the numbers 6100-6149 and the first was called 'Royal Scot' which gave its name to the entire class. The following 24 engines were also named after regiments in the British Army, but the next 25 engines carried names of old locomotives, some dating from the earliest locomotives of the 1830s. Later they were renamed after more army regiments. A further 20 'Royal Scot' locomotives, Nos. 6150-69, were built by the LMS itself at Derby workshops in 1930, also mostly named after regiments although three carried the names 'Royal Air Force', 'The Girl Guide' and 'The Boy Scout'.

The 'Royal Scots' were impressive machines with large 1.75m (5ft 9in) diameter parallel boilers carrying 17.57kg/sq cm (250lb/sq in) pressure, which, with three cylinders of 457mm×660mm (18in×26in) and 2.06m (6ft 9in) diameter driving wheels, gave a power output sufficient to work 492 tonne trains at around 105km/h (65mph) on the easily graded main line between London and Crewe. They could even tackle the steep climb over Shap with 14 coach loads of about 413 tonne single-handed, keeping to a schedule calling for average speeds of 88km/h (55mph) with top speeds of about 121km/h (75mph). The 'Scots' were noted for their feats of heavy haulage rather than high speed. Certainly they did not feature in such high-speed exploits as the LNER Pacific 'Flying

Designed and built in a shorter time than perhaps any other steam locomotive in history, even in wartime, the 'Royal Scot' Class represented a desperate gamble by the LMS to meet the competition of the rival LNER on the lucrative Anglo-Scottish routes. Despite production without testing a single prototype, the class proved to be strong and reliable, well equal to their task. This is the first of the class No. 6100 'Royal Scot' (below) when built in 1927; now rebuilt with a taper boiler and smoke deflectors, it is preserved at Diss in East Anglia, England.

Scotsman's' 161km/h (100mph) with a light-weight special train in 1934, or the Great Western Railway's six-coach express 'The Cheltenham Flyer' which, by 1932, was running the 124km (77 miles) from Swindon to London at an average speed of 115km/h (71.4mph) with a 'Castle' Class 4-6-0 of broadly similar power to the 'Royal Scots'. At that time 'The Cheltenham Flyer' was the fastest train in the world, for the German high-speed diesel trains running at 161km/h (100mph) and American runs at the same speed with steam and then diesel traction came in following years.

In 1933 a 'Royal Scot' locomotive and representative LMS train made a tour of North America and was exhibited at the Chicago World Fair. The locomotive carried the number 6100 and name 'Royal Scot', but was originally No. 6152, and the exchange of identities became permanent. The locomotive was fitted with a larger tender, and to conform to North American practice was equipped with a large electric headlight, bell and a cowcatcher. The train name, 'The Royal Scot', was displayed on the front of the smokebox. The route of the tour took the train over 17,699km (11,000 miles) from Montreal, and included Denver and Vancouver.

In everday service on the LMS the 'Royal Scot' locomotives took over the principal expresses including the Anglo-Scottish day-time expresses, named 'The Royal Scot' and 'Mid-day Scot' from 1928 until the mid-1930s when new, more powerful, 'Princess' and 'Coronation' 4-6-2s gradually took the fastest and heaviest trains. Nevertheless the 'Scots' continued to play an important part on LMS express duties. By the 1940s they were becoming expensive to maintain and gradually all were extensively rebuilt with taper boilers and other new parts in which form they survived until 1962-65 when they were withdrawn, with the exception of two, Nos. 6100 and 46115 (carrying its BR number), which have been preserved.

One other locomotive has always been included in the 'Royal Scot' Class, No. 6170, but it has been one on its own. It was originally built with an experimental high-pressure boiler but after a pressure tube exploded on trial soon after building it was stored and later rebuilt with a normal locomotive boiler but of a new design. Rebuilt, it was in many ways a predecessor of the later rebuilding carried out on the 'Royal Scots'.

Despite its somewhat diminutive size alongside the giants of the American railroads, 'Royal Scot' created enormous interest among the public on the North American continent (above) when it was shipped there in 1933 for a 11,000 mile tour of the country, culminating in exhibition at the Chicago World Fair. It was fitted with a large electric headlight, warning bell and cow-catcher to conform with American practice.

Railways at War

Just as in peacetime railways provide essential services for passengers and freight, so in wartime they have proved to be a vital part of the war machine. Naval and aviation experts might look askance at the claim that the railways had a major influence over the course of both world wars, but history has shown that the army which keeps its railways intact and mobilized wins.

Railways first became involved in war during the American Civil War of 1866—which also saw the famous episode with 'The General', popularly known as the Great Locomotive Chase—and in the various European wars thereafter, between 1870 and 1900, military leaders were not slow to utilize the mass-moving ability of the railways. The British General Kitchener owed his success against the Dervishes very largely to the railways upon which he concentrated, but the Russians suffered in their conflict with Japan because their single supply line, the Trans-Siberian Railway, was overlong and unreliable.

In the South African War of 1900-01, all the principal battles were fought around railheads, and by the time the First World War broke out in 1914 the main combatants had carefully-laid plans for the immediate requisition of the railways and mobilization of troops. Indeed, the early success of Germany in the First World War was very largely due to the immense, clockwork-like efficiency of the German railways, which had for many years been worked on semi-military lines, and the inability of the French to retaliate because

Military commanders were quick to exploit railways. This Naval gun (below) was adapted for rail use in the Boer War in 1900. Later more sophisticated equipment appeared. The train of innocent-looking huts on flat wagons (above) in fact concealed armoured guns and their crews.

their railway system had been fragmented by pre-emptive strikes.

In Britain, too, it had been realized that a single train could carry as many men and as much equipment as a complete convoy, and although, because of the lack of land frontiers, few military railway installations had been provided on the scale of those in Germany, the efficiency of the peacetime planning was such that within eight days of the outbreak of war the first British Expeditionary Force was embarked at Southampton, involving the provision of 334 special trains from all

parts of the country for nearly 70,000 men and over 20,000 horses, as well as their equipment and stores, without serious interruption of normal train services.

During the First World War, and again during the 1939-45 conflict, the railways carried extra traffic in addition to that created by the military; bulk loads of such vital supplies as coal and iron ore, which would normally in peacetime be conveyed by coaster, were sent instead by the greater safety of rail, while general restrictions on the use of motor vehicles compelled a wholesale switch to rail of both passenger and freight traffic. Ambulance trains had to be run, as well as trainloads of completed munitions, and all this while attempting to maintain some form of normal passenger service for the forces returning home on leave and those involved in war work. And even as the railways strove to carry all this extra traffic their workshops were asked to cut maintenance and new construction to a minimum so that staff could be redeployed onto military and munitions work!

During the First World War, 22 Army and 4 Navy ambulance trains were in constant use in Britain, while 34 more were provided for use in France and Egypt, and 19 for the American armies in Europe.

Compared with the railways of mainland Europe, Britain's railway system suffered little material damage during the First World War, and it was able to send over 600 locomotives and more than 40,000 freight vehicles, many of them specially built in the railway workshops, to support the forces overseas in France, Egypt and Salonika.

Trains were used for attacking as well as defensive roles; the heavily-armed converted flat wagon (above) is part of a camouflaged armoured train used in the First World War. In both World Wars, the railways played a vital role in the movement of the sick and wounded. Special ambulance trains were provided complete with doctors and nursing staff like the group on the platform at Waterloo in April 1918 (below).

A feature of the prolonged trench warfare of the 1914-18 War was the number of narrow-gauge railways which were hastily laid in a network of lines right up to the battle front to bring in men, ammunition and supplies, and remove the wounded and those due for leave. These railways were generally laid at great speed across the ground with a minimum of engineering work, and just as quickly removed when no longer needed.

The end of the First World War left the railways of Europe in a decidedly indifferent state, and it took some of them two decades—ironically, almost to the eve of the next conflict—to recover. But the lessons of 1914-18 had not been forgotten, in Britain at least, and as the implications behind Nazi Germany's territorial ambitions became increasingly clear in 1937-38, the First World War Railway Executive Committee, now composed of the General Managers of London Transport and the four group companies, was revived and asked to prepare plans for the protection of staff and equipment, the provision of additional and emergency equipment, and the arrangement of lighting restrictions. This last item was a new element, but vital, for nobody was under any illusions; this time, when it came, the enemy would attack not by land or sea, but in the air. By 1939 some form of confrontation seemed inevitable, and the railway administrations throughout Europe prepared for war as best they could, preparing shelters and evacuation plans, and training staff in air-raid procedures. Throughout Europe, the damage was much greater and more widespread than in the First World War, and this time Britain was no exception; but incredibly, and thanks largely to their high state of preparedness and generally high standards of maintenance, the railways across war-torn Europe kept rolling amidst quite horrific scenes of destruction. In Britain, as elsewhere in Europe, the railway works were

The 19th-Century engineers built their railways and rolling stock to last forever, and this predilection for strength paid dividends the world over when the railways were thrown into the mayhem of war; locomotives and rolling stock worked for years with virtually no maintenance. Despite receiving a direct hit which lifted it off the track, this Netherlands Railways 4-6-4T (above) remains basically intact and could well have been repaired and returned to traffic.

once more turned over to war work; but this time it was mechanized warfare, and in addition to arms and munitions they turned out tanks, field guns, aircraft, even complete boats and landing craft. Official figures released after the war showed that during hostilities Britain's railways stepped up output by a staggering 46 per cent—and this while some 25 per cent of its workshop facilities were being used for other purposes, and 15 per cent of its staff released for service in the forces!

Once again, and despite enormous pressures of other work, Britain alone among the Allies began to turn out steam locomotives for use overseas; from 1941 it was decided to concentrate all new construction on one type of locomotive, the London Midland and Scottish 'Stanier' Class 8F 2-8-0, a modern design but solid and reliable, with a relatively low axle loading and therefore high route availability, important for use over indifferent track. Later, a simplified 'Austerity' version was

produced in large numbers, and later still American-built 'Liberation' 2-8-0s and 2-10-0s began to arrive in Europe and South East Asia in large numbers. Many, although only built for a short life, survived for many years on the various railway systems of the world, particularly in Asia, on which they were left when the war was over.

The biggest hazard to the railways came from aerial attack, and railway administrations were therefore very strict about blackout precautions; all passenger trains had to be totally blacked out at night, and steam engines had to carry tarpaulins between cab and tender at night to shield the glare from the firehole door, making cabs very cosy in winter but quite intolerable in summer.

London's Underground railway system played a unique role in the Second World War, carrying millions of Londoners across the City in relative safety, even at the height of the blitz.

At first, the main fear was the possibility of

Scenes of heartbreaking devastation such as this bomb-damaged station at Freiburg in Germany (left) became all too common to railwaymen throughout Europe in the Second World War. Yet such was the speed and tenacity of the clearing gangs that it was often only a few hours before the tracks were clear again.

Railways at War (continued)

flooding, and at the outbreak of war huge electrically-operated floodgates were installed on those parts of the system which ran beneath the Thames, or were close to main sewers or water mains, so that affected sections of tunnel could quickly be isolated from the remainder of the system. Weighing over 10 tonne, and designed to withstand 787 tonne water pressure, the doors could be closed within 30 seconds of an alert; the mechanism was fully interlocked with the signalling equipment to avoid any possibility of a train being inadvertently trapped in the closed section, and a small air-lock type hatchway was provided for the use of any employees caught on the wrong side of the doors.

But perhaps the most important role of the Underground during the war was the provision of shelter from air raids for large numbers of the working population. More extensive and deeper then most systems, the tube stations in particular were virtually immune from all but the worst of the bombing; in all, 79 stations were fitted out as shelters, providing accommodation for 75,000 people or 100,000 in emergency, although at the height of the blitz, on the night of September 27, 1940, as many as 177,000 were sheltering on the Underground. With such large numbers to cope with some organization was necessary, and, as time went by, bunks, medical posts, canteens and libraries were provided, served by special trains run during the slack hours. It was calculated that each 1.8m (6ft) of platform length could accommodate six people—three in bunks and three on the platform itself.

In addition to their use as shelters for the public, some stations were equipped as emergency civil and military headquarters;

London's deep level tube lines proved a great asset in wartime; throughout the height of the blitz trains ran virtually unaffected on the Underground sections while many of the station platforms became overnight shelters for nearly 200,000 Londoners.

during the blitz Churchill's War Cabinet met regularly in the offices at the disused station at Down Street, while the running tunnels of the closed Aldwych branch of the Piccadilly line were used to store the more valuable treasures from the British Museum. Even the tunnels on the incomplete extensions of the Central line were pressed into use; the trackless tunnels were converted into an aircraft component factory, with a workforce of 2,000.

From 1940 to 1944 most of mainland Europe was under German occupation, but the various railway authorities continued to provide a service as best they could although much equipment was torn out and removed to Germany by the occupying forces. But it was the British and American liberation forces and the retreating German armies, fighting every inch of the way, who caused the most damage. More than two-thirds of the 3,218km (2,000 miles) of the Netherlands railways, for example, were destroyed, mainly in the seven months between September 1944 and liberation in May 1945, during which time the Netherlands Government, in exile in London, ordered Dutch railwaymen in the occupied territories to stop work so as to hamper the movement of the German forces as much as possible. It was found that the staggering number of over three million sleepers had been removed, together with 206,682 tonne of steel, three-quarters of the overhead equipment on the electrified lines and all the latest

London's termini, with their huge glass roofs were easy prey for the bombers. St Pancras suffered a direct hit, the bombs piercing both the roof and the platforms to explode in the cellars beneath. True to the railway tradition of improvization, the platforms were merely shortened (below) and service resumed.

Britain's railways may have been harassed from the air, but they were spared the total destruction of front line battle such as this pile of twisted metal and rubble (left) at Rotterdam Maas.

electric and diesel-electric rolling stock. Most of the older locomotives and rolling stock had been damaged beyond repair. Nearly 200 bridges, including all the major river crossings, had been damaged or destroyed, as had 80 per cent of the signalling equipment. This picture, to a greater or lesser extent, was repeated right across Europe, from Denmark in the north to Italy in the south, in North Africa, and in the Far East.

Although assailed from the air, Britain alone escaped occupation, and with the preparations for the invasion of Europe in June 1944 her railways were carrying more traffic than ever before—or since. As the build up of men and materials along the South Coast gathered momentum in the spring and early summer, regular train services to the South Coast were restricted to make way for the increasing number of special trains. No less than 13,000 special trains were run in the four weeks prior to D-Day—and 17,500 in the following four weeks, as well as return workings with ambulance trains and trainloads of prisoners of war. This was also the summer of the V1 flying bomb and, later, V2 rocket attacks, but by the end of 1944 Britain's railways—the four group companies plus London Transport—had kept passenger and freight services running whilst also providing no less than 178,362 special trains, an increase of 92 per cent over the previous year, and more than 200 per cent more than in 1940.

The Netherlands Railways system, which abounds in bridges crossing the numerous waterways, suffered incredible structural damage. In an effort to halt the advancing Allied armies, the German engineers destroyed the staggering total of nearly 200 bridges. This bridge near Arnhem (above) was felled, as was the girder bridge near the border town of Venlo (left). Demolition of bridges by breaking the span at the centre, as on the Moerdyk bridge (below left) not only renders them useless, but impedes reconstruction.

Streamlining and Air-smoothing

Streamlining, the covering of a locomotive with a smooth metal casing of generally rounded shape, was adopted by a number of countries for their principal express passenger locomotives in the 1930s. In theory, this would reduce wind resistance and achieve a saving in fuel. However, these effects became significant only at very high speeds and depended more upon the streamlining of the rest of the train than the locomotive. The word became synonymous with 'speed', but the weight of the casing, and its inconvenience, were high prices to pay for the publicity!

It was early this century that some French locomotives appeared with 'wind cutting' features, such as conical smokebox doors and vee-fronted cabs. Later, the French produced some more recognizably streamlined engines. But it was in Germany that streamlining was first applied for really high speeds. In 1934 three 4-6-4s, Nos. 05.001/2/3, were totally enclosed in casings which reached down to rail level. The fast runs of these locomotives between Berlin and Hamburg included two occasions when speeds of 189km/h and 199.5km/h (118mph and 124mph) were achieved.

In Britain a half-hearted venture was made by the Great Western Railway in 1935, when a 'Castle' and a 'King' were fitted with domed smokebox doors and various other 'streamlined' embellishments. These features were removed from the two 4-6-0s after a short period, although 'King Henry VII' retained its vee-fronted cab until withdrawal. Later that same year, though, the 'streamline era' began in earnest with the LNER 'Silver Jubilee' express, running between London and Newcastle. The new Class A4 Pacific locomotives, of which 35 were built, featured a wedge-shaped front, claimed to be most effective in the twin requirements of reducing wind resistance and throwing exhaust steam and smoke clear above the locomotive. The coaches were smooth-sided, with plating between the bogies and rubber sheeting covering the gaps between the coaches.

Gresley streamlined the last four of his six P2 Class 2-8-2 express locomotives in 1936-37. And when, in 1937, two Class B17 4-6-0s were modified for hauling the 'East Anglian' express, and the experimental 4-6-4 No. 10000 was rebuilt, these were similarly treated. Of the LNER streamlined locomotives, only the A4s and the 4-6-4 retained their casings to the end of their careers.

Streamlining reached the LMS in 1937 with the new Pacific built for the Euston-Glasgow 'Coronation Scot' express. The locomotive, No. 6220 'Coronation', sported a bullet-nosed casing, similar to the German 4-6-4s. In all, 24 streamlined and 14 non-streamlined locomotives were built, but for economy reasons the streamlining was removed during 1946-49.

'Air-smoothed' rather than streamlined describes the Southern Railway Pacifics of 1941. The 'Merchant Navy' locomotives had a smooth casing each side and a flat 'roof' along the length of the boiler. Thirty were built and, from 1945, a series of 110 similar, but smaller Pacifics carrying 'West Country' or 'Battle of Britain' names. In 1956, British Railways commenced rebuilding the 'Merchant Navies' and, later, 60 of the smaller engines were also modified. During this rebuilding the air-smoothed casings were removed.

The last European pre-war streamlined locomotives were six 4-4-2s, built in 1939 for the Belgian Railways Brussels-Ostend service.

During the mid-1930s the fashion had caught on in the USA. Some railroads were already using diesel power, but both 4-6-4s and 4-8-4s hauled many important expresses in the 1930s and 1940s. The best of the steam-hauled streamliners ran on the Chicago, Milwaukee, St Paul and Pacific—'The Milwaukee Road'. Four oil-fired Atlantics were built from 1935 for the Chicago-St Paul/Minneapolis 'Hiawatha'. This was the world's only steam-hauled service to demand continuous running at 160km/h (100mph). Before long the train grew in size and the Atlantics were succeeded by Class F7 4-6-4s, one of which reached a speed of 210km/h (125mph). Probably the most impressive streamlined locomotive of all was the Pennsylvania Railroad's No. 6100, an enormous 6-4-4-6.

Nearly all the American railroads adopted a streamlined look for their major expresses, simply because the appearance became synonymous with speed and modernity. Typical is the Burlington Railroad 'Denver Zephyr' (above).

Oliver Bulleid insisted that his remarkable Pacifics were not 'streamlined' but merely air smoothed with a lightweight casing. One of the survivors, No. 21C123 Blackmore Vale, is seen (left) at work on the preserved Bluebell Railway in Sussex, England.

'Flying Scotsman' and 'Mallard'

Which are the world's most famous locomotives? Best-known of all is surely 'Flying Scotsman', and the streamlined 'Mallard'—holder of the world speed record for a steam locomotive—is hot favourite for second place.

Both 4-6-2s ran on the London and North Eastern Railway, but their claims to fame are very different. While 'Flying Scotsman's' reputation was earned by several notable events in a 40-year working life, 'Mallard's' rests on a single exploit of high-speed running, which included a few seconds at 203km/h (126mph)!

'Flying Scotsman' was the third of a series of express locomotives, which eventually totalled 79. Designed by Nigel Gresley for the Great Northern Railway, the locomotive entered service early in 1923, after the GNR became part of the LNER. Then numbered 1472N, it was named in 1924 for display at the Empire Exhibition in London. The name chosen was that of the main daytime express running between London (King's Cross) and Edinburgh. When that train began to run the 632km (393 miles) non-stop, 'Flying Scotsman'—carrying its now-familiar number 4472—received one of the new corridor tenders, which allowed a fresh crew to take over while the train was running at speed. Appropriately, No. 4472 hauled the train out of King's Cross at 10.00am on the first day of non-stop running, May 1, 1928.

A favourite performer on the 'Flying Scots-man' train, No. 4472 next made news in 1934 during speed trials for the LNER's proposed streamlined express service. The Pacific, with four coaches, ran 299km (186 miles) from King's Cross to Leeds in 152 minutes at an average speed of 117km/h (73mph) and returned two hours later, hauling six coaches, in 157 minutes. On the return journey the first officially recorded speed of 160km/h (100mph) in Britain was attained.

During the 1940s and 1950s the Pacifics of Class A3, as they were known, were generally overshadowed by more modern types. But at the end of their careers some returned to the most exacting duties. During the years 1957 to 1962, 'Flying Scotsman'—now numbered 60103—often headed the fast expresses between King's Cross and Newcastle or Leeds. At least once, it even hauled the normally A4-powered (but no longer non-stop) 'Flying Scotsman' express. During this period the locomotive was improved by the fitting of a double chimney; later, German-style smoke deflectors were fitted to assist in lifting the softer exhaust clear of the locomotive.

On February 14, 1963, 'Flying Scotsman' retired and began a new career in private ownership. After restoration to something like its pre-war appearance it undertook a round of special train working which covered almost every part of the country. By 1966 the abolition of watering facilities made necessary the acquisition of a second tender, modified to

Gresley's streamlined LNER A4 Class Pacifics with their distinctive wedge-shaped front end, are renowned throughout the railway world, and none more so than 'Mallard', holder of the world speed record for steam of 203km/h (126mph), attained in July 1938 and never yet equalled. Here (left), in its later days as British Railways No. 60022 and sporting commemorative plaques, 'Mallard' hurries past Potters Bar with the London-Edinburgh Elizabethan express.

carry 6,000 gallons of water. Thus equipped, No. 4472 was able to repeat a feat it had first performed exactly 40 years before. On May 1, 1968, 'Flying Scotsman' once again hauled a train from King's Cross at 10.00am (departing alongside the diesel-hauled express of the same name) and ran non-stop to Edinburgh.

In the year after this amazing journey, No. 4472 was shipped to North America. Its tour of the USA and Canada was beset with financial difficulties and at one time it was thought that the Pacific might have to remain on that side of the Atlantic. However, a group of enthusiasts brought it home in 1973 and 'Flying Scotsman' has continued to work special trains and to win new admirers.

Built in 1938, 'Mallard' was one of the last of 35 streamlined A4 Pacifics. Since the A4s appeared, in 1935, there had been rivalry between the LMS and the LNER in the realm of speed. Records of 181, 182 and 183.4km/h (112.5, 113 and 114mph) had been set—the last by an LMS Pacific. Then, on Sunday July 3, 1938, a seven-coach train, which included a coach equipped for measuring the locomo-

tive's performance and hauled by No. 4468 'Mallard', took part in what was ostensibly a routine braking test. But some exceptional speeds were anticipated.

The LNER 'race track' was the 24km (15 miles) downhill stretch from Stoke Summit to Tallington, a few miles north of Peterborough. Starting near Grantham, 'Mallard' climbed hard to pass the summit at 119.8km/h (74mph) and accelerated down the other side. Speed rose rapidly to 160km/h (100mph) in 4.8km (3 miles) and raced past the previous best of 183.4km/h (114mph). Faster still went the A4 until, finally, for a few seconds the speed touched 203km/h (126mph). This set a world record which has never been equalled and the event was commemorated later by the fitting of plaques on each side of the locomotive.

'Mallard' was withdrawn in 1963 and repainted in its original blue livery. After several years on display at London's now-closed Clapham Transport Museum, No. 4468 moved with other exhibits to Britain's new National Railway Museum at York in 1975 where it is now on display.

Possibly the most famous engine in the world (above), 'Flying Scotsman' has had a chequered career. Surprisingly, it is the only member of the large A3 Class to have been preserved and at one stage was nearly marooned in America when an exhibition train it was leading ran into financial difficulties. It is pictured here after restoration to its original LNER livery and the fitting of Westinghouse air brakes and a bufferbeam bell ready for its trip to the United States and Canada.

How a Steam Engine Works

Steam locomotive design is subject to severe constraints. Not only must the mobile steam-raising plant and the engine be contained within the dimensions set by the railway loading gauge, but the locomotive must be stable as a vehicle in all conditions and throughout its range of operating speeds.

Heat for steam raising is generated by a furnace in a firebox at one end of the boiler. Only a small proportion of the water in the boiler is in direct contact with the hot firebox walls. The heat is therefore distributed over the whole length of the boiler by tubes which convey the hot gases of the fire from the firebox to the smokebox at the opposite end, where they escape up the chimney.

Steam forms in the space between the water and the top of the boiler. It is collected at a point as far as possible above the surface of the water, often in a dome mounted on top of

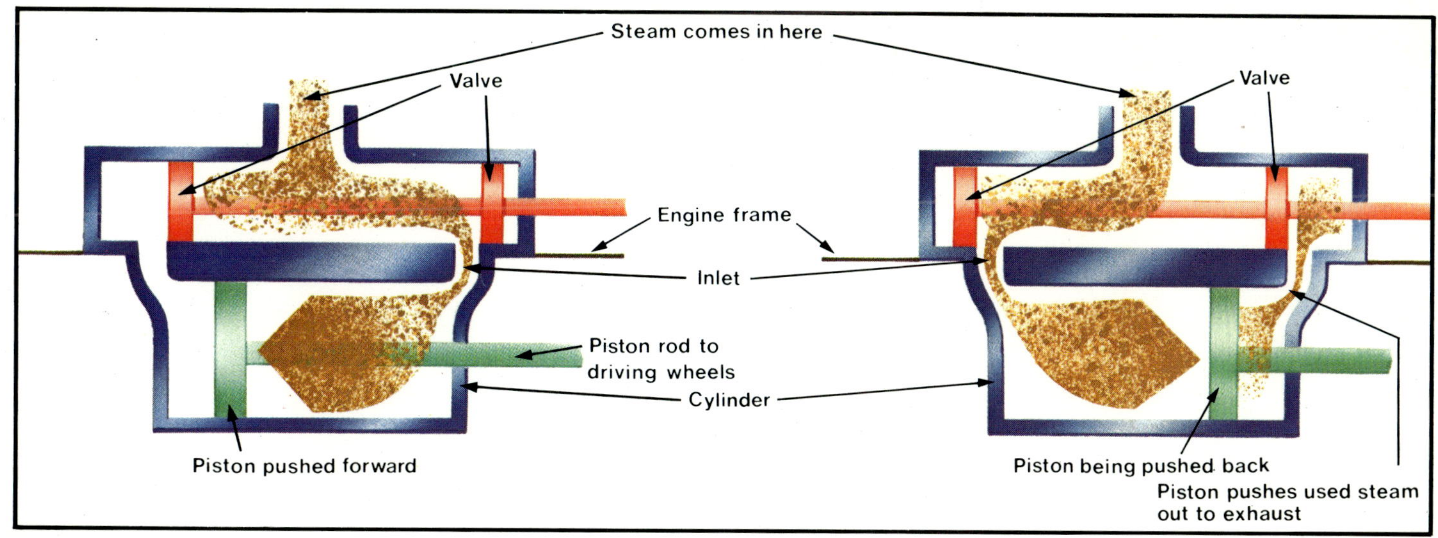

the boiler barrel. In some boilers, extra space is provided above the water at the firebox end by building them with a taper from the rear towards the front. A valve to control the supply of steam is fitted at the point of collection inside the dome or in the smokebox. It is controlled from the cab and known as the regulator.

Heat is a form of energy, and the steam entering the engine should be as hot as possible. Instead of passing direct from the boiler to the cylinders it often does so by way of a superheater. This is a system of tubular elements fitted inside large flue tubes which run the length of the boiler and connect to the smokebox and the firebox like the boiler tubes already mentioned. The superheater elements are therefore in contact with a stream of hot gases flowing from the fire along the flue tubes to the smokebox and the steam eventually leaves them at a temperature of some 330°C.

A locomotive may have two, three or four cylinders. When there are only two they are often between the frames and not easily seen from outside. Three-cylinder and four-cylinder designs have two of their cylinders outside the frames. Inside the cylinders the heat energy in the steam is converted into mechanical energy. A piston in each cylinder is attached to a piston rod which passes through a steamtight gland in the front cylinder cover. Ports in the cylinder allow steam to enter at one side of the piston or the other as they are uncovered in turn by the valve gear.

The pressure of the steam on entering the cylinder pushes the piston to the opposite end. At the end of the piston stroke the port through which steam has been entering is closed and the second port is opened to apply steam pressure on the other side of the piston and push it back. The piston rod, moving to and fro with the piston, is linked by a connecting rod with a crank on the driving axle so that the reciprocating movement of the piston

is converted into rotation at the wheel.

During each piston stroke the steam which has done its work on the previous stroke flows out into a blastpipe and so into the smokebox. Issuing with force from the blastpipe and escaping to atmosphere through the chimney, the steam creates a partial vacuum in the smokebox. Air to fill the vacuum flows over the fire and through the boiler tubes into the smokebox, creating a draught which helps combustion of the fuel in the firebox.

The movement of the valves is controlled by a system of rods and links driven from the axle. A reversing lever or handwheel in the cab allows the valves to be positioned at starting so that the locomotive moves forward or backward as required. It also adjusts the valve travel while the locomotive is running. In this way the valves can be made to cut off admission of steam soon after the beginning of each piston stroke. The steam already in the cylinder, however, continues to expand and exert pressure on the piston. Once a train is on the move and very high tractive effort is no longer required, economy in steam consumption can be achieved by 'notching up' the valve gear to give early cut-off.

Another method of making maximum use of steam is by compounding. This means that after working at high pressure in one cylinder steam is not exhausted direct to atmosphere but passes into another cylinder of larger volume, where it works again at lower pressure before being discharged through the chimney.

Towards the end of the steam era in the years after the Second World War outputs as high as 4,474kW (6,000hp) were recorded in test conditions in the United States. The fundamental problem of the steam locomotive, however, was the time spent in preparing it for work and servicing it between journeys. It cannot compete with the round-the-clock availability of electric and diesel power.

This cutaway drawing of an ex-South Eastern and Chatham Railway class P0-6-0T shows the basic components common to all steam locomotives. The diagrams (above right) show the cycle of a steam engine cylinder and its associated valve gear.

Steam around the World

There have been so many and varied steam locomotives used throughout the world since Richard Trevithick's first steam locomotive made its inaugural run in South Wales in 1804 that a complete picture would fill this book. In a brief review, one can only select a limited number of locomotives of particular interest or importance to illustrate some of the variety of steam locomotive development.

Many railway systems throughout the world commenced operation using British-built locomotives, often the products of Robert Stephenson and Son of Newcastle. That company's reputation having, no doubt, been enhanced by its success at the Rainhill trials in 1829, Stephenson locomotives pulled the first trains in Germany (1835), Belgium (1835) and Canada (1837), whilst in Russia the firm not only built the first locomotives but also engineered the whole of the first railway between St Petersburg and Pavlovsk. Robert Stephenson and Son also supplied early locomotives to the United States of America, although there the honour of producing the first locomotive fell to another British firm.

Britain did not long enjoy monopoly of locomotive construction but, until the end of steam, continued to supply locomotives to distant parts of the world. The expansion of railway systems during the growth of the British Empire in the 19th and early 20th centuries created a guaranteed market for British locomotive builders, and famous companies such as Vulcan Foundry, the North British Locomotive Company and Beyer Peacock supplied locomotives to all continents.

British influence is still easily distinguishable on the railway systems of the African continent, where steam traction still survives. Even before the former German African territory of Tanganyika was absorbed into the British Empire at the end of the First World War, Cecil Rhodes had dreamt of a 'Cape-to-Cairo' railway, but his dream has not been fulfilled and a gap remains to this day between Uganda and the Sudan. The gauge selected for the difficult African terrain was 1.067m (3ft 6in), but a generous loading gauge enabled massive locomotives to be built larger and heavier than anything constructed for the standard gauge system in Britain. One of the largest classes of locomotive operated by South African Railways is the Class 15 F, a 4-8-2 mixed traffic locomotive equally at home hauling express passenger trains such as the Blue Train or on goods work. Even larger are the Class GEA and GMA 4-8-2+2-8-4 Beyer-Garratt locomotives; Beyer-Garratts are also used extensively by Rhodesian Railways and East African Railways, whilst as recently as 1968 new 2-6-2+2-6-2 Garratts were built for the .610m (2ft) gauge in the Port Elizabeth area of South Africa.

Large locomotives are also the order of the day on the main lines of the Indian sub-continent, where a gauge of 1.676m (5ft 6in) was chosen. An early Governor-General, the Marquis Dalhousie, determined to avoid the break of gauge problems that had occurred in Britain and laid down that a common gauge should be used throughout the country, only to weaken thereafter and authorize the construction of narrow-gauge lines of a metre or narrower width in remoter parts. The generous 1.676m (5ft 6in) gauge, however, permit-

Chinese Railways are among the few in the world still building steam engines. The system itself is still being extended, and only in China can one see the unique sight of a newly-built steam train (right) running over a newly-laid railway line.

Despite electrification and dieselization of its trunk routes, steam still survives on some South African branches. The combination of 1.067m (3ft 6in) gauge tracks and mountainous terrain calls for sheer power rather than speed. This massive 4-8-2 (right) looks the part, with huge 'elephants ears' smoke deflectors, and the mandatory headlight and 'cowcatcher'.

European steam scenes: Henschel-built German Federal Railway Class 01 Pacific No. 01 128 of 1935 vintage waits (far left) for the signals to clear at Lichtenfels, while Italian Railways 2-6-0 No. 625-042 (left) darkens the Mediterranean sky.

Because of their unique combination of high tractive effort and low axle loading the Beyer-Garratt articulated locomotives were suited to the lightly-laid lines of the African and Indian continents, but they found work too, in Europe. This is a Spanish Railways Beyer-Garratt 2-8-2+2-8-2 (right).

In South East Asia today, railways often provide the only means of transport for the mass of the population. This is an Indonesian Railways rack-fitted 0-4-2T (right) in Central Java. In towns, the stations are quite open and often the centre of commercial activity, with crowds wandering freely about the running lines. Such is the scene (far right) as a morning train noses gently into Jakarta Tanahabang station.

ted the construction of large and powerful locomotives, particularly after the bulk of the railway system came under government control in 1922. Amongst the most common of Indian locomotives in recent years has been the Class WP 4-6-2, early versions of which were built in Britain but which after 1950 were also constructed at the Chittaranjan locomotive works in India. Freight has long been the forte of the Class XD 2-8-2 locomotives originally designed in the 1920s. Indian steam locomotives are, in their final years, painted in more colourful liveries than ever before, each region having adopted since independence distinctive colours applied wholly or in part to locomotives in the regional stock.

In contrast to the broad-gauge main-line locomotives, India still enjoys narrow-gauge mountain services, one of the most famous of which must be the .610m (2ft) gauge Darjeeling Himalayan Railway on which 0-4-0STs climb up into the mountains through spirals and sharp curves on gradients as steep as 1 in 20. This is no narrow-gauge preserved 'toy' railway, but a working line serving the community through which it passes.

Another part of the former British Empire which suffers, far more so than in India, from break of gauge problems is Australia. Before the formation of the Commonwealth of Australia, the separate states acted as independent 'nations' and unfortunately chose differing gauges for their developing railway

Many European and overseas railways used British-built locomotives with their distinctive clean lines. This ancient Portuguese Railways tender engine (above) pictured at Campahna, Porto, was built by Beyer-Peacock around the turn of the century. Somewhat older, and looking as if it has come straight from the Wild West, is this Baltimore and Ohio Railroad wood-burning 4-4-0 'William Mason', now preserved at Baltimore (right). The huge spark-arresting chimney, oil headlamp and cowcatcher were all quite typical of the period.

systems. Because of the different gauges throughout Australia it was only possible in 1962 to travel by through train between Melbourne and Sydney. Probably the most useful Australian standard-gauge locomotive was the C17 Class 4-8-0 introduced by the Queensland Railways in 1920, further examples of which were later constructed (in England and Australia) for use on the ex-South Australian Railway's line to Alice Springs and on the east coast line to Brisbane. They were at home on express passenger, suburban passenger, goods or branch-line work and the last of the class remained in service until 1969.

More modern in appearance was the streamlined 4-6-2 Class C38, introduced on the new South Wales Railway in 1943. Thirty locomotives of the class were constructed, the last of which was delivered in 1949, and the early locomotives were clearly distinguishable by their partial streamlining: the original locomotive (No. 3801), after earning its place in history by hauling the first through train from Sydney to Perth on the standard gauge in 1970, has been preserved for posterity and restored for special workings in the green livery adopted after the end of the Second World War. The later members of the class were not given streamlined casings.

Large though the locomotives in the British Commonwealth may be, they do not compare in size with the massive steam locomotives built for use in the United States of America. Early American railway history is epitomized by the 4-4-0 locomotives so common in 'cowboy and Indian' films, about 20,000 of which were built in the latter half of the 19th century. Later, as trains grew longer and heavier, more powerful types were required, culminating in the construction of the Union Pacific 'Big Boy' 4-6-6-4 introduced in 1941 for use in the mountainous districts near Cheyenne. One of the class, No. 4012, has been preserved at Steamtown Locomotive Museum in the USA.

The 'Big Boys' were primarily freight

The partition of Germany at the end of the Second World War left both the West German (DB) and East German (DR) systems operating the same type of locomotive and rolling stock. This ex-Prussian Railways Class P8 4-6-0 (left) is DB Class 038 No. 038 509-6, climbing the steep gradient from Lautlingen to Ebingen. The sister locomotives trapped in East Germany were reclassified 38.10 by the DR. Germanic in every detail from its smoke deflectors down to the distinctive headlamps is the East German DR Class 03.2 Pacific No. 03 2105 (below).

The famous streamlined A4 Class Pacific 'Sir Nigel Gresley' (above). The railways of the USA were among the earliest to embark on wholesale dieselization. This 2-8-2 of Denver and Rio Grande Western Railroad on the turntable (right) was hustled into retirement. Steam still survives on Czechoslovakian Railways. A 2-10-0 heads out of Prague (left).

One country in which whole railway systems disappeared before even the diesels came, is Eire. The entire locomotives, carriages, wagons and track of County Donegal Railways system were sold for scrap at prices which would make present day enthusiasts wince. In its final years 2-6-4T 'Foyle' (left).

In France modernization has taken its toll on the steam locomotives. This is a smartly turned-out 0-6-6-0 Mallet (right). The least likely country to find steam traction is Switzerland, with its almost total reliance on electrical power, much of it hydro-generated. This preserved Pilatus Railway steam railcar (left) built at Winterhus in 1889 has put in many years of hard work.

locomotives, although it was not unknown for them to be used on passenger services and they were designed for speeds up to 112.6km/h (70mph). Designed for higher speeds were the famous streamlined express locomotives introduced in the USA in the 1930's before the advent of the all-conquering diesel. Of these, amongst the most famous are the Chicago, Milwaukee, St Paul and Pacific Railroad 4-6-4s introduced in 1938 for the Hiawatha service between Chicago and St Paul that required 100mph running, and the Pennsylvania Railway Class T1 4-4-4-4s introduced in 1942. 'Streamliners' were also introduced in Canada in the 1930's; 'Royal Hudson' 4-6-4s were built by the Canadian Pacific Railway in 1937 and 'Selkirk' 2-10-4s introduced by the CPR for service in the Rockies in the following year. The first 'Royal Hudson'—No. 2850—achieved its royal accolade by hauling the royal train of King George VI and Queen Elizabeth in 1939.

In Britain the 'streamliner' craze affected both the London and Midland and Scottish Railway and the London & North Eastern Railway in the 1930s, when the 'Coronation' and A4 Pacifics were introduced by the companies respectively when competing for Scottish traffic. On the Southern Railway, its last Chief Mechanical Engineer, O.V.S. Bulleid, introduced streamlined 'Merchant Navy' and 'West Country' and 'Battle of Britain' Pacifics during the Second World War, construction of which continued even after the formation of British Railways in 1948. From 1956, however, many of the locomotives were rebuilt by British Railways in a more conventional style and the streamlined casings were removed.

However, many of the 'West Country' and 'Battle of Britain' locomotives remained in service in their streamlined state until withdrawal and a West Country Pacific has been preserved in Southern Railway livery on the Bluebell Railway. The Great Western Railway (GWR) made only half-hearted and singularly unsuccessful attempts to modernize its standard express locomotives by experimentally adding a bullet nose to a 'Castle' and a 'King' Class locomotive. These additions were soon removed, and the preserved members of each class are not so adorned, although both 'King' Class No. 6000 'King George V' and 'Castle' Class No. 7029 'Clun Castle' vary from the original designs by retaining the double chimneys added by BR to improve efficiency.

In Britain these two locomotives form part of an impressive collection of preserved locomotives, some kept privately and others officially by British Railways; the collection appropriately includes the last steam locomotive to be built for British Railways, Class 9 2-10-0 No. 92220 'Evening Star', which was constructed at Swindon in 1960 and turned out in Brunswick green adorned with a GWR style chimney and nameplates.

Throughout the world, steam locomotives have been, or are rapidly being, replaced by diesel and electric machines. They will, however, continue to be held in high regard by railway enthusiasts of all ages, even when they have ceased to be used in day-to-day service and are to be found only on 'preserved' lines or hauling enthusiasts' specials. Although the days of the steam locomotive throughout the world may be numbered, it will never be forgotten.

Spanish Railways tend to be isolated from the remainder of the European system both geographically and because of its differing track gauge, but this did not deter the development of some powerful and efficient steam locomotive types; the pair of RENFE 2-8-2s climbing towards Bujedo (below) with a heavy southbound freight in May 1968 are both oil fired.

Bridges and Viaducts

Almost a century has passed since the collapse of the Tay Bridge in 1879 shocked the world, and yet it is still remembered as a unique disaster. For, in general, most members of the travelling public do not give a second thought to the safety of bridges, placing implicit faith in the soundness of the thousands of bridges and viaducts on the railways of the world.

Many of the bridges and viaducts still in daily use in Britain have already celebrated their centenaries, and others are fast approaching that landmark. The Royal Albert Bridge, soaring 30.48m (100ft) above the waters of the River Tamar at Saltash between Cornwall and Devon, was designed for the Cornwall Railway by Isambard Kingdom Brunel. Opened for traffic in 1859, the bridge was a development of his earlier design, used successfully to bridge the River Wye at Chepstow in 1852. Brunel's plans were governed by a strict Admiralty requirement that there should be adequate headroom for even the tallest of sailing ships, and no undue obstruction. This he resolved by designing two 137.2m (450ft) tubular trusses in the form of huge oval wrought-iron tubes springing from masonry piers on each bank and supported by a centre pier whose foundations lie 27.4m (90ft) below high-water mark in the middle of the river. Suspended from each side of each tube are giant suspension chains, and these in turn support the deck. Like its counterpart, the Royal Albert Bridge was built of wrought iron, and although it has received only minor modification and strengthening since construction, it remains in use today carrying trains of much greater weight than can ever have been contemplated by its designer.

Britain's earliest great wrought-iron railway bridge was designed by Robert Stephenson for the Chester and Holyhead Railway to bridge the Menai Strait between what was then Caernarvonshire and Anglesey. As at Saltash, the Admiralty insisted on sufficient clearance above water level for tall sailing ships, and the Britannia Tubular Bridge was therefore designed as two wrought-iron box-section tubes, supported side by side on masonry towers 36.6m (120ft) above water level, with each tube carrying within it one line of railway track. Opened in 1850, the bridge was in continuous use until May 23, 1970 when a fierce fire irreparably distorted the tubes, and it has now been rebuilt as a single-track steel-arched structure of modern design but using the original piers.

Despite its modest geographical size, Britain is well endowed with massive engineering works. One of the longest is in Scotland, the new Tay Bridge built across the Tay Estuary to the designs of W. H. Barlow in 1887 to replace Thomas Bouch's ill-fated structure that formed part of the North British Railway main line for only 18 months before its 'high girders' came crashing down into the angry waters of the Firth of Tay at the height of a storm on December 28, 1879, taking with it to its doom a Burntisland-Dundee train, its passengers and crew. The subsequent inquiry found evidence of sub-standard work in the structure, and although it was never positively established what initiated the fatal collapse of the centre 13 girders, Thomas Bouch, only the year before knighted in recognition of his work, was disgraced.

At the time of the disaster Bouch had been preparing plans for an even greater structure across the Firth of Forth, but his proposals were shelved after the collapse of his Tay Bridge. The crossing of the Forth was an undertaking even more daunting than the crossing of the Tay; plans were prepared for the North British Railway by Sir John Fowler

Crossing the Alps was a colossal challenge to the 19th century railway engineers and their work resulted in some very spectacular viaducts and tunnels. Curving across the lofty stone-built Landwasser viaduct to plunge headlong into a tunnel through the sheer rock face of the mountain is a steam-hauled special (right) on the metre-gauge Rhaetian Railway in South-East Switzerland.

The Royal Albert Bridge at Saltash, striding high above the River Tamar between Devon and Cornwall so as to clear the tall masts of the 19th century sailing ships, was opened in 1859. One of the last works of Isambard Kingdom Brunel, builder of the Great Western Railway, this turn-of-the-century view (left) shows the wrought-iron structure before it was joined by the concrete and steel road suspension bridge which now stands alongside.

and Benjamin Baker and, chastened by the Tay Bridge experience, they produced a plan for a massive bridge based on the cantilever principle. Work began in 1883 and the bridge was ceremonially opened by the Prince of Wales (later King Edward VII) on March 4, 1890. Dominant features of the bridge are the three massive 109.7m (360ft) high cantilever towers linked by the two main spans each of 521m (1,710ft). Clearance above high water is 45.7m (150ft), and the lofty approach spans are formed of girders on masonry piers. One of the towers is built on Inchgarvie Island, from which Baker carried out his initial wind-pressure experiments, but the foundations for the other two towers had to be built 30.48m (100ft) down on the murky bed of the River Forth, no easy task in an era which knew little of welding, electric pumps or reinforced concrete. Such is the size of the bridge and the complexity of its 51,000 tonnes of steelwork that repainting is a continuous process, the painting gangs taking three years to complete the task before promptly starting all over again!

The cantilever principle was used again in Scotland for the construction of the Connel Ferry bridge on the Ballachulish branch, opened in 1903. Designed by Sir John Wolfe Barry to give a clear 524ft span across the deep, fast-flowing waters from Loch Etive, the structure was originally designed to carry both rail and road traffic, but the motor car has reigned supreme since the single track branch was closed in 1966.

Another British bridge to come to an ignominious end was the Severn Bridge, opened by the ex-Great Western and Midland

Heading across a graceful brick and lattice girder bridge east of Sevi in Sardinia is a 2-6-2T (above) with a Mandas-Arbatax special. Echoing in line the base of his famous tower in Paris, Eiffel's graceful Maria Pie bridge carries a Portuguese Railways 2-6-4T high above the River Douro (below).

Severn and Wye Joint Railway in 1879. In thick fog on the night of October 25, 1960, two tank barges carrying petroleum collided with one of the piers of this 1268m (4,161ft) long bridge and the force of the collision and subsequent explosion caused one pier and two of the 22 spans to collapse into the River Severn, 21.3m (70ft) below. The cost of repairing the bridge—used mainly as an alternative route when the Severn Tunnel was being repaired—proved prohibitive and the remainder of the structure was subsequently dismantled. Also now demolished is the once-nearby Crumlin viaduct which until 1965 carried the Newport, Abergavenny and Hereford railway across Ebbw Vale in south Wales at a height of 60.96m (200ft).

But despite its position at the heart of the industrial revolution, not all Britain's 19th century bridges were of brick, iron and steel; in Devon and Cornwall Brunel built a large number of graceful wooden viaducts for the GWR, and the last, on the Truro-Falmouth branch in Cornwall, was not replaced until 1934.

Britain's railway bridges may be the most varied in the world, but in terms of sheer height and length they are handsomely exceeded elsewhere.

The longest bridge in the world is the Huey P. Long bridge over the Mississippi River near New Orleans in the USA. It is no less than 7.24km (4.5 miles) long, the flat, flood-prone nature of the surrounding country and the need for ample headroom above the river necessitating long approach spans. The centre spans over the river are cantilevered, the

centre section of almost 274.3m (900ft) being flanked on each side by smaller spans of 161.5m (530ft) each.

The greatest cantilevered span in the world is also to be found on the North American continent, across the US border in Canada. The centre span of the Quebec bridge across the St Lawrence River is 548.6m (1,800ft) long, 27.4m (90ft) longer than those of the Forth Bridge. But its construction proved more troublesome, taking 16 years to complete, delays being caused first by the collapse of one of the main towers and then by the fall into the river of the massive central span during raising operations, as the result of which an entirely new span had to be constructed. It was not finally opened for traffic until 1917.

More famous, although with a slightly smaller span, is the Sydney Harbour Bridge in Australia, completed in 1932 after earlier cantilever designs had been rejected. Originally designed to carry four railway tracks as well as a roadway, the bridge was planned in conjunction with new cross-city suburban railways recommended by a Royal Commission on the 'Improvement of the City of Sydney and its Suburbs' as early as 1908. Neither the railway—now reduced to two tracks—nor the road pass over the great steel arch that is the most obvious feature of the structure, but are instead carried through the bridge on a suspended deck.

Equally as impressive in its location is the Victoria Falls railway bridge on the borders of Rhodesia and Zambia. Cecil Rhodes is said to have deliberately chosen the location of the bridge, which was intended to be part of his 'Cape to Cairo' railway, so that the spray from the falls would reach the railway carriages as they passed 122m (400ft) above the river. The main span is 152m (500ft) long, and it is to be hoped that it will emerge from its present limbo to become once again a great tourist attraction when relations between the two countries linked by the bridge improve.

The Crumlin Viaduct was the loftiest railway bridge in Britain, but its height is easily exceeded by that at Fades, near Clermont-Ferrand in France, the highest in the world. Built between 1901 and 1909 for a single-track railway, the 144m (472ft) span stands 131m (430ft) above the floor of the River Sioule at its highest point, the lattice girder being supported on slender granite piers themselves 100.5m (330ft) high. Elsewhere in France, the Garabit Viaduct (designed by Eiffel, a gentleman better known for his tower) carries the railway over 122m (400ft) above the valley floor on a 164.8m (541ft) span, and in Portugal the same designer was responsible for the graceful Maria Pie arch over the Douro.

Bridges and viaducts built of brick and stone cannot match the sheer size of iron and steel structures, but mention must be made of the 55.2m (181ft) centre span of Ballochmyle Viaduct in Ayrshire, possibly the largest masonry span in the world, and of the numerous long viaducts such as that at Welwyn on the ex-Great Northern main line and that across the Ouse valley on the Brighton line which almost enhance the countryside with which they have blended over the decades. Even garish modern-day concrete mellows with age, as can be seen on the West Highland line at Glenfinnon, or high in the Alps in Switzerland and Austria.

Horrified by the collapse of his Tay Bridge in a gale, the North British Railway discarded Bouch's plans for a crossing of the Forth. Instead Fowler and Baker built a massive cantilever bridge (above) which would withstand the severest weather known to man.

Like the Royal Albert Bridge at Saltash, completed over 70 years earlier, the Sydney Harbour Bridge (left) employs the "fixed" suspension principle, with the deck carrying both road and rail suspended from the main arch girders.

Tunnels

In May 1830, just a few months before the opening of the Liverpool and Manchester Railway, a short, passenger-carrying steam-powered line opened in Kent, between Canterbury and Whitstable. This line, now closed, had a 925m (1,012yd) tunnel beneath Tyler Hill at Canterbury, and although it has been alleged that a tunnel was unnecessary, and only constructed to satisfy local residents who considered a tunnel a necessary part of any proper railway, it was certainly the first passenger railway tunnel to be opened. It was built to a rather more restricted loading gauge than subsequent structures, and in later years locomotives with specially cut-down cabs and chimneys had to be used.

The decade from 1830 saw the framework of Britain's railway network beginning to take shape; by 1842 lines had been constructed from London to most of the main centres of population. As planned, both the Great Western Railway (GWR) line to Bristol and the London and Birmingham Railway crossed major hill ranges and required the construction of tunnels on a scale hitherto unattempted.

The engineer for the London and Birmingham line was Robert Stephenson, and he proposed to build a 2,195m (2,400yd) tunnel at Kilsby. This was much longer than had ever previously been contemplated for locomotive haulage, and opponents of the railway system confidently predicted the suffocation of the first passengers to use it. Partly to allay such

Some early tunnel builders adorned the entrances to their work to reassure nervous passengers, whilst others, realising the strategic value of a tunnel to an invading army, slowly fortified them. The castellated northern portal of Clayton Tunnel (right) owes its existence to both. At the time of its construction it was the largest tunnel of the Brighton line, hewn entirely through chalk, and although it may seem unlikely today, the Brighton Company was anxious both to reassure its customers and to defend it from an invading army which might have come swinging in through the Weald! Equally ornate in the classical style was the portal of Watford Tunnel (right).

Tunnels through soft or unstable ground need to be lined with bricks or stone, and to have properly-constructed tunnel mouths with retaining walls. But tunnels blasted through solid rock need no such refinements, for they provide their own lining and natural tunnel mouth. Red Sucker Tunnel (right) on the Canadian Pacific Railway in Ontario is a fine example as two CP diesels wheel by with a heavy freight.

fears, although he had every confidence in the structure himself, Stephenson incorporated in his design two massive ventilation shafts of 18m (60ft) diameter and more than 30.5m (100ft) deep. Objectors to the tunnel were delighted when quicksand was encountered in such volume as to cause temporary abandonment of the works, but Stephenson was not daunted and the tunnel was completed in 1837.

Isambard Kingdom Brunel, who had been appointed engineer of the Bristol Railway at the age of 27 in 1833, faced similar opposition when he laid out the Great Western Railway main line between Paddington and Bristol. On this magnificently engineered line, used today by British Rail's 200km/h (125mph) High Speed Trains, Brunel proposed a tunnel nearly 3km (2 miles) long at Box on a gradient of 1 in 100. Work commenced on the tunnel in September 1836 and the line was opened to traffic, completing the link to Bristol, in June 1841. Brunel deliberately designed the tunnel to enhance the countryside through which it had been built, and the entrances were graced with huge classic porticos in Bath stone which even today impress passengers as they plunge from the rolling countryside into the tunnel.

The Severn Tunnel is the longest in Britain, burrowing under the River Severn to link the county of Avon in England with Gwent in Wales. Parliamentary powers for the 6.4km (4 miles) long tunnel were obtained by the GWR in 1872; at its lowest point it was to be 40m (130ft) below river level. Construction work commenced in the following year, and the next decade was one of continual struggle with water; twice water from underground streams burst into the workings and brought tunnelling to a standstill, and although the line through the tunnel was eventually opened for traffic in December 1886, even today powerful pumps are kept continuously at work to keep seepage under control.

British tunnels pall into insignificance when compared with the later major works throughout Europe, particularly those on lines traversing the Alps. The first attempt to link the railway systems of France, Switzerland and Italy commenced in 1857 when work started on the 12km (7.5 mile) Mont Cenis Tunnel between Modane and Bardonecchia; it was opened in December 1870, but celebrations at the French end were somewhat subdued by the prospect of imminent defeat in the Franco-Prussian War. The tunnel closed between 1877 and 1881 while it was extended to avoid landslide problems, and it was again closed temporarily at the end of the Second World War.

To give a more direct link between Italy and Germany, work commenced on the construction of the Gotthard line and tunnel in 1872.

The St Gotthard Tunnel, 14.65km (9 miles 562yd) in length, is now so heavily used that consideration is being given to the construction of a relief tunnel, despite the enormous cost of such an undertaking. A considerable part of the traffic on this all-electric line, operated by Swiss Federal Railways, consists of cars and their occupants being ferried through the tunnel from Switzerland to Italy or vice versa rather than face Alpine roads.

Even greater in length is the Simplon Tunnel, which at 19.47km (12 miles 537yd) is the longest double-line tunnel in the world. Work commenced on this extension of the Jura-Simplon Railway in 1898 and the first bore opened in 1906, with the second following in 1921. Ten years earlier, in 1911, the Lötschberg Tunnel, at the head of the Kander Valley on the Berne-Simplon line, was opened. The western portal of this 14.9km (9 mile 140yd) long tunnel is within sight of the ski resort of Kandersteg. Both lines were operated with electric traction from the outset, as are all railways through the Alps today.

In America the longest tunnel, over 11.3km (7 miles) in length, is near Seattle, while in Japan new tunnels have been built as part of the development of the Shinkansen high-speed lines, and an undersea tunnel is under construction to link the system with the island of Hokkaido.

Britain's chance, with France, to regain the lead in the 'tunnel league' with the construction of a railway tunnel under the English Channel—'the chunnel'—has yet again faded for the foreseeable future with the decision to suspend construction work, although proposals for a cheaper scheme are under discussion. Nevertheless, it is in Britain that the world's longest railway tunnel is situated; the London Transport Northern Line underground tunnel between East Finchley and Morden, via Bank, is over 27.35km (17 miles) in length.

Austerities

'Austerity' was as much a word of the 1940s as 'streamlined' had been of the previous decade and, likewise, was applied to a particular type of locomotive. A dictionary definition of austere is 'severely simple'—an apt description of the 'Austerity' locomotives built by the British, American and German systems during World War II.

In the early part of the war the British Ministry of Supply ordered LMS Class 8F 2-8-0s to be built for use by the forces. As the war progressed, a requirement arose for locomotives for service in Europe, coinciding with a shortage of labour available for locomotive construction. A simplified version of the 2-8-0 was developed by R. A. Riddles, who was responsible for obtaining railway equipment for military purposes. A considerable saving in materials was achieved by the use of plate or cast iron instead of steel castings, while the locomotive manufacturers involved devised production techniques to save thousands of man-hours per locomotive. Between them the North British Locomotive Company and Vulcan Foundry built 935 of the new 2-8-0s during 1943-45. A version with ten

and 533 further 2-8-0s. Many of the Austerity 2-8-0s remaining on the European mainland were taken over by the national railways. On British Railways they were widely dispersed over all Regions, except for the Southern, and large numbers remained at work until the mid-1960s. Curiously, none of the BR 2-8-0s or 2-10-0s is preserved. However, a former Swedish Railways WD 2-8-0 is in service on the Keighley and Worth Valley Railway, and 2-10-0 No. 600 Gordon—which remained in military service until the late 1960s—is popular with visitors to the Severn Valley Railway. Many of the 0-6-0STs have been employed by the National Coal Board and other industrial railways in the post-war years, in which period more were constructed. Several are preserved or are still employed on industrial systems.

There were two other sources of 'austerity' locomotive during the 1939-45 war, Germany and the USA. At the same time as the British 2-8-0 was being developed, the Ministry of Supply ordered 2-8-0s from America. These were of the same general size and capacity, except for a wider firebox, but their trans-

coupled driving wheels was also developed, and 150 were built by North British. The 2-10-0s had wide fireboxes, better suited to burning low-grade coal, and their lighter axle-load allowed a wider area of operation over lines likely to be in poor condition through lack of maintenance. The third type of locomotive was based on Hunslet's sturdy 0-6-0 saddle tank for industrial use. Hunslet and other manufacturers—Barclay, Robert Stephenson, Vulcan Foundry, Hudswell Clarke and Bagnall—built 377 of the 0-6-0STs for the British Ministry of Supply in 1943-46.

After the war most British 'Austerities' returned to England. Two hundred 2-8-0s and 75 0-6-0STs joined the LNER in 1946, whilst in 1948 British Railways purchased 25 2-10-0s

atlantic origin was apparent when they entered service in Britain in 1942-43. Later they went overseas alongside British-built 'Austerities', but they did not return to Britain after the war.

A more lasting impression was made by the American 0-6-0T shunting locomotives. Several European railways retained examples after the war, among them the Southern Railway, which purchased 14 in 1946. Classified simply 'USA', they worked in Southampton Docks until the early 1960s and four are now preserved.

German 'austerity' locomotive building was carried out on a massive scale, particularly during the years 1942-44. All told, nearly 11,000 2-10-0s were built, of three or four

Although developed by opposing factions, the German and Anglo/American Austerity designs revealed many common features: standardisation, versatility and ease of maintenance were all of the utmost importance. It was hardly surprising that both sides opted for small wheeled 2-8-0 or 2-10-0 types with large, easily accessible twin outside cylinders, steel parallel boilers, large enclosed cabs and simple high running plates. Over 6,000 of the German Class 52 'Kriegsloks' (left) were built, many surviving the war years to work both on the German Federal system and other Central European lines, while the Americans built equally large numbers of 'Liberation' 2-8-0s and 2-10-0s for use by the Allied armies in Europe. They too became distributed throughout the railway systems on which they worked, and some like this British example (above) acquired such local flavourings as vacuum brakes and oil lamps.

types, commencing with Class 50UK, based on a pre-war design. Most numerous of the 'Kriegsloks' (war locomotives) were the 6,000 Class 52s. Relatively few Class 52s remained serviceable in Germany when the war ended and in West Germany these had been reduced to a handful by the end of the next decade. However, the class was widely dispersed and its members saw many years' service with various central and eastern European railways.

In Britain, the LMS Stanier Class 8F 2-8-0 was at first adopted for war production because of its simple design and high route availability, and many of the class had adventures abroad before returning to the British Railways fold after the war (left). From 1943 the railway workshops began to turn out the first of over 900 locomotives still based very much on the Stanier engines, but of simplified, pre-fabricated construction, and with parallel steel boilers. Perhaps the ugliest of all the austerities were the Southern Railway Q1 'Coffeepot' 0-6-0s (left), designed by Bulleid in 1942 for heavy shunting and freight work, and unique among austerities in having inside cylinders, a prefabricated smokebox with multiple-jet blastpipe, cast 'box-pox' wheels and absolutely no running board whatsoever.

Nationalization

Although many of the early railways were projected by entrepreneurs and supported by private enterprise, it was not long before governments and other official bodies began to show more than a passing interest. For as the railway companies grew in size and stature they were seen in some eyes as a growing threat, both financially and militarily, to the authority of the states concerned. To have them under State control was economically, politically and militarily attractive.

With the exception of Belgium, where the railways have been State-owned ever since the first line was opened in 1835, the countries of Western Europe, together with the United States, met the problem by discouraging amalgamation and fostering instead fierce competition between the existing companies, and it was not until after the First World War, with the changed economic climate and new competition from road and air, that the major European railways passed one by one into State ownership.

The German railways system had a chequered career in this respect; the German State Railways (Deutsche Reichsbahn) were formed on April 1, 1920, but made independent again on October 11, 1924, only to be renationalized on January 30, 1937. And after the Second World War, with the splitting of the system between east and west, the eastern part of the system, under Communist control, continued as the DR, while that in Western

Japanese National Railways

Germany became the German Federal Railways (Deutsche Bundesbahn). In neighbouring Switzerland the Swiss Federal Railways (SBB) was formed over the years from 1901 as various states acquired individual lines, and today it is an entirely autonomous authority supported by the various cantons, or states. The railways of France were nationalized on August 31, 1937, to form the French National Railways (SNCF), while in Belgium a new administration (SNCB) took over from the original State authority in July 1926. Steps to place the Netherlands railways in public ownership began on January 1, 1938, but the process was delayed by the Second World War and its aftermath and was not completed

until 1951. In Denmark, on the other hand, the State interest dates from 1862, and now 80 per cent of the railways are owned and operated by the Danish State Railway system (DSB).

Of the Mediterranean countries, Italy was the first to come into State ownership, in 1905, while the State railways of neighbouring Greece, Hellenic Railways, were gradually built up from 1920. The Spanish National Railway system was formed on February 27, 1943, so that by 1945 the railways of Britain, together with those of Luxembourg, were virtually the only national systems in Europe not to be State owned, although both were, because of wartime conditions, under State control. And they were never to return to private ownership, for the Luxembourg National Railways (CFL) were formed on June 16, 1947, while the 'Big Four' in Britain, the GWR, SR, LMS and LNER, were nationalized and merged to form British Railways on January 1, 1948.

Elsewhere in the world State ownership has been very much the rule from the early days. In the Eastern bloc countries many of the railway systems were State-owned long before they passed into Communist control; in the Czarist Russia of 1913 as many as 25 of the 38 lines were already State-owned, the remainder coming under public control after the Revolution in 1917, while the railways of Hungary and Romania came into State ownership in 1868 and 1888 respectively. The Chinese People's Republic Railways were formed in 1908 and have been expanding steadily ever since, while the Japanese National Railways came into being in 1906.

Even before the Revolution in 1917, and the setting up of the Socialist Republic, well over half of the railways of Czarist Russia were State-owned. Without the fierce, sometimes unfair, competition of road transport found in almost all Western countries, the railways of the Eastern bloc have not suffered the financial constraints imposed on many of the Western World's Nationalized systems. The Russians have electrified a major part of the Trans-Siberian route; this is (above) one of the stylish, but still obviously Russian, new TEP-60 Co-Co electric locomotives.

Amtrak

Canadian National Railways

Of the old British Commonwealth countries, the South African Railways (SAR) were formed in 1910, while the State railways of Australia and New Zealand have been under public control virtually from the outset. In Canada an interesting dual State/private ownership situation has grown up. In 1923 Canadian National Railways (CN) was formed by the amalgamation of several State-owned railways and now works in competition with the Canadian Pacific Railway (CP), originally set up to complete the Montreal-Vancouver trans-

Finnish Railways

Netherlands Railways

continental railway, opened on June 28, 1886, but now with tracks throughout southern Canada, as well as some across the border in the northern United States.

India, like Britain, had a very strong history of private enterprise speculatively-built railways, and it was not until after independence that the Indian Railway Board was formed in 1951.

Nowadays, even the fiercely independent, anti-State ownership railroads of Northern America are having to accept Federal assistance and, with it, some directives as to how money will be spent.

Some of the eastern seaboard companies, in particular, with their dense commuter traffic and smaller freight potential, have suffered huge losses; on February 1, 1968, in an attempt to form a more economic unit, the Pennsylvania and New York Central Railroads merged to form the Penn Central Co., and from the end of the same year the New York, New Haven and Hartford Railroad joined the grouping, as a result of which it now owns over 20,000 miles of track—720 of which are electrified—in 16 different States. Likewise, in March 1970 the Chicago, Burlington and Quincey, Great Northern, Northern Pacific and Spokane, and Portland and Seattle Railroads all combined to form the huge Burlington and Northern Railroad which, with 24,519 miles of line, is larger than all of British Railways and approaching the size of the German Federal system.

To remain in business, many of the American railroads were obliged to severely curtail or even abandon their passenger services, and to maintain a basic long-distance network an Act of Congress in 1970 set up the National Railroad Passenger Corporation—Amtrak—as a Government-subsidized private corporation to operate inter-city services. Over 20 railroads have elected to join Amtrak and allow their system to be used by its trains in return for a fee, instead of operating a passenger service of their own. Because of the complexities of operation, and the indifferent state of much of the rolling stock it inherited, Amtrak got off to a poor start, but it now operates about 250 trains each day over 38,000km (23,600 miles) of track, serving 450 towns.

The Chinese People's Republic Railways were formed as long ago as 1908, and this now vast State system has been growing steadily ever since. Perhaps the last country in the world to be building both modern new steam engines and new lines on a considerable scale, China uses her railways as the strategic distributor of food and materials in much the same way as Western societies use motorways. This diesel locomotive (above) is heading one of the first trains across a new bridge on the new line to Kunming opened in 1974.

Standard Engines

Nationalization and state ownership of railways did not immediately bring about uniformity of motive-power types. In Britain, for example, about 1,500 steam engines of existing designs were built after Nationalization. But work on a series of 12 new types was being carried out under the new British Railways Chief Mechanical and Electrical Engineer, R. A. Riddles. The team designing Britain's last main-line steam engine was asked to analyse and compare differing techniques and to 'standardize the best'. A tall order!

Like Riddles, his two chief assistants were former LMS men, so it is not surprising that many of that company's practices were embodied in the new locomotives. But responsibility for certain common parts and the co-ordination of design for particular classes, as well as construction, was shared between workshops of each of the former 'Big Four' companies.

The basic theme of the 'Standards' was ease of maintenance and the use of well-tried ideas. Common features included a taper boiler with Belpaire firebox, single chimney, two outside cylinders and Walschaerts valve gear. High running plates gave easy access around the wheels and between the frames.

First of the 999 Standards to appear, in 1951, was the Pacific No. 70000 'Britannia', forerunner of a class of 55. For lighter work there were 10 less powerful Clan Pacifics and 172 Class 5 4-6-0s. The 280 smaller tender locomotives comprised four types of 4-6-0 or 2-6-0. Largest of the tank engines were the 155 Class 4 2-6-4Ts, then came two classes of 2-6-2T, totalling 75 locomotives.

Finally, in 1954, the last two types entered service. Arguably the most successful of the Standards was the Class 9F heavy freight engine with—for Britain—the unusual 2-10-0 wheel arrangement. The last of no less than 251 9Fs was also the last steam locomotive built for British railways. It emerged from Swindon Works in March 1960 as No. 92220, named 'Evening Star'. Although the 9Fs were designed for hauling heavy freight and mineral trains, they were frequently employed on fast freights and occasionally appeared on passenger trains. There is a famous—perhaps notorious!—occasion when one is reported to have touched 145km/h (90mph) running down gradient with a heavy express passenger train. That's quite an achievement for a 2-10-0 freight locomotive with driving wheels only 5ft in diameter!

The most numerous of the BR Standard engines were also the largest, the handsome and powerful Class 9F 2-10-0s, of which 251 were built. Last of the Class to be built was also the last steam locomotive built by British Railways and was named, appropriately, "Evening Star" (above).

In the latter days of steam traction, many of the larger railway administrations, notably the Germans, standardized on successful locomotive types. In Britain a complete new range of types were designed and built from the outset as "standard" engines, using as many interchangeable parts as possible. This Class 3 mixed traffic 2-6-0 No. 77001 (right) was one of these types.

The other type to appear in 1954 was something of an 'odd man out'. This was a solitary 4-6-2, more powerful than the Britannias, with three cylinders, Caprotti valve gear and a double chimney. No 71000 'Duke of Gloucester' had potential for development, but the advent of diesels eliminated the need for new, front-line express passenger steam locomotives.

The work of the Standards was varied. In most areas they replaced older types, and the smaller tender engines generally performed well, working side-by-side with other modern types. If one application can be singled out for special mention it has to be the allocation of Britannias to the London (Liverpool Street)-Norwich service in 1951. Motive power staff took to the new locomotives and together they worked well on the accelerated expresses for almost ten years until the diesels took over.

Few modifications were made to the Standard designs, of which the most drastic was the fitting of Italian Franco-Crosti pre-heaters and boilers to ten of the 9Fs. But the experiment did not suceed in its aim to economize on coal and the locomotives were converted to orthodox working. Other 9F variations were the fitting of double chimneys to the last 70 or so and the similar modification of a few others, while one was equipped with a Giesl chimney. American Berkeley mechanical stokers were tried out on three examples. Some of the small 4-6-0s also gained double chimneys, and 30 Class 5 4-6-0s had Caprotti valve gear.

Hardly had the last Standard entered service when the first examples were withdrawn. One of the earliest to go was 'Duke of Gloucester', in 1962, and six other classes had become extinct by the midsummer of 1967. A year later, Britannia No 70013 'Oliver Cromwell' took part in working the final special before steam traction ended, in August 1968. Twenty-two Standards, representing most of the tender types and including several 2-6-4Ts, are preserved. Among them are 'Oliver Cromwell', 'Duke of Gloucester' and—most appropriately—the first and last of the Standards, 'Britannia' and 'Evening Star'.

First of the British Railways Standard engines to appear was the Pacific No. 70000 'Britannia' (above), the first of a hard working class of locomotives which subsequently worked in every Region of the country.

Three of the 12 BR Standard designs were merely tank engine versions of the smaller mixed traffic tender engine designs. Largest were the handsome and compact Class 4 2-6-4Ts, (left) used mainly for suburban passenger work.

Early Diesels

Even in the 'Golden Age' of steam from 1900 to 1914, the first tentative trials of diesel traction were taking place. In 1912 the North British Locomotive Co. built a 1,000hp diesel-mechanical unit with a direct-drive Diesel-Klose-Sulzer engine. And in the following year an Atlas diesel-electric railcar was introduced on the Mellersta-Sodermanlands railway, becoming the first diesel vehicle in money-earning service.

Development of diesel engines in the First World War brought greater strength and reliability, and in 1924 a small German-built diesel-hydraulic was tested. In America, GEC/Alco/Ingersoll turned out their first diesel locomotive, a 300hp shunter.

The late 1920s were a time of growing financial depression, and few companies were keen to venture into the unknown realms of novel forms of traction. Nevertheless, Armstrong-Whitworth, of Scotswood-on-Tyne, an established firm of steam locomotive builders, secured an order in 1929 for a 600hp diesel-hydraulic shunter for the Buenos Aires Great Southern Railway, and armed with this experi-

Although there were many earlier successful diesels, it was the feats of the German 'Flying Hamburger' (below) twin diesel railcar in 1933 that first brought public attention to the possibilities of diesel traction in Europe. Built in 1932, the two-car high-speed diesel-electric unit entered regular service in May of the following year between Berlin and Hamburg on a schedule which demanded an average speed of 125 km/h (77 mph) throughout.

rugged and basically simple 'Universal' main-line unit which would be capable of hauling a wide range of both passenger and freight trains at speeds up to 112km/h (70mph). A most progressive proposal for the period was that the locomotive should be used in conjunction with a rake of coaches and a control trailer for push-pull work. Turned out in 1933 and powered by an Armstrong-Sulzer 8LD28 8-cylinder vertical engine, the prototype performed well for a year until a crankcase explosion brought about its premature demise.

ence turned out Britain's first diesel-electric 0-6-0 shunter in 1932. Powered by an Armstrong-Sulzer 6LV22 vertical six-cylinder engine of 250hp, it had one frame-mounted traction motor driving the six coupled wheels by means of a jackshaft. It had a single cab at one end, and the engine and equipment was mounted in a long bonnet which had sloped sides to allow adequate forward vision. It underwent prolonged and basically successful trials on the LNER, LMS and SR before being sold to a private company in 1935, and in many ways set the standard for the later LMS/English Electric shunters, derivatives of which remain in use throughout the world today.

Encouraged by the success of their shunter, Armstrong-Whitworth set about designing a

Meanwhile, the Germans had not been idle. In 1932 the Deutsche Reichsbahn unveiled its 'Fliegender Hamburger' (Flying Hamburger), a two-car high-speed articulated 850hp diesel railcar which from May 15, 1933, entered regular service between Berlin and Hamburg, at an average speed of 125km/h (77mph). In Britain the LNER was impressed and considered purchasing German units for its high-speed services, but Chief Mechanical Engineer Gresley persuaded the directors that his new streamlined A4 Pacifics could match their performance on indigenous fuel, and the brief romance with main-line diesel traction in Britain came to an end until after the War.

But in the USA the advantages of diesel traction were being demonstrated quite dramatically; on October 22-25, 1934, a streamlined diesel set covered the 5,227km from Los Angles to New York in 56 hours 55 minutes at an average speed of 91.8km/h (57mph), demonstrating decisively the advantages of diesel power over steam for sustained output on transcontinental services. In the following month the first scheduled streamlined diesels began regular operation, and these 'Zephyrs' proved to be immensely popular. In 1941 the first main-line diesels specifically for freight operation began to appear in the USA, and from then on, although workshops were still busy building 'Liberation' steam locomotives for the Allied war effort, domestic services, both passenger and freight, were increasingly dieselized.

In the immediate post-war years all four British main-line companies realized the need to develop new forms of traction; the LMS, LNER and SR all placed orders for prototype main-line diesel-electric locomotives, while the GWR, always the eccentric, opted for a gas-turbine prototype from Brown-Boveri in Switzerland.

The 'Flying Yankee' (below), an impressive looking diesel used on Maine.

The London, Midland and Scottish Railway in Britain was one of the first to realize the potential of diesel traction, not for passenger work but for prolonged shunting. With traction motors driving locomotive-size wheels through gearing and conventional steam-locomotive-style coupling rods, diesel shunters could move impressive loads and work virtually round the clock, bursting into life at the flick of a switch. This 400 hp 0-6-0 shunter (left) proved to be the prototype for thousands.

Modernization and Rationalization

Ironically, because the railways of Central Europe—with the exception of those of neutral Switzerland—had been so badly damaged during the war, they received much more financial aid and new equipment in the immediate post-war period than those of Britain, whose railways had managed to keep their wheels turning throughout the 'blitz'. In contrast to Britain's railways, which were basically only patched up after the war, with no new schemes started in the immediate post-war period, the European railway systems set about the task of rebuilding with enthusiasm; the SNCF (French National Railways) pressed ahead with electrification, setting up the still-extant world rail speed record of 330.8km/h (205.6mph) on March 28, 1955, with one of their new 1,500V dc electric locomotives, while the Deutsche Bundesbahn (German Federal Railways) embarked on an

ambitious plan to electrify 6,114km (3,800 miles) of track. In the Netherlands steam traction was abolished in the early 1950s, and over half of the 3,218km (2,000 mile) system electrified, while the badly-damaged Italian State Railways planned to complete electrification by 1956.

By the mid-1950s, therefore, Britain's railways, having also suffered from a chronic lack of investment since nationalization, were quite clearly outdated and less well equipped than their French, German, Italian and Dutch neighbours, and in urgent need of refurbishment. In the war-free United States, large-scale dieselization got under way in the 1940s.

In 1955 the British Government announced a massive £1,240 million Modernization Plan to sweep away steam power by 1970, and to provide new electric and diesel motive power,

While Europe was preoccupied with war, the American Railroads pressed ahead with dieselization. The new form of motive power allowed the development of luxury, air-conditioned trains for long-distance travel. An early example is this massive Union Pacific/Chicago North Western 14-car unit 'City of Denver' (above). War and its aftermath brought a reprieve for steam traction right across Europe; it was 1959 before steam gave way to electric traction (top) on the London-Dover leg of the prestigious 'Golden-Arrow' London-Paris Pullman express.

new rolling stock, signalling systems and stations. Sadly, some of the Plan's more ambitious schemes were subsequently dropped as a result of political and financial pressures, but nevertheless the transformation over the following few years was considerable; in little more than a decade all 18,000 steam locomotives, some of them less than five years old, were replaced by about 4,500 diesel locomotives, 5,000 diesel-railcar vehicles, 300 electric locomotives and over 800 electric multiple units.

Lines proposed for electrification included the remaining steam-worked Southern Region lines in Kent, the main line from London (Waterloo) to Southampton and Bournemouth, most of the Eastern Region suburban lines in Essex, the main line from London (Euston) to Crewe, Manchester and Liverpool, the Glasgow suburban lines and the main line from London (King's Cross) to Doncaster, Leeds and York. All but the last, which was dieselized instead, have been carried out, although the King's Cross suburban lines have recently been electrified.

All remaining lines were to be worked by diesel locomotives or railcars. The Plan also called for the adoption of continuous brakes on all freight wagons—an area in which British practice had been curiously backward compared to North America and mainland Europe—but proposed the continuance of the British vacuum brake system rather than the air brake used elsewhere. The enormity of the task was such that it was never completed, and British Rail have now rather belatedly adopted the air brake as standard for freight stock, although there are still vacuum-braked

and unbraked freight vehicles in use.

Even as the Modernization Plan schemes came to fruition in the early 1960s, it became obvious that the switch of passenger and freight traffic to road, and particularly the rise in popularity of the private car, experienced in the United States in the 1950s, was beginning to affect the railways of Europe. In 1963 British Rail announced a Reshaping Plan, designed to cut losses by axing unremunerative services, and over the next decade the railway system in Britain, once the most complex in the world, was reduced to 17,700km (11,000 miles) in length, mostly by the abandonment of rural branch lines and routes which duplicated the remaining services. In some cases, the pruning proved to be too severe; in recent years several suburban lines have been re-opened and electrified, while in Scotland the boom in North Sea oil traffic has necessitated relaying some lines.

The need to rationalize services and equipment in the face of road and air competition has forced the railway systems of all the major European countries to review their services, and the German, French and Swiss authorities have all announced plans to reduce railway mileage. In North America and Canada several railroads have been entirely abandoned, some as a result of bankruptcy, while others have become freight-only lines, allowing the sale of station buildings and the adoption of lower maintenance standards. Most remaining long-distance passenger services in the United States are operated by Amtrak, the Government-backed authority which pays the various railroad companies for operating rights over their tracks.

The Decline of Steam

In the 1950s the railways of western Europe and North America were engaged on modernization programmes which would eventually replace steam with diesel or electric traction. The development of the steam locomotive in the USA had reached its peak with streamlined express passenger locomotives and giant, articulated freight locomotives like the Union Pacific 'Big Boys' in the late 1930s and early 1940s. After the war, diesel locomotives were built in large numbers and quickly took over long-distance passenger train working. Over four-fifths of all traffic was handled by just over 24,000 diesel locomotive units in 1954 and within a few years the remaining 12,000 steam locomotives all but disappeared from the main railroads. A similar process took place in Canada, but with only some 4,500 steam locomotives between them the Canadian National and Canadian Pacific Railways completed the change-over almost entirely during the 1950s.

Most European railways were by this time changing over to more modern forms of traction, or preparing to do so. Some, including the French and Dutch, looked to electrification for some or all of their main lines, while others introduced diesels. Britain started a little later than most and was even building steam locomotives up to 1960. But in 1957-58 main-line diesel locomotives began to join diesel and electric multiple unit trains in displacing the steam engine. By the early

By the early 1960s, steam locomotives all over Europe were disappearing fast, to be replaced by gleaming new diesels. For a time, the old and the new had to work side by side from the same depots, as in this view (below) of a new English Electric diesel at Devon's Road depot, London, flanked by two steam engines dating from 1924. Railway managements tried to hasten such scenes as the last steam-hauled train (bottom) of the Belgian Railways getting a suitable send off in 1966.

1960s it was becoming clear that British Railways would not only catch up but eliminate steam in what many people considered to be almost indecent haste.

On British Railways as late as 1962 there were many complete classes of steam locomotive, some of them 40 or more years old, still going strong. The next six years, though, saw the total withdrawal of steam engines, and two phenomena of the 'sixties—large-scale breaking up of locomotives by outside contractors, and the growth of the 'preservation era'. The first was caused by the inability of railway workshops to deal with the large number of withdrawn locomotives, steady streams of which were towed to breakers' yards in the Midlands, North East, Glasgow and South

Wales areas. The last area contains the best-known of the yards, that of Woodhams at Barry. Almost one-third of the 260 locomotives received there have since been sold for preservation and many of them are once more in working order. Ironically, the rapid withdrawal of steam locomotives and the simultaneous closure of many branch lines stimulated the growth of the preserved railways. As far as they were concerned, the availability of small tank engines and other types of locomotive in reasonable condition was very welcome!

On the main lines it was interesting to see how the famous express locomotive classes fared as new motive power entered the scene. Whereas the ex-GWR 'King' Class 4-6-0s were withdrawn straight from front-line service in 1962, coinciding with the introduction of 'Western' Class diesels, the ex-LMS 'Coronation' Pacifics often appeared on menial duties until they became extinct in 1964. Some of the streamlined A4s displaced from East Coast expresses in 1962-63 were transferred to the Glasgow-Aberdeen run where they

The three powerful French Railways 141 R Class 2-8-2 locomotives belching smoke defiantly (above) at Boulogne shed in October 1965 were among the last to work on the SNCF, while the Gresley A4 class streamlined Pacific "Kingfisher" (below), banished to Scotland when the Deltic diesels took over the London-Edinburgh route, eventually went the way of the Great Western Railway 4-4-0 (left) being cut up at Swindon works.

had apparently been leading the way in modernizing and improving their services? As many British railway enthusiasts discovered, steam engines were still to be found as close to hand as northern France and Germany. The remaining French steam locomotives, of which the Class 141 R 2-8-2 was the dominant type, were withdrawn during the early 1970s. Steam ended on the SNCF with the withdrawal of four 2-8-0s in September 1975. In West Germany, however, steam lingered on for a while, but by the late summer of 1976 the remaining locomotives, all 2-10-0s, were concentrated in a small area. The last steam workings, between Rheine and Emden, ceased in 1977.

enjoyed three more years of express passenger working. Finally, the 'Merchant Navy' Pacifics put up some of their best performances in the hands of keen crews in their final years before the Waterloo-Bournemouth line was electrified in July 1967.

The various regions of British Railways eliminated steam working individually, the first being the Western Region in March 1966 when the exclusively steam-worked Somerset and Dorset line was closed. The end came on August 4, 1968, when all the remaining steam engines in the Manchester area of the London Midland Region were withdrawn. All, that is, except four locomotives (three of which are now preserved) which took part in the official last steam special from Liverpool to Carlisle and back on Sunday August 11. On that day the era of the steam locomotive on Britain's main-line railways closed. It was a sobering thought that no less than 17,000 steam locomotives had been withdrawn from service in the previous decade, some of them only a few years old and far from life-expired.

But what of those European railways which

Diesels Today

With the exception of the People's Republic of China, where new steam engines are still being built, almost all the major railway systems of the world are converting to diesel or electric traction—or, more commonly, a combination of both. For despite the many electrification schemes of recent years, the greater part of the world's railway mileage remains unelectrified and dominated by the diesel, despite its high maintenance costs and increasingly expensive fuel.

The wholesale conversion of the American railroads to diesel power in the 1940s did not have an immediate effect elsewhere; indeed, both in Britain and on mainland Europe, the early 1950s proved to be an 'Indian Summer' for steam, while the private contractors continued to have full order books for new steam engines for Commonwealth and African railways.

But the increasing cost of coal and labour in the later 1950s, and the then deceptively cheap price of oil, accelerated the switch to diesel power; in Britain the 1955 Modernization Plan

diesels of 1947 with the 3,300hp of the powerful English Electric 'Deltic' Co-Cos introduced in 1961—power output was more than doubled in under 15 years. Like the original LMS diesel 'twins' Nos. 10000/1, the 22 English Electric 'Deltics' were specifically built for high-speed passenger work, and they have rapid powers of acceleration and a maximum speed of 160km/h (100mph) for use on the London-Edinburgh East Coast main line. Power is supplied by two 18-cylinder Napier 'Deltic' 1,650hp engines.

The other locomotives on British Rail with 160km/h (100mph) capability are the 50 single-engined 2,700hp English Electric Class 50 locomotives, although almost all of the BR main-line locomotive fleet is passed for 144km/h (90mph) running.

The most powerful diesel locomotive to run on British tracks was the Hawker-Siddeley 4,000hp Co-Co prototype 'Kestrel', introduced in 1968. Powered by a single Sulzer 16LDA engine, it was the first locomotive in Europe to have such a powerful single engine,

Despite extensive electrification in recent years, all the major European railway systems still rely heavily on diesel traction. This is a French Railways Bo-Bo diesel No. 67001 (far left). The English Electric Deltic prototype (left) was specifically developed for high speed work on the British Rail East Coast route from London to Yorkshire, Tyneside and Edinburgh. Derived from marine engine practice, the powerful and successful twin Napier Deltic engines develop 3,300 hp.

brought a spate of new diesel locomotives and bus-engined diesel multiple-unit types, while in both France and Germany diesel locomotives and multiple-units were becoming steadily more numerous.

In Britain many of the early 'pilot' scheme diesels were less than successful, and although in general only the more successful types were carried into series production, it was another decade before British Rail had sufficient reliable locomotives to be able to withdraw the more errant varieties. With experience came reliability and the ability to build larger, more powerful plants into the confined space of the engine room and yet keep within acceptable axle loadings. Some idea of the progress achieved can be gained by comparing the 1,600hp of the first LMS Co-Co

but although it proved successful in traffic, performing happily on both passenger and freight duties, its all-up weight of 126 tonnes incurred a heavy route restriction, and in 1971 it was re-gauged and sold for further use on Russian railways.

The most powerful units in use today are the American General Motors '50' Do-Do locomotives, which have a huge single engine of 6,600hp, but only a $23\frac{1}{4}$ tonne axle-load, thanks to the use of eight powered axles. General Motors have applied the same principle to their Metre and 1,067mm gauge Do-Do which can develop an impressive 3,600hp.

In Europe, the Danish State Railways have a fleet of Nohab-built 3,300hp Co-Cos with General Motors two-stroke engines, whilst the French have 45 4,000hp diesels in traffic. In

1972 Rheinstahl Transport Technik of West Germany built some massive 5,400hp locomotives with two MAN 2,700hp engines for the People's Republic of China; used singly, these engines were first tried in the German Federal Railways Class 150 diesel-hydraulics.

In recent years diesel-electric transmission has been preferred to diesel-hydraulic, but the Western Region of British Railways for a long time preferred the latter, building over 70 'Warship' Class B-B locomotives, a similar number of larger (and more handsome) 'Western' Class C-C units, and over 100 of the smaller Beyer-Peacock 'Hymek' B-B locomotives. British Rail subsequently decided to standardize on electric transmission, and all the diesel-hydraulics are now withdrawn.

Another British innovation, in 1963, was the English Electric-built electro-diesel. This was not really a diesel locomotive at all, but a 1,600hp 750V dc electric locomotive fitted with a 600hp auxiliary diesel engine to power the traction motors when the locomotive was working over unelectrified siding or branch lines. What was really novel about the electro-diesel was that, using its multiple-unit control gear, it could also propel multiple-unit stock push-pull fashion. Developments in rolling stock design in recent years have relaxed previously-conservative thinking about propelling long rakes of trailer coaches from the rear with merely a driving trailer at the front, and the practice is now to be found in Britain, Holland, Belgium and Germany. A further development, used by BR on its Edinburgh-Glasgow shuttle, and by the Netherlands and Belgian Railways on the Amsterdam-Brussels run, is the use of two locomotives, for higher speed, positioned one each end of a rake of locomotive-hauled stock. And indeed both the British diesel-electric High Speed Train and the German gas-turbine TEE trains, both of which work at 200km/h (125mph), are merely a further development of this principle, with streamlined power cars at the outer ends of variable rakes of rolling stock.

Because of the greater train weights and more ample loading gauge, the giants of the diesel world are mainly to be found in the United States. On the US railroads, at least, the Do-Do is far from extinct, like this massive example of the genre (above) from General Motors.

Severe loading gauge restrictions preclude European railways from developing titans akin to those across the Atlantic, and their engineers have had to resort to other means. One of the most ingenious and versatile locomotives is the 'electro-diesel' (left), a cross between an electric locomotive and a diesel developed by British Rail.

How a Diesel Locomotive Works

The engine of a diesel locomotive is classified as an internal combustion engine, like that of a motorcar. Power at the crankshaft is produced by the explosion of a fuel/air mixture in the cylinders. A fundamental difference from the petrol engine, however, is that the explosions are not triggered by sparking plugs but by heat generated by very high compression.

Just before the start of each power stroke of the engine, fuel is pumped into the cylinders in a very fine spray and mixes with air which has been drawn in on the previous stroke. The air is compressed by the rising piston and reaches a temperature of some 980°C. When the fuel is injected the mixture ignites and the sudden expansion of the hot gases forces the piston down on its next stroke.

Air is not simply sucked into the cylinders by the descending pistons, but is forced in by a high-speed fan, or turbocharger. The charging process raises the air temperature, making it less dense, so that some of the benefit of turbocharging is lost. Between the turbocharger and the cylinders, therefore, the air often passes through an intercooler, where the extra heat is given up to water.

The amount of fuel delivered by the fuel pumps can be regulated to control the engine speed and power, but the speed of the engine is not directly related to the speed of the locomotive. It must often run fast to provide the necessary power while the train is running slowly because of the load and gradient. Something equivalent to the motorcar gearbox is required between the engine and the wheels. A fluid flywheel and mechanical gearbox are used in low-power shunting locomotives but above about 224 kW (300hp) the transmission has to be electric or hydraulic.

In a diesel-electric locomotive the mechanical power of the engine is converted into electric power by means of a generator coupled to its crankshaft. Current is conveyed by cables to electric motors geared to the axles, where reconversion to mechanical power for moving the locomotive and its train takes place.

The power developed by an electric motor

1 Driver's seat
2 Assistant Driver's Seat
3 Driver's control desk
4 Main, auxiliary and train heating generator
5 Sulzer diesel engine
6 Engine air inlet filter box
7 Turbocharger
8 Charge air intercoolers
9 Silencer and exhaust outlet
10 Lubricating oil heat exchanger
11 Lubricating oil filter
12 Radiator fans
13 Electric motors for fan drive
14 Roof mounted radiators
15 Air filter panels
16 Translucent fibreglass hinged roof doors
17 Train heating boiler
18 Boiler flue outlet
19 Fire extinguisher CO_2 bottles
20 Traction motors
21 Resilient gearwheel
22 Three-axle cast steel bogies
23 Air brake cylinders
24 Handbrake
25 Horns
26 Walkways
27 Radiator header tank
28 Radiator drain tank
29 Main fuel tank
30 Boiler water tanks
31 Engine fuel oil feed tank
32 Batteries

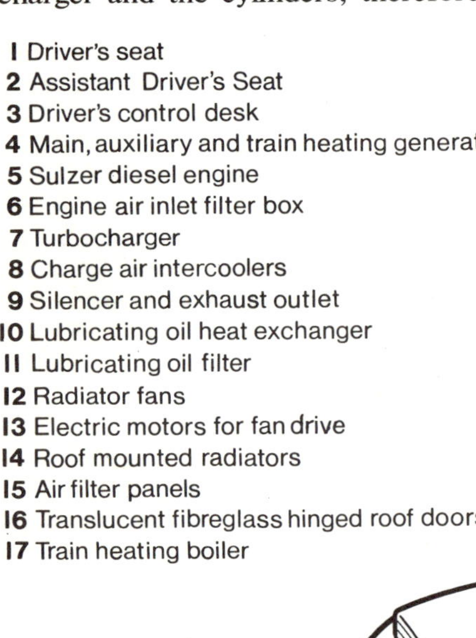

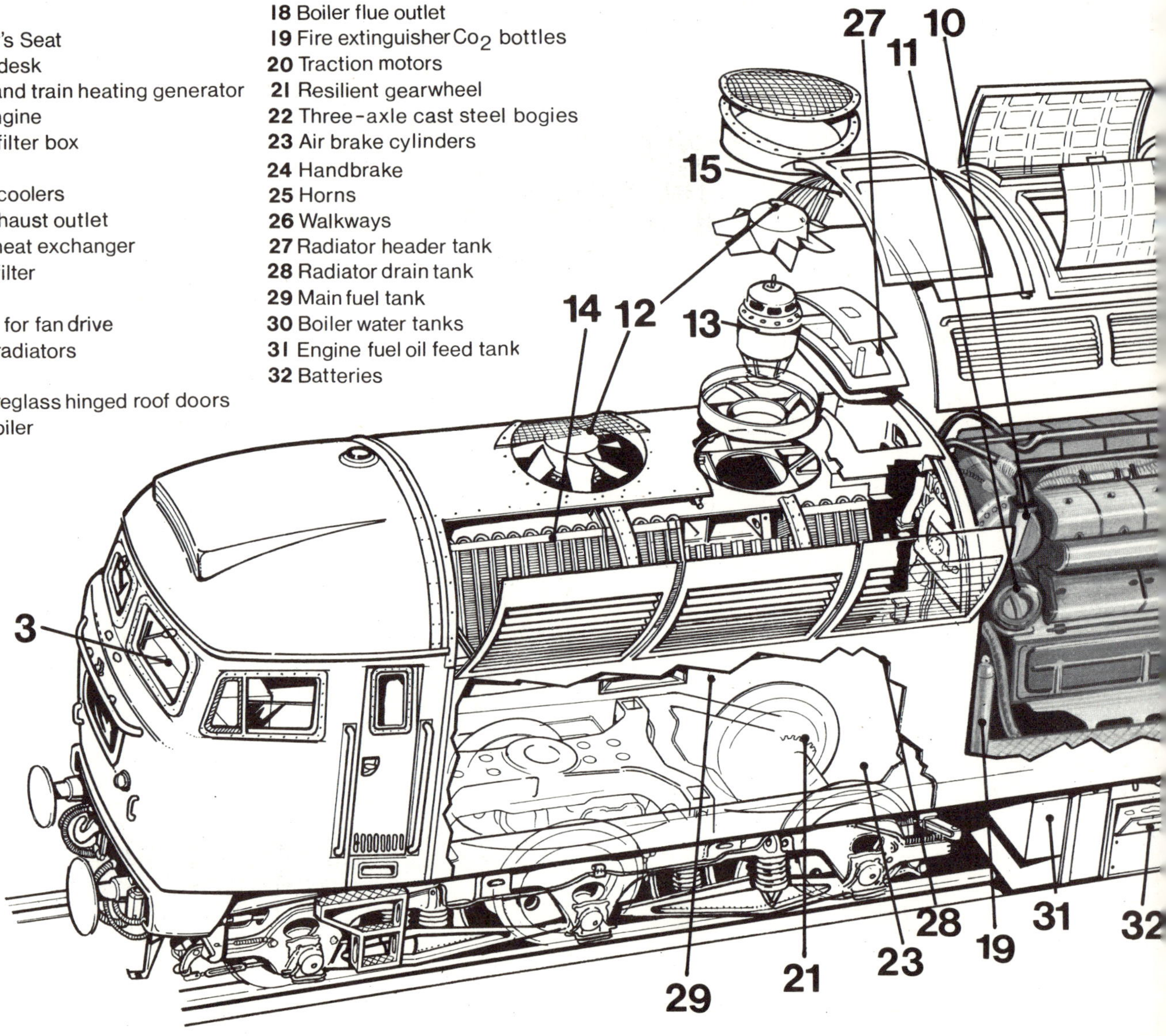

is the product of voltage and current. At starting the current is high and the voltage is kept low. As speed rises the current falls, and so to continue developing the same power the voltage must be raised to overcome the opposing voltage developed by the motors at their higher speed. For efficient use of engine horsepower at any train speed, the control equipment of a diesel-electric locomotive automatically juggles with the generator output to provide the relationship of volts and amperes (current) appropriate to the needs of the moment. If these adjustments were not made some of the power produced by the engine would be wasted, or the engine would be overloaded and possibly stall.

The alternative to electric transmission is an hydraulic system. Here the engine drives a bladed wheel, or impeller, which circulates oil inside a casing. Also in the casing is a turbine wheel on an output shaft, which is coupled to the locomotive axles. As the oil circulates it strikes the turbine blades and the output shaft revolves.

The method by which the power from the engine running at a speed fixed by the setting of the driver's controller allows the train to run at a speed which absorbs all the power available can be followed by considering a single 'droplet' of oil. Receiving energy from the impeller, it gives energy up to the turbine, but before its circuit of the system is complete it strikes against fixed blades attached to the inside of the casing. Gaining further energy from the impact, it again imparts energy to the turbine. This effect is maximum when the impeller is running fast and the turbine is stationary, and provides the high turning effort, or torque, needed to get the train moving. As the train accelerates and the difference between input and output speeds narrows, the torque falls away. The whole arrangement is called a torque converter.

The maximum power that can be handled by hydraulic transmission is about 1,490kW (2,000hp). Many main-line diesel-hydraulic locomotives therefore have two diesel engines each driving the axles of one bogie through its own transmission. The hydraulic system has been highly developed in Germany, but the trend worldwide is now towards diesel-electric traction because latest developments enable some 4,470kW (6,000hp) to be generated with one engine.

This exploded diagram of a British Rail Class 47 Co-Co diesel-electric locomotive shows the equipment and general arrangement of a typical main line diesel locomotive.

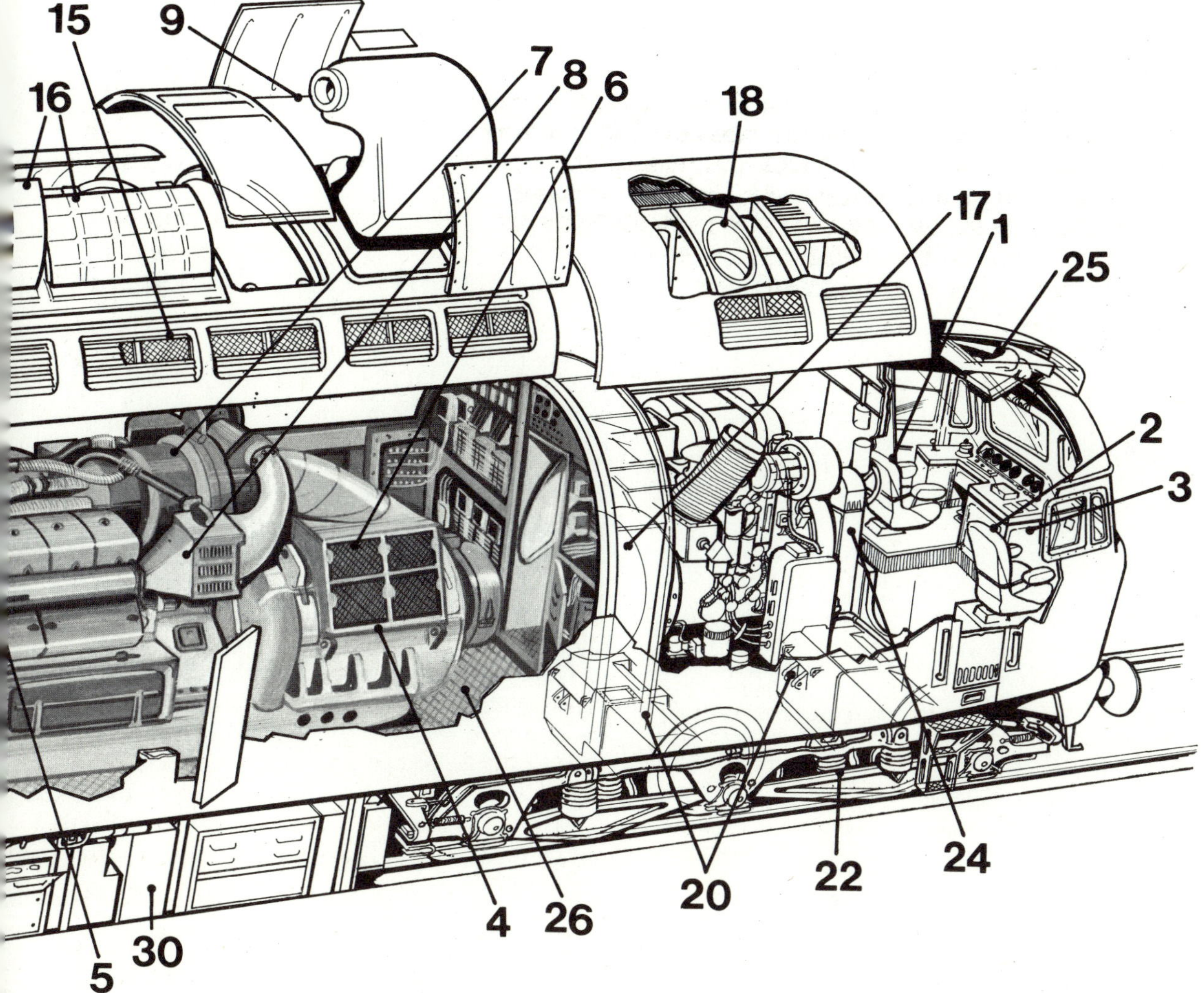

Early Railway Carriages

The first railway pioneers of the 1820s were faced with providing the complete railway, for, apart from primitive track and early experiments with steam traction, railways were new. For passenger coaches in Britain and much of Europe the railway builders took as their example the road coaches of the period. Road coaches usually had a body with a door on each side, and padded seats rather like two benches facing one another, and together seating up to six passengers. The doors usually had a window which could be lowered and sometimes there were additional windows, often in the form of a quarter circle on each side of the doors. There were more seats on the roof so that passengers paying a lower fare travelled outside. A rack on the roof carried luggage, and a boot at the back of the coach would be used for carrying valuable consignments and mail. Apart from the coach driver there was also a guard who was usually armed.

The first railway carriages had most of these features except that train guards did not need

Early railway carriages were derived directly from contemporary road carriage design, creating 'compartment' type coaches still used on some railways today. At first, they were simply wagons with seats and roofs; although short and archaic, this Midland Railway first class coach, built about 1860 (above) was quite well appointed. With just three compartments on a short, four-wheeled wooden frame, it has no brakes and retains the roof luggage rack of its road contemporaries.

to be armed. It was soon realized that railway carriages did not have to be quite so restricted in size and weight as horse-drawn coaches, for steam locomotives could haul much heavier loads. The first railway carriages were thus built with what in effect were three or sometimes four road-coach type bodies, each with their own pairs of facing seats and entry doors, on one four-wheeled underframe, thus originating right from the start the compartment-type carriage which still survives on a few railways today. Luggage was carried in racks on the roof and the guard or brakesman sat in a seat high up at the coach end so that he could see forward over the roofs for lineside signals or hand signals from the engine crew. Passengers were not allowed on the roof

First class passengers could usually be assured of enclosed, glazed accommodation and upholstered seating. Second class passengers could hope for a roof, but third class merely open wagons with bench-type seats. The Great Western Railway broad gauge six-wheeled coach (above) dating from 1840 is of special interest as it is one of the earliest examples of the use of metal panels for the bodywork instead of wood.

because of the danger from bridges.

Only the carriages for the wealthy were well upholstered, with glass windows. These were first-class carriages. Carriages for the less well off were called second class and were usually closed types with wooden bench seats across the compartment. They often had only one opening in the upper part of the door, which might have glass or just be left open. Some railways did not carry the poorest working class or labouring people at all. Other railways provided third-class open coaches without roofs and often without seats, and with holes in the floor to let out rainwater. By 1844 the British Parliament had stepped in with an Act making all railways treat third-class passengers better, with covered carriages run on

trains which had to keep up average speeds of at least 19km/h (12mph) and with fares at not more than 1d a mile.

In Europe most of the early railways also used compartment-type coaches at first although some introduced coaches with open balconies at the ends, leading through doors at each end of the body into a long passenger saloon with pairs of seats on each side of a central passageway running right through the coach. Sometimes the seats were of plain wood but some were padded with upholstery.

The saloon passenger car with open-end balconies was used almost from the start in America. Distances were much greater than in Britain and much of Europe, and primitive toilet facilities were provided in the early American passenger cars. The saloon interiors and open balconies allowed free access through the train. These early American cars were also notable for having pivoted trucks carrying the wheels at each end of the under-frame. These trucks, or bogies, usually having four wheels, could turn or rise and fall slightly to cope easily with uneven track. The four- and six-wheel rigid wheelbase coaches used

In the early days, the purchase of a first class rail ticket not only bought better accommodation, but often a faster journey, for on most railways—as, indeed, on some lines still today—the fastest trains were first class only. Second class trains would be slower, while third class trains often positively dawdled while wagons were shunted and loaded. These interesting prints, published in 1834, four years after the Liverpool and Manchester Railway had opened, show (top) a L & M first class train with covered, enclosed coaches, the mail coach, and a flat wagon carrying private road coach, and (above) a second class train on the same railway with covered but open-sided coaches, which were pleasant enough in summer, but decidedly draughty in winter!

universally in Britain, and to a large extent in Europe, during the 1850s and 1860s were very hard and stiff and needed good track if they were not to derail.

The Great Western Railway in England at first adopted a track gauge much wider than the rest of the country or anywhere else in the world. With a distance between the rails of one track at 2.13m (7ft) its coaches were wider than those of other railways, without being unstable. In the 1830s and 1840s most railway carriages in Britain were between 1.8m and 2.13m (6ft and 7ft) wide but Great Western broad-gauge coaches were 2.7m (9ft) wide at first, and by the 1860s were 3.2m (10ft 6in) wide, giving far more room inside. Some compartments were divided into two halves.

In these early days carriages did not have heating in winter, and lighting was by oil lamps inserted through holes in the roof covered by hinged lids. Often the lamps, even in first-class coaches, were placed on top of the partitions to light two compartments. In coaches without internal partitions, or in open saloon cars, one or possibly two lamps provided the only light for the whole car.

Travel in the open third class coaches could be quite trying, particularly in inclement weather, or when the line passed through lengthy tunnels, and by the 1850s many railways were beginning to provide enclosed accommodation, albeit of a somewhat austere nature; this GWR broad gauge third class carriage, built for the Culm Valley line, is particularly short, but shows the small windows and the solitary centrally-mounted roof oil lamp to light all three compartments.

Corridor Coaches

The end balcony saloon passenger cars common in America automatically provided access within the car and through the train. With the compartment type of coach with side doors it was not possible to pass from one coach to another except at stations. There were not even toilets on British trains for general use until the 1880s, although Queen Victoria's saloons and certain private saloon coaches available for hire by the wealthy had such refinements by 1860. The first train toilets in ordinary coaches in Britain were placed in small compartments between the normal passenger compartments with the facilities only available to the half-dozen or so passengers next door.

To extend toilet facilities to all passengers in a coach the Great Northern Railway, whose train services ran from London through Peterborough northwards to Leeds and York, brought into service in the early 1880s some six-wheel first-class coaches with a side corridor linking the four compartments to toilets at each end of the coach. There was no means of passing from one coach to the next. In Switzerland at around the same time some coaches were given open-side balconies to link the compartments, which, while giving spectacular views of the mountain scenery, must have been unpleasant with rain or driving snow sweeping across the balcony.

and the East Coast route from King's Cross introduced new corridor trains with dining cars, and for the first time passengers of all classes could walk through the train from one coach to the next. These Anglo-Scottish trains had the flexible gangways between the coaches in the centre of the ends of the coaches, a much more sensible arrangement than the Great Western's side gangways which could not be coupled if a coach was turned. The GW soon adopted centrally-placed gangways. These pioneer corridor trains were not the first in Britain where passengers could walk through from coach to coach, for this had been possible in Pullman cars a few years before, as we shall see, but they were the first of what became the standard main-line corridor trains.

By 1900 other new features had been introduced to improve passenger comfort, including steam heating from the locomotive which warmed radiators under coach seats, and electric lighting which was replacing gas, itself having replaced oil lights from the 1870s. The new corridor coaches were also generally larger than the older non-corridor coaches they replaced, being built to the maximum allowed by the British loading gauge of around 18.29m (60ft) length and 2.7m (9ft) wide over the body. The Great Western went one better,

By the ealy 1900s, most main line coaches in Europe were mounted on bogies, with side corridors serving individual compartments and, usually, with flexible gangway connections to adjacent vehicles. This South Eastern and Chatham Railway corridor brake composite coach is typical of the period, although the raised 'birdcage' roof lookout for the guard is an unusual feature.

During the 1880s, as we shall see later, refreshments and meals were introduced to one or two British trains for first-class passengers but they had to join and leave the dining car at intermediate stations. In 1892 the Great Western (GW) took up the side corridor introduced by the Great Northern Railway 10 years before, but extended it to provide covered side gangways between coaches. The first GW corridor trains did not have a meal service and the corridors were for the use of the guard only. A year later the railways operating the West Coast route to Scotland from Euston

for with generous clearances left by the broad gauge, finally abolished in 1892 when remaining 2.13m (7ft) lines were converted to the standard 1.44m (4ft 8½in) gauge, it built some fine new corridor coaches in 1905 no less than 21.3m (70ft) long and 2.9m (9ft 6in) wide. These coaches were unusual in having a staggered corridor changing sides half-way. Moreover, they had end and centre doors and access to compartments was only by the corridor, a new feature for side-corridor coaches. They also had high elliptical roofs built to the maximum height allowed to pass under bridges. Before this many coaches still

had low roofs, a relic from the days when guards had to see over the train to the engine. By 1900 most railways gave their guards enclosed side lookouts from the guard's van, but a few still had a roof-mounted covered lookout.

For some years before and after 1900 some railways used a special form of roof known as the clerestory, which was raised in the centre and with small windows along the side of the raised section between the lower and upper parts of the roof. Sometimes the raised centre section swept down to meet the coach ends. This type of roof was extensively used in America and Southern Africa until the 1930s and in certain countries in Africa is still fairly common.

In Europe, coach developments occurred about the same time as they did in Great Britain. Flexible gangway connections between coaches appeared in France by 1889, and by 1900 corridor coaches had begun to appear on longer distance and international trains. In America certainly there were inter-coach gangways, but most cars for day use had central passageways with seats on each side rather than side corridors with compartments.

Such was the pace of development in railways by 1900 that carriage design soon became dated. But no other railway had to face the daunting task confronting the Great Western Railway in Britain when it finally abandoned the broad gauge in 1892. This was the incredible scene after the last broad gauge trains had run, with well over 200 redundant coaches awaiting their fate at Swindon works.

The Pullman Story

Although by the end of the 1850s it was not yet possible to travel right across America by train, many journeys needed overnight travel. Although a few cars had been adapted for night-time sleeping, an American cabinet-maker, George Pullman, thought that better accommodation was necessary. He built sleeping cars with fold-up berths hinged above the windows which could be closed up against the roof by day and lowered to form an upper berth by night. The lower berth was formed by pairs of daytime seats drawn forward to meet each other. Curtains gave privacy from the central passageway. Pullman also introduced better heating, lighting and ventilation and much improved standards of accommodation, but in return passengers had to pay an extra fare to Pullman. Pullman cars gradually spread to many American railways, owned and operated by the Pullman company but hauled by locomotives of the railway concerned. Sometimes the Pullmans ran in ones or twos, and sometimes as complete trains. Pullman also introduced a dining car in 1868

At first, Pullman cars were run as individual luxury coaches in otherwise normal service trains, but during the first decade of the present century complete all-Pullman trains began to appear on some British railways. This all-Pullman express (below) on the London, Brighton and South Coast Railway was the forerunner of the famous 'Brighton Belle', London-Brighton non-stop Pullman, worked electrically from 1933 and only finally withdrawn in 1972.

cars were slightly smaller. In fact they were built in America and shipped to Britain to be re-erected like a kit. They had massive clerestory roofs, domed at the ends, end balcony entrances, toilets and hot-waterpipe heating from a boiler at one end of the car, looked after by the attendant. Lighting was from paraffin lamps. Even though cars were provided on the Midland for all three classes and were far better than the small six-wheel non-corridor compartment coaches without heating or toilets, the British travelling public did not like them. Possibly it was the long open interiors where all passengers could see and hear all the others, or possibly because of the supplementary fare. As in America it was a Pullman car which provided the first dining car on a British train when in 1879 an American-built car was introduced between King's Cross and Leeds.

During the late 1870s Pullman cars first appeared on the London-Brighton line, eventually becoming sufficiently popular to warrant an all-Pullman train. It included a car

and parlour cars for daytime travel. Soon, the name Pullman became synonymous with luxury train travel.

In 1874 the general manager of the Midland Railway in England was so impressed with Pullman travel that he introduced Pullman cars to Britain, at first in complete trains of parlour cars and sleepers arranged for daytime travel, and later singly with the sleepers used on the overnight trains between London St Pancras and Scotland. The day cars introduced new standards of travel to Britain. The cars were long, carried on bogies just like those used in America, although the British

supplying light refreshments. One of the Brighton-line cars in 1881 was notable for being lit by electricity, while a new Pullman train, built for the Brighton service in 1888, was lit throughout by electricity. It also had enclosed vestibules at the car ends instead of open balconies and flexible enclosed gangways between cars, the first, other than on one or two special saloons, in Britain.

Gradually Pullman cars in Britain were used only for daytime journeys as the railway companies themselves took over or introduced their own sleeping cars. By the first years of the present century Pullmans were

largely confined to the short routes between London and Brighton and Bournemouth, but gradually they were extended to a few other services, even to what today are London underground services.

During the 1920s and 1930s Pullmans were mainly found either on the routes of the Southern Railway, where many of the trains were named, often including 'Belle' in the title, or on the LNER, which ran Pullman trains from King's Cross. Most famous of the Southern all-Pullman services was still that to Brighton which became an all-electric train in 1933 called the 'Brighton Belle', and lasted until 1972. Pullman cars at this period were noted for personal service to passengers, with meals and refreshments at their seats and attendants to help at all times.

During this period also daytime Pullmans spread to Europe, where they operated in conjunction with the International Sleeping Car Company. They were even found in such places as Egypt and on narrow-gauge lines in Switzerland.

By the 1960s gradual improvements in travel comfort by ordinary trains began to make Pullmans unnecessary. Pullman-style travel is now obsolete.

The American influence on this 1876 Pullman 'Drawing Room Car' (above) for the Midland Railway is almost complete; the open layout, deep clerestory roof, style of windows, ornate panelling and open end verandahs were all typical of contemporary American practice. Over the years, British Pullmans became more European, but retained their distinctive open layout, large, deep windows in flat sides and inward-opening doors.

Unusual Coaches

From the early days of railways eccentric engineers had tried to devise ways of attaching or detaching coaches from non-stopping trains at intermediate stations. They never succeeded in attaching coaches, but from the end of the 1850s slip coaches, uncoupled from a train at speed, were used on several lines to serve stations while the main train carried on without stopping. At that time it needed nothing more than the coupling link to be lifted off the hook of the last coach of the main train by the guard on the slip coach pulling a rope, after which he applied the handbrake to bring the coach gradually to a stop at the station. Sometimes the slip coach was

'Slipping'—detaching coaches for intermediate stations from a non-stop train whilst it was on the move—was a mainly British practice, although some other railways of the world used slip coaches on an experimental basis. Each slip portion, which of course could not be connected by gangways to the remainder of the train, had to have a special slip coach at its head equipped with slip couplings and brake hoses (left) so as to detach the coaches without applying the continuous brake on the main train. Each portion had its own guard who, having released the coupling, controlled the brake on the slipped portion as it fell away from the main train (above) and brought it to a stand at the appropriate station.

diverted on to another track so that the signalman had to be quick in changing points after the main part of the express had passed before the slip coach approached. Sometimes the slip coach stopped by accident, or by instruction, outside the station and had to be hauled in by horse or a shunting engine. It was only possible for passengers to arrive at a station this way. To pick up passengers, express trains had to call at the station. Slip coaches were only used where a large number of passengers wanted to get off at a particular station. Sometimes the slip coach went on to call at other stations or on to a branch line.

When automatic vacuum or compressed-air brakes became standardized after 1889 a special hose coupling was used on the brake pipes for slip coaches, so that the brakes would not be applied on the main train, which they would do if the train became uncoupled accidentally. The Great Western Railway (GWR) was the largest user of slip coaches in Britain although several other railways had them. Most famous of GWR expresses to have slip coaches was the Cornish Riviera Express which in the 1920s and 1930s often had as many as four slip sections, some with more than one coach, while the front part of the train ran on non-stop from London to Plymouth.

With the onset of diesel locomotives from the late 1950s, the time difference in stopping a complete train instead of running through a station was so small that slip coaches hardly saved any time and were an operating nuisance. The last one ran in September 1960. Special coaches were needed for slip working, with a guard's compartment fitted with the slip coupling and brake controls. Slip coaches were not unknown in countries outside Britain but nowhere else enjoyed such general use.

Double-deck coaches are used on some railways in various parts of the world, particu-

larly where the loading gauge is generous. The original road coaches from which railway carriages were developed were double-decked in that passengers sat on the roof, but on most railways passengers were not allowed on the roofs of rail vehicles. Some lines not restricted by bridge heights tried out properly built double-deck coaches early on though they were confined to local services. At various times in the last 100 years of railways double-deck coaches have come and gone, with claimed advantages and disadvantages. During the last 40 years some European railways have tried double-deck suburban coaches with the lower deck slung low between the bogies. Entrance doors have usually been placed in two groups, and a major problem is the jam of passengers trying to get on and off, which lengthens station stops and delays trains. Additional doors would reduce seating capacity so that a conventional single-deck train would carry as many passengers. Some suburban railways in North America and Australia have also used double-deckers but with mixed results. Indeed as one US railroad was abandoning with glee its last double-deckers in the early 1960s another line was welcoming its new two-level cars! Even in Britain, with its more restricted loading gauge, the Southern Region tried a 1½-deck train with alternate high- and low-level compartments interlaced between each other. Again delays at stations stopped further development.

One type of coach, using the two-deck principle, which has been more successful is the dome lounge-observation car, used in a few countries on long-distance express trains which run through areas of outstanding scenic beauty. The upper deck is usually laid out with arm-chairs, and windows which in some cars go right over the top to form the roof. Passengers have a clear view all round and usually forward as well, for the observation roof is

often a little higher than the ordinary coaches. The lower floor is sometimes devoted to a bar or perhaps other train services such as a secretary's office. In recent years dome observation cars have been used on certain trains through the Rocky Mountains in Canada and along the Rhine valley down to Switzerland, while both in France and Germany single-deck railcars, with all-over glass roof, are used for excursions to give the same type of view.

Observation cars have been used on a few express trains since the last century, particularly in North America and Britain. Open-end balcony cars had a natural end observation platform when marshalled at the back of a train, but when vestibules were enclosed specially-built observation cars with windows all round the car end to give good views were provided by some railways. They were not always in regular use, and in Britain appeared only on certain trains for short periods. The LNWR used them on certain trains running in the North Wales mountain areas just before the First World War, the LNER had two on the King's Cross-Edinburgh 'Coronation' trains in 1937-39, and the 'Devon Belle' Pullman trains, which ran between Waterloo and Ilfracombe between 1947 and 1952, had observation lounges. Observation cars from all these services survive today on preserved steam-operated tourist lines in Britain.

Railway Headlines

1825 September 27: Stockton and Darlington Railway opened; first public railway using steam locomotives. About 64km (40 miles) of public railway in use.

1826 First-class passenger coach 'Experiment' introduced on the Stockton and Darlington. Bodywork similar to that of road stage-coach, but with rail wheels.

1827 Fusible plugs, to protect boiler, first used. Hackworth's 'Royal George' locomotive introduced, with vertical cylinders driving directly to wheels, and restricted blast pipe to encourage draught.

1828 Delaware and Hudson Railroad opens in USA using British-built 'Stourbridge Lion' locomotive. First railways in France and Austria. Stephenson's 'Lancashire Witch' with inclined cylinders.

1829 Stephenson's 'Rocket' wins Rainhill Trials for a locomotive design for the Liverpool and Manchester Railway. Success mainly due to use of multiple tube boiler.

1830 May 3: Canterbury and Whitstable Railway opened. September 15: Liverpool and Manchester Railway opened. 'Rocket' travels light for 17.6km (11 miles) at 58km/h (36 mph). Stephenson's 'Planet' establishes conventional form for future locomotives, with horizontal cylinders at front end under smokebox, single cranked driving axle and one-piece boiler/firebox assembly with multiple tubes.

1831 Glasgow and Garnkirk Railway opened. First bogie coaches introduced in USA.

1832 Street tramways in New York. France opens first railway. Piston valves first tried. 'Petticoat' blast pipe introduced.

1833 St Helens and Runcorn Gap Railway opened. First six-wheeled goods engine with wheels of front two axles coupled with 'coupling rods' to gain greater adhesion.

1834 July 4: Bodmin and Wadebridge Railway opened. September 22: Leeds and Selby Railway opened. December 17: Dublin and Kingstown Railway opened. First fixed running signals used to control train movements on Liverpool and Manchester Railway. First railway in Ireland.

1835 First railway in Belgium opened. State-owned from outset. First railway in Germany opened at Nurnberg.

1836 February 8: London and Greenwich Railway opened. April 20: Narrow-gauge Festiniog Railway opened in North Wales. First sleeping cars introduced on Pennsylvania Railroad, USA. First railways in Canada opened.

1837 July 4: Grand Junction Railway opened. July 13: London and Birmingham Railway opened. August 18: Paisley and Renfrew Railway opened. Electric telegraph in use; Morse indroduces single-needle telegraph and Morse Code.

1838 Britain passes Act of Parliament to permit transmission of mails by train. May 21: London and Southampton Railway opened. June 4: First section of broad-gauge Great Western Railway opened between Paddington and Maidenhead. Over 800km (500 miles) of railway open in Britain. First railway opened in Russia.

1839 G. Bradshaw publishes first edition of worldwide 'Bradshaw's Railway Timetables'. May 29: York and North Midland Railway opened. June 1: London and Croydon Railway opened. June 18: Eastern Counties Railway opened. September 16: Midland Counties Railway opened. Davidson's first battery-driven electric vehicle demonstrated at Edinburgh. First railways in Italy and Netherlands opened.

1840 May 11: London and Brighton and North Midland Railways opened. June 4: Birmingham and Gloucester Railway opened. September 23: Chester and Birkenhead Railway opened. 3,842km (2,388 miles) of railway open in Britain, 661km (411 miles) in France, 867km (539 miles) in Germany, 7,297km (4,535 miles) in USA, and 43km (27 miles) in Russia.

1841 January 4: Great North of England Railway opened. June 30: Great Western Railway, built to broad gauge, opened throughout from London (Paddington) to Bristol. June 9: Thomas Cook organizes

1859—Royal Albert Bridge under construction.

first railway excursion. First semaphore arm signal introduced by Gregory on London and Croydon Railway. Sanding gear fitted to locomotives for greater adhesion.

1842 Stephenson link motion valve gear introduced. June 13: Queen Victoria travels by train for first time. Railway Clearing House opened. First railways in Poland. December 1: South Eastern Railway opened.

1843 First interlocked signal lever frame, devised by Gregory, in use at Bricklayers Arms, London.

1844 First railway in Switzerland opened. May 10: Midland Railway formed by amalgamation. Gladstone's Railway Act makes it compulsory to provide passenger accommodation at one penny per mile on at least one train each way every day—the 'Parliamentary' train. Walschaerts radial valve gear introduced.

1845 May 5: Guildford and Woking Railway opened—with wooden rails and 'Prosser's Patent Guide Wheels'! December 23: Manchester and Leeds Railway opened. Royal Commission on Gauges appointed. Dial-type pressure gauges perfected in Germany.

1846 Royal Commission on Gauges recommends adoption of 1.435m (4ft $8\frac{1}{2}$in) gauge as 'future standard'. 'Railway Mania' in Britain; 272 Acts of Parliament passed for new railways. First side tank engine completed. May 30: South Devon Railway opened with 'atmospheric' trains, drawn along by suction from fixed pumping stations. July 16: London and North Western Railway formed by amalgamation. First railways in Hungary and Jugoslavia opened.

1847 High pressure (120lb/sq in) boiler used on 'Jenny Lind' locomotive. First six coupled bogie locomotive completed in USA. First railway in Denmark opened.

1848 Trials with first mechanical continuous brakes. First railways in Spain and Guyana opened.

1849 Bogie tank engines introduced on Great Western Railway.

1850 Over 10,614km (6,600 miles) of railway open in Great Britain. September 26: North London Railway opened. First railway in Mexico opened.

1851 Absolute block system of train working introduced on South Eastern Railway. Steel locomotive tyres perfected by Krupp at Essen. Railways reach Chile and Peru.

1852 Rack system introduced for mountain railways. Great Northern Railway claims main line completely equipped with distant signals, first introduced 1846. Newall's continuous mechanical brake patented.

1853 First railways in India and Pakistan.

1854 First railways opened in Victoria, Australia, Brazil, Egypt and Norway.

1855 Railways come to New South Wales, Australia.

1856 Saxby's first interlocked signalling frame. First railways in Portugal, Sweden and Turkey. Ramsbottom safety valves introduced.

1857 Fire-brick arches used in boilers on Scottish North Eastern Railway. Coal burned instead of coke. Railways opened in Argentina.

1859 G. M. Pullman introduces first 'Pullman' car in USA. Giffard injector patented and applied to locomotives for first time. May 4: Cornwall Railway opened. First railway in Luxembourg.

1860 Ramsbottom patents water scoop for refilling tender from track water troughs at speed. Adopted in America as 'track pans'. First compressed air brake patented. Railways reach South Africa. 14,595km (9,069 miles) of railways opened in United Kingdom, 9,410km (5,847 miles) in France, 11,558km (7,182 miles) in Germany, 49,288km (30,627 miles) in USA, and 1,077km (669 miles) in Russia.

1861 Train introduces first London Street Tramway. First railway in Paraguay.

1862 Belpaire-type fireboxes introduced. Algeria gets first railway. Experiments with steel rails. First trains in Finland. April 12: Great locomotive chase in USA.

1863 January 10: First underground railway, the Metropolitan, opened in London. New Zealand gets first railway.

1864 Continuous compressed air brakes tested on London, Chatham and Dover Railway. Fairlie double-ended, twin-boiler articulated locomotive patented. First railway in Indonesia.

1865 Ceylon gets first railway.

1866 First railways in Bulgaria.

1867 First section of New York elevated (the El) railway built. Originally cable-worked. Pullman Palace Car Company founded in America. Steel rails in general use.

1868 Emergency communication throughout train compulsory in USA. First successful street tram-

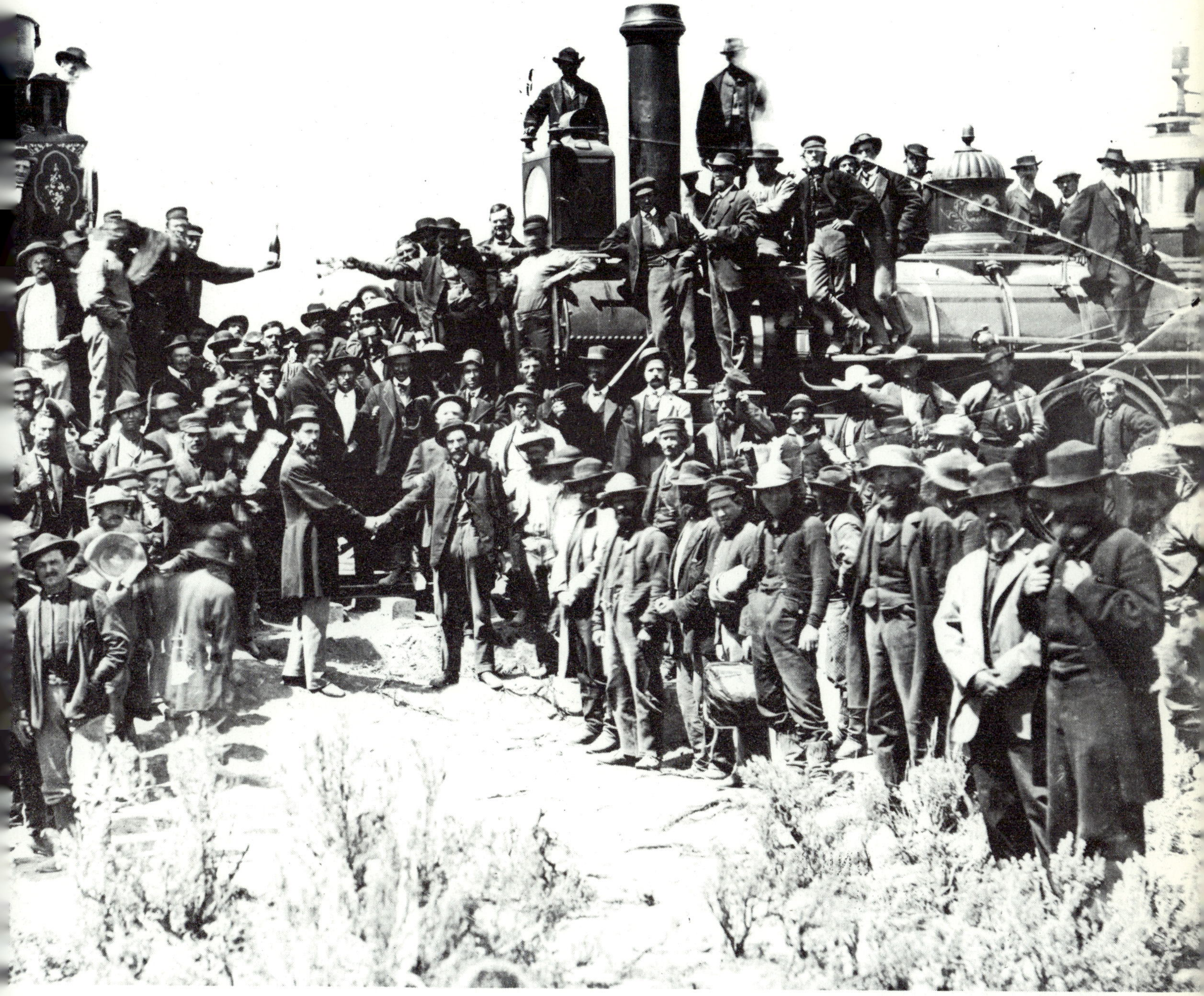

1869—(above) railroads meet to form transcontinental railway in USA.

way in Britain opened in Liverpool.
1869 Board of Trade approves outside continuous communication cord system for British railways. Westinghouse straight air brake patented. Construction of Union Pacific and Central Pacific. Railroads meet near Ogden to form first transcontinental line in USA. Rigi rack railway opened it Switzerland. Greece, Honduras, Romania, Uruguay get first railways.
1870 Stevens patent tappet interlocking for signal frames. Sykes

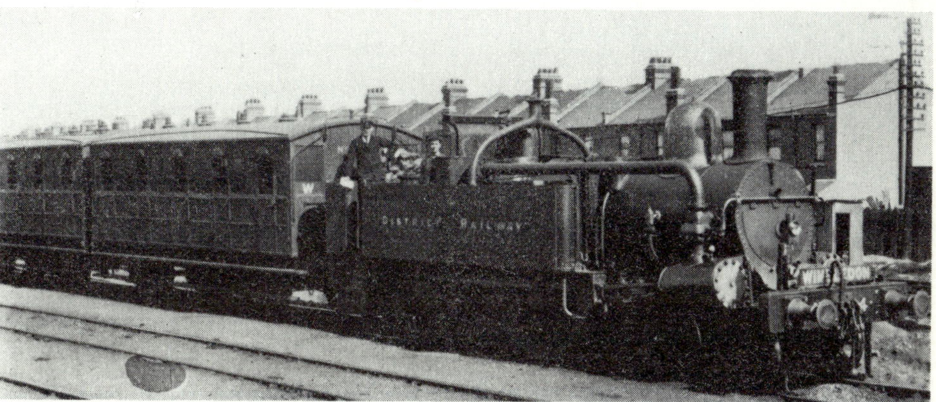

1863—(above) locomotive which operated on the first underground railway.

adds electric interlocking to mechanical frame.

1871 Mont Cenis tunnel opened 13.67km (8.5 miles) long. Railways opened in Ecuador.

1872 Electric track circuits in use in USA. Westinghouse continuous automatic air brake introduced. Japan gets first railway.

1873 First sleeping cars introduced in United Kingdom. Bolivian railways opened.

1874 Pullmans introduced to Britain on Midland Railway. Brighton Railway uses 'speed indicators' on engines. Railways in Colombia.

1875 Sykes lock and block signalling system introduced on London, Chatham and Dover Railway. Comparative brake trials at Newark.

1876 Oil-gas lighting introduced on Metropolitan Underground Railway, London. Trains reach Tunisia.

1877 Railways in Burma, Venezuela opened.

1878 Tyer's electric tablet system for signalling on single-line railways. Gresham introduces automatic vacuum brake.

1879 Von Siemens electric railway demonstrated at Berlin Exhibition. David Joy introduces his radial valve gear. Dining cars introduced in Britain. December 28: Tay Bridge disaster.

1880 First trains in Guatemala, Nicaragua. 25,036km (15,557 miles) of railways open in United Kingdom, 23,599km (14,664 miles) in France, 32,515km (20,205 miles) in Germany, 150,000km (93,272 miles) in USA, and 17,708km (11,003 miles) in Russia.

1882 El Salvador gets first railway.

1883 Corridor coaches introduced on North Eastern Railway. August 3: Magnus Volk's electric railway opens at Brighton. First railway in China.

1884 Inner Circle underground railway completed. Steam heating of carriages introduced. Westinghouse electro-pneumatic signalling.

1885 Railways opened in Malaysia and Vietnam. November 7: Canadian Pacific Railway completed from Atlantic to Pacific.

1886 Severn Tunnel opened. Steam sanding introduced on Midland Railway. Railways in Angola, Mozambique.

1887 Hugh Smellie introduces the 'extended smokebox'.

1888 First railway races in Britain from London to Scotland. Eritrea gets first railway.

1889 Regulation of Railways Act required by law use of absolute block signalling, interlocking of points and signals and continuous automatic brakes on all passenger railways in Britain.

1890 Daimler tries petrol locomotive. First electric tube railway, City and South London, opened. Costa Rica gets first railway.

1891 First electric street tramway opened in Leeds. Great Eastern Railway builds an 0-6-0 goods engine in 10 hours at Stratford. First railway in Israel.

1892 Broad-gauge finally abolished on Great Western Railway. First railways in Philippines.

1893 Liverpool Overhead Railway opened, the first electric elevated railway. Mechanically-worked automatic signals used from outset. First trains in Thailand.

1895 Railway Races from London to Aberdeen between East Coast and West Coast companies; London to Edinburgh covered in 6hr 18min at average speed of 100km/h (62.3 mph). First trains in Lebanon, Syria.

1896 November 29: Volk's 'Daddy longlegs' sea railway opened. Abandoned in 1901.

1897 Sprague introduced multiple-unit control gear on electric trains in USA. First superheating experiments in Germany by Schmidt. First railways in East Africa, Rhodesia.

1898 Conversion of London's Underground railways to electric traction begins. Waterloo and City electric tube line opened. Railways in Zaire.

1899 First electro-pneumatic signalbox in Britain opened on Great Eastern at Granary Junction, Bishopsgate. First railways in Sierra Leone and Korea.

1900 Ethiopia, Somaliland and Sudan get first railways. First railway electrification in France. 29,039km (18,044 miles) of railways open in Great Britain, 36,799km (22,867 miles) in France, 51,958km (32,287 miles) in Germany,

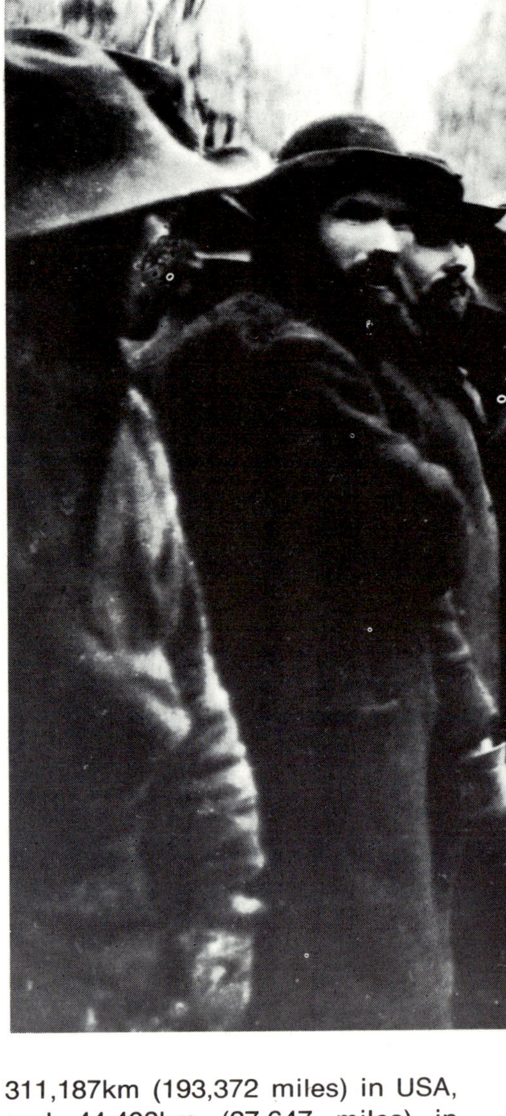

311,187km (193,372 miles) in USA, and 44,492km (27,647 miles) in Russia.

1901 First electric trams in London. Corridor trains for all classes introduced on LNWR. Nigeria and Ghana get railways.

1902 Automatic semaphore signals controlled by track circuits installed between Andover and Grately on LSWR.

1903 Mersey Railway electrified throughout on 650V dc third and fourth rail system, becoming first surface railway to be converted. First multiple-unit electric trains on Central London Tube Railway.

1904 GWR claim record for 'City of Truro' as first locomotive to exceed 160km (100mph). First automatic ticket machines (mechanical) introduced on Central London Railway. Trans-Siberian Railway completed,

1885—(above) last spike of the Canadian Pacific Railway is hammered in.

1899—(above) workers at the northern end of the Simplon tunnel.

and Jordan Railway opens. German railways begin to electrify.

1905 First railway in Zambia opened. Lentz poppet valves introduced in Germany.

1906 Simplon Tunnel, over 19km (12 miles) long, opened. First main-line electrification in Switzerland. GWR introduces prototype mechanical cab-signalling equipment, forerunner of Automatic Train Control.

1907 H. W. Garratt patents design of articulated locomotive. Automatic signalling introduced on London Underground.

1908 GWR introduces first Pacific (4-6-2) locomotive 'Great Bear'. Midland Railway electrifies Lancaster-Morecambe-Heysham line on 6,600V ac overhead system. First application in Britain of high-voltage alternating current electrification.

1909 First Garratt articulated locomotives built for use on Tasmanian Government Railways. Upper quadrant signals introduced by Metropolitan Railway LBSCR opens first section of 'Overhead Electric' line from Victoria to London Bridge. Equipped on 6,600V ac overhead system. First of London's suburban electrifications.

1910 Superheating in general use. Railway to Hong Kong opened.

1911 Earls Court underground station gets first-ever escalator—and Morocco gets first-ever railway.

1912 North British build experimental 1,000hp diesel unit.

1913 L & Y experimental electrification of Bury-Holcombe Brook at 3,500V dc overhead. First revenue-earning diesel. First section of LNWR suburban electrification at 750V dc complete.

1914 Outbreak of war halts electrification plans throughout world.

1915 LSWR introduces electric trains on its Thames Valley suburban lines, using 600V dc third rail system. Forerunner of later Southern Electric system. May 22: World's worst-ever rail disaster at Quintinshill, Scotland. 227 killed.

1916 Manchester-Bury line electrified at 1,200V dc with protected side-contact conductor rail; earlier overhead section converted. Newport-Shildon line electrified at 1,500V dc overhead.

1917 Railways came to Iran.

1919 Power interlocking frame and three-position American-style signals installed at Victoria Station, London.

1920 First (two-aspect) automatic colour-light signals installed on Liverpool Overhead Railway. Italians adapt Caprotti poppet valve gear for steam locomotives. Iraq's first railway opened.

1921 Air-operated automatic doors introduced on London Underground trains.

1922 First Gresley Pacific introduced.

1923 123 separate railway companies in Britain 'grouped' into the 'Big Four'—the GWR, SR, LMS and LNER. First three-aspect (red, yellow, green) colour-light signal.

1924 Diesel firsts: in Britain, small diesel-hydraulic tested on LNER; in USA, 300hp diesel built by GEC/Alco.

1925 First diesel-electric locomotives in USA on Jersey Central Railroad. Beyer-Garratt built first locomotive for LNER.

1927 First railways in Nepal. LMS introduces 'Royal Scot' Class locomotives. GWR introduces 'King' Class locomotives. Post Office tube railway opened, with automatic, driverless trains. Weir Report recommends adoption of 1,500V dc overhead electrification as future standard.

1928 May 1: World's longest non-stop train service, London-Edinburgh, 632km (393 miles), inaugurated.

1930 First railway in Cambodia.

1931 Manchester-Altrincham line electrified at 1,500V dc on overhead system.

1932 'Flying Hamburger' diesel-electric high-speed train introduced. First relay interlocking power frame on LNER.

1933 Southern Railway electrifies London-Brighton line throughout at 750V dc. First complete main-line electrification. LMS introduced diesel-mechanical shunting engines. All London's Underground and Tube railways grouped under new London Passenger Transport Board.

1934 October: Streamlined diesel-electric trains introduced between Los Angeles and New York, 5,226km (3,248 miles). Journey time: 57 hours. First railway across Congo. LMS introduces steam turbine-driven 'Turbomotive'.

1935 First Gresley streamlined A4 Class Pacifics on LNER.

1936 Dover-Dunkirk train ferry introduced. Through coaches between London and Paris.

1937 Southern Railway electrifies London-Portsmouth main line. LMS introduces Stanier streamlined 'Coronation' Class Pacifics.

1938 July 3: Gresley streamlined Pacific 'Mallard' creates still-extant world speed record for steam engines of 203km/h (126mph). Mongolia gets railways.

1939 Germans claim record of 214km/h (133.5mph) for diesel traction. War. Railways throughout Europe in front line. First mechanized goods marshalling yard opened at Toton.

1941 Brown Boveri builds first gas turbine locomotive for Swiss Federal Railways. Bulleid 'Merchant Navy' Class Pacifics introduced with all-welded boilers, chain-driven valve gear and lightweight 'air-smoothed' casing.

1944 Hundreds of American-built 'Liberation' 2-8-0s shipped to Britain and Europe for Allied invasion.

1945 Peace. But Europe's railways lie smashed and in disarray.

1947 First British main-line diesel locomotive introduced on LMS. Albania gets first railway.

1948 January 1: Britain's 'Big Four' railway companies nationalized. British Railways comes into being. Summer: Large-scale locomotive exchanges to compare performance and reliability of classes.

1949 Southern Region introduces experimental double-deck suburban train, but it takes too long to load. Canadian Pacific Railway announces that all steam locomotives will be replaced by diesel electrics. Pulverized coal-burning gas turbine locomotive on test in USA. First railway in Saudi Arabia completed.

1950 Swiss-built (Brown Boveri) 2,500hp gas turbine locomotive introduced on Western Region of British Railways. 7,000th locomotive built at Crewe Works, England. Liberia opens first railway.

1951 First British Standard steam locomotive 'Britannia' completed.

1952 First British gas turbine goes into service. October 8: Harrow and Wealdstone disaster. 112 killed.

1954 June: Manchester-Sheffield 1,500V dc overhead electrification opened. October: Steam gives way to diesel on Canadian Pacific transcontinental routes.

1955 British Railways announce huge modernization plan. June 29: French electric locomotive reaches 330km/h (205mph) on test.

1956 British Railways decide to adopt 25,000V ac overhead system of electrification for all new schemes. First Modernization Plan diesels built in Britain.

1957 December 4: Lewisham collision. 90 killed.

1958 First 25,000V ac locomotive

1957—(above) the scene after the Lewisham train crash, one of the worst collisions in railway history.

tested on British Railways.

1959 Thanet lines to Ramsgate and Dover electrified on 750V dc conductor rail system. First 25,000V ac passenger trains between Manchester and Crewe.

1960 Last steam locomotives withdrawn on Canadian Pacific. Class 9F 2-10-0 'Evening Star', last steam engine built by British Railways, completed at Swindon.

1961 English Electric build experimental gas turbine 4-6-0 GT3. Last steam engines on London Transport railways withdrawn. English Electric 'Deltics' introduced on East Coast line.

1962 BR introduce prototype electro-diesel locomotive.

1963 Beeching Plan recommends abandonment of many of Britain's railway lines. Experimental plastic-bodied coach introduced by BR.

1964 Gresley streamlined Pacific 'Dwight D Eisenhower' presented to USA; record-breaking sister locomotive 'Mallard' preserved. 160km/h (100mph) schedules introduced in Britain. New railways

opened in Swaziland. New Tokaido line opened in Japan.

1965 Freightliners introduced for container traffic.

1966 London Manchester/Liverpool 25,000V ac overhead electrification opened throughout. April 18: Experimental French gas turbine set reaches 239km/h (148.5mph).

1968 August 11: Last steam trains on British Railways. Hawker Siddeley 'Kestrel' prototype introduced.

1969 Paved track introduced. Union Pacific Railroad introduces first GM 6,600hp Do-Do diesel-electric locomotive.

1970 May 24: Stephenson's Menai Bridge destroyed by fire.

1971 British air-conditioned coach exhibited in Moscow. Hawker-Siddeley 'Kestrel' sold to Soviet railways.

1972 April 30: 'Brighton Belle' service withdrawn. Prototype High Speed Train on trial.

1973 High Speed Train sets a new world record of 230km/h (143mph) for diesel traction.

1974 London-Glasgow main line 640km (398 miles) electrified at 25,000V ac. German Federal Railways prototype electric multiple-unit achieves 215km/h (134mph) on test between Beilefeld and Hamm.

1975 150th Anniversary of opening of Stockton and Darlington Railway. 18,000km (11,185 miles) of railways in Britain, 34,000km (21,128 miles) in France, 28,000km (17,399 miles) in Western Germany, 530,000km (329,342 miles) in USA, 136,000km (84,510 miles) in USSR.

1976 October 4: British Rail High Speed Trains commence intensive 200km/h (125mph) services between London, Bristol and Cardiff.

1977 Amtrak borrows Swedish, French and Japanese electric locomotives for tests on Boston-New York-Washington corridor.

1978 May: British Rail introduces diesel High Speed Trains on London-Edinburgh route to fastest-ever timing of $4\frac{1}{2}$ hours for 632km (393 miles). First production tilting electric Advanced Passenger Trains begin tests on West Coast Route.

Royal Trains

Queen Victoria came to the throne of England in 1837 just as the first of the great trunk railway routes in Britain were being opened or built. Yet even though the Great Western Railway was open between Paddington and Maidenhead in 1838, with Slough station conveniently near Windsor Castle, it was another four years before the Queen travelled by train between Windsor and London. Indeed her aunt, the Dowager Queen Adelaide, wife of King William IV, was the first member of the royal family to travel by rail. The Great Western Railway had built a royal saloon coach in readiness for royal patronage. Queen Adelaide also travelled on the London and Birmingham Railway and that company adapted one of its first-class bed-carriages for the purpose. This was a four-wheel coach with two full compartments and one half compartment. One of the full compartments was convertible for sleeping by stretchers placed across the gap between the seats and cushions filling the space to give a continuous bed. The compartment was not quite wide enough for a person to lie full length, but a boot outside the end of the coach, adjoining the compartment, normally containing mailbags, was adapted to form an extension from the inside of the coach. Queen Adelaide's coach can be seen in the National Railway Museum at York.

Once Queen Victoria had sampled rail travel she made many journeys, not only between London and Windsor but also to Ballater in Scotland when she stayed at Balmoral Castle, and to Gosport for Osborne House on the Isle of Wight. Most of the railways on which the Queen travelled regularly built royal saloons for her Majesty.

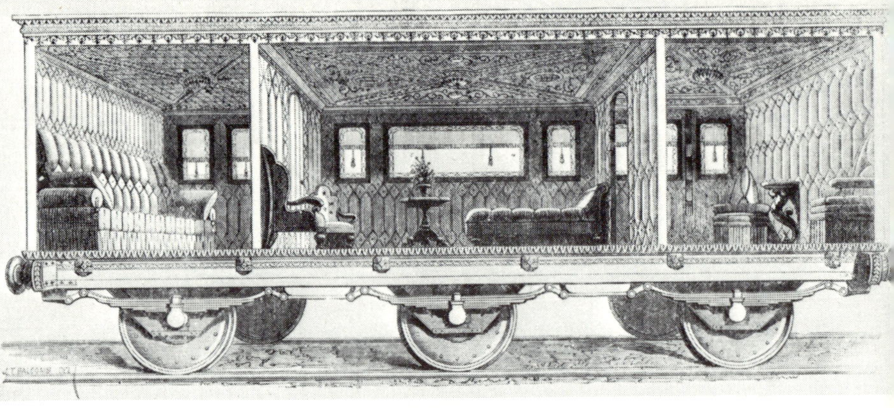

For almost a century, from the advent of railways to the widespread adoption of the motor car, railways were the main mode of travel for the Royalty and National leaders of the world. Most major railways had a Royal or Presidential saloon, and some regularly-patronised lines had complete Royal Trains, with various saloons for individual members of the Royal Family. The cutaway drawing (above) shows the interior of the lavishly-furnished special six-wheeled saloon built by the Great Eastern Railway in 1850 for the then Prince of Wales. This four-wheeled vehicle (below) was the special saloon provided in Colombo for the Prince of Wales' world trip in 1875.

These saloons were far more luxurious than ordinary coaches with well-padded and richly upholstered armchairs and quilted walls and ceilings in the coaches themselves. Often the royal saloons were the first to have new fittings to improve passenger comfort, for example toilet facilities and beds, long before such features were included in ordinary coaches. In 1869 the London and North Western Railway (LNWR) built a pair of six-wheel saloons for the Queen, one for day use and the other for night-time. They were permanently coupled and linked by a flexible enclosed gangway, the first use of a corridor between coaches and not seen in ordinary service until the late 1880s. This pair of saloons were later rebuilt on a long single underframe as one coach and in this form it also survives at York. So too do the LNWR royal saloons of 1903 built for King Edward VII. These two vehicles were much less ornate than those for the late Queen. They formed part of a completely new royal train and one or two coaches of this period survive in use in the royal train today although the principal royal saloons in use now for royal journeys were built by the London Midland and Scottish in 1941 or by British Rail in the 1950s and were among the first to have air-conditioning.

Normally when the present Queen travels by day for fairly short journeys by rail only one royal saloon is used with perhaps two or three other coaches for her staff. Occasionally

an ordinary first-class coach or Pullman car has been used. For long overnight journeys to Balmoral the entire royal household needs to be moved including the Queen's personal staff, secretaries and other officials, which means running a train of up to 14 coaches, including dining and sleeping accommodation.

Special precautions have always been taken over the running of the royal train. In the early days of railways, when train signalling methods were in the primitive stage, there was a real risk of collisions and derailments. It would not have done for the royal train to be involved in an accident. Operating instructions for the royal train meant that no other train could run on the same line for a specific period before or after the royal train, trains in the opposite direction had to slow down,

points had to be padlocked in the proper position for the royal train for at least half an hour before it was due, shunting had to stop in adjoining sidings, and a pilot engine had to run about 20 minutes ahead of the royal train to prove that the line was clear and nothing other than the signals could be changed until the royal train had passed. Men were placed at about 800m ($\frac{1}{2}$ mile) intervals along the lineside to keep watch. Even today when ordinary safety standards are high some of the old precautions survive. The running of a royal train today in Britain is still organized with great care and advised to the staff concerned by a special coded notice.

Other countries of the world, whether monarchies or republics, have special saloon cars or complete trains for the head of state. Usually the state saloons are much more ornate than ordinary coaches, but it is ironic that today many of the state saloons are rather old, and improvements in the coaches used by ordinary passengers in such matters as good riding and improved sound and heat insulation have overtaken the equipment in the State trains. In some countries ordinary first-class coaches are now provided when the head of state travels and this is likely to be the trend in the future for daytime journeys. Certainly we are unlikely to see again new saloons richly decorated with gilt fittings and equipped regardless of cost, like those built for some of the world's richest rulers in the past.

Restaurant Cars and Sleepers

Despite some of the long rail journeys in North America and Europe, and even in Britain, the provision of meal services on trains did not really start until at least 50 years after the pioneer railways were built in the 1820s and 1830s. If passengers wanted to eat on a journey they had to take food with them, or buy it at refreshment rooms at the larger stations where the train stopped. Meal stops on the longer journeys were allowed in the timetable. The stops were often no longer than 20 minutes, in which time the passenger had to order and eat a three- or four-course meal. Other passengers could buy luncheon baskets containing a cold meal to eat on the way.

The first dining car was a Pullman, built in America in 1868, but another 11 years passed before the first dining car appeared in Britain, a converted Pullman car placed in service during 1879 between King's Cross and Leeds. Even so dining cars did not become more widespread until the late 1880s and, since trains in Britain were still without through corridors between coaches, passengers either had to change into and out of the dining car at intermediate stops or sit in it all the way. Only first-class passengers were at first allowed in dining cars. In the early 1890s corridor trains with dining cars for all classes of passenger appeared on the main East Coast and West Coast routes between London and Scotland. The Great Western was a few years behind the other railways in having dining cars because until late in 1895 all trains to the West and Wales had to stop at Swindon under contract with the operators of its refreshment room!

In Europe the first dining cars appeared in the early 1880s, particularly on the Orient Express from Paris to Constantinople (now Istanbul). This train was operated by the Compagnie Internationale des Wagons-Lits et des Grands Express Européens (the International Sleeping Car Company), which gradually introduced sleeping and dining cars on many services in Europe.

By the early years of the present century dining cars were becoming an accepted part of travel, on long-distance trains all over the world. Cooking was normally done on a stove heated by anthracite or by gas. Some of the meals were large, consisting of five or six courses, all of which were prepared and cooked in the small kitchen, often no more than 15ft×6ft, in the dining car. In the 1930s electricity was introduced to a few British dining cars but today propane gas, carried in portable cylinders, is often used.

In Britain and in other parts of the world for journeys which used to take perhaps four to

Inevitably, the advent of Pullman Cars, with their luxurious seating and general appointments, encouraged a general improvement in the standards of ordinary rolling stock. By the turn of the century, several railways were providing facilities equal to that of Pullman in their ordinary first class coaches; this 1907 view (above) of a British Midland Railway dining car reveals Edwardian decor and luxury that for the period was probably second to none.

five hours with steam locomotives, and which today with high-speed diesel or electric trains take only two to three hours, the need for full meal service is declining, and more buffet cars serving drinks and light refreshments or quickly-cooked hot snacks are being provided. Freezers now allow pre-cooked frozen meals to be carried on buffet cars, and with modern micro-wave ovens, which can heat up food in only two or three minutes, individual hot meals can be provided to order. Refreshment cars in Switzerland, for example, provide a choice of up to six main courses which can be served within a few minutes. The food is cooked and prepared in the first place at the main kitchens in the supply depot serving the buffet cars.

Although it was possible to sleep in some of the very early first-class carriages by making a bed across the seats, this arrangement was not used widely. The first proper beds in railway carriages were those in special family or invalid saloons from the 1860s which could be hired for private use by wealthy passengers. But in America the first Pullman sleepers were built at the end of the 1850s and were introduced in Britain in 1874. Sleeping berths were arranged along the sides of the car, which had a central passageway, and two berths, one above the other (the top one folding against the roof during the day) were fitted in each section. A year earlier the first sleeping car in Britain had been placed in service by the North British Railway. It was a six-wheeler with two compartments of three seats in each which pulled forward to make separate beds.

Modern dining and catering cars in Europe, Japan and America (left) surpass Pullman standards of comfort and service in their fight with the airlines for business traffic.

Sleeping cars were first introduced in America as early as the 1850s, and in Britain and Europe in the 1870s. Nowadays regular networks of overnight 'sleeper' trains criss-cross Britain and Europe. Many expresses offer comfort equal to that of a high class hotel; generally, a standard compartment module is used with a single bed for first class passengers, or double- or triple-decked, as in this cutaway view (below) of a Wagons-Lits car, for second class or tourist traffic.

Passengers had to provide their own sheets and blankets. In the 1880s the Great Western built what is accepted as the forerunner of the present-day sleepers with individual compartments across the car served by an internal side corridor. Passengers slept on a berth that took the place of the ordinary long bench type seat in a day coach, rather than across a pair of facing seats. At this time in Britain sleeping cars were only for first-class passengers. Not until 1928 were third-class passengers provided with sleeping accommodation and then only in bunks, four to a compartment in two pairs one above the other and supplied only with rug and pillow. First-class cars by then had full bedding. Cars were fitted with washbasins, hot and cold water, and pressure ventilation, while light refreshments could be obtained from the attendant.

Today in Britain first and second-class cars are distinguished by having single or double berths, but both have full bedding. In Europe many of the sleeping cars are still operated by the International Sleeping Car Company. The cars are ingeniously laid out with one, two or three-berth compartments often interlaced, one partly over another, to make best use of space, yet giving passengers privacy of individual compartments. Some railways in Europe operate couchette cars, usually with six berths to a compartment, in vertical groups of three. In other parts of the world sleepers vary from multi-berth compartments to private rooms. On some railways, today's long-distance trains are like top-class hotels on wheels, with full service on the move.

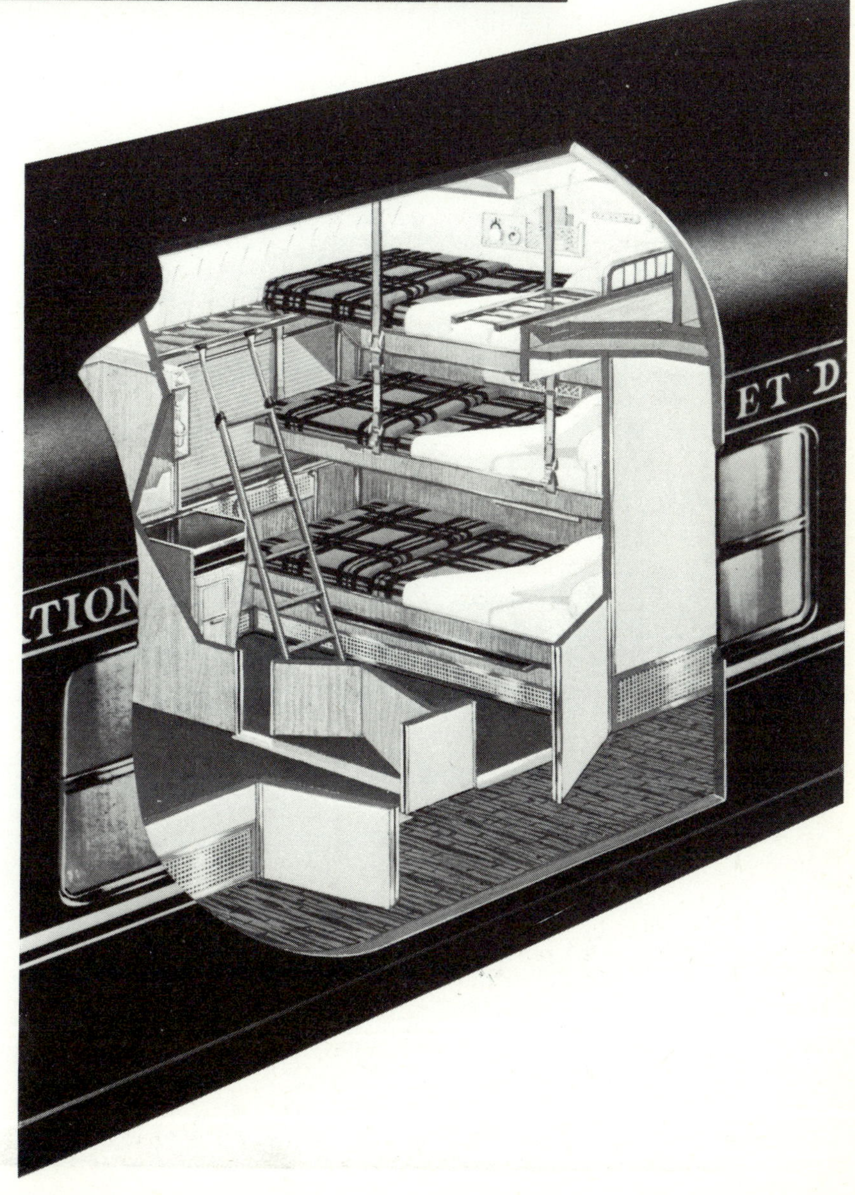

Bigger and Better Coaches

The First World War brought changes in railway operation and equipment in many parts of the world. While railway carriages had gradually become larger, to the maximum allowed by the space between platforms, lineside structures and bridges, during the first decade of the present century, materials used in construction and fittings had not changed much. Wood was still extensively used for building coaches and lighting was still largely by gas. After the First World War steel was used much more and electricity became standardized for lighting. The clerestory roof, common in many parts of the world, gave way to the high elliptical roof, although in a few countries because of climatic extremes it continued to be built to provide more ventilation in hot weather.

Steel-bodied coaches had started to appear in America around the turn of the century, and were used for underground railways in Britain about the same time. During the 1920s steel panelled coaches, though with wooden body frames on steel underframes, began to be built for British main-line service. Yet since timber was cheaper than steel, and despite the safety advantages of steel, British coaches continued to be partly built of wood, sometimes with steel outer panels for smoothness.

This was the era of the streamlined train, when it was realized that projections from the coach side, like the mouldings covering joints in the timber or wood window frames, as well as the large domed clerestory roof, all helped to add to the air resistance of a train, besides trapping dirt. Even the space below the underframe between the trucks or bogies was covered by a fairing to reduce wind resistance of underfloor equipment. In North America,

Britain and Europe generally it was the age of the crack express, usually named and sometimes with such services as hairdressing, ladies' rest lounges for mothers with young children, secretarial services, even cinemas on a very few trains. Interior decor on some trains in Britain and America was startling, with multi-colour seating materials or interior paintwork to give what were known as jazz effects; they were not liked by all passengers!

In Europe it was the period of the train deluxe, with many luxury services provided by the International Sleeping Car Company on international routes with daytime Pullman cars as well as sleepers or diners. It was also a period in which the railways began to lose their monopoly as passenger carriers, which they had had for almost 100 years in some parts. The first commercial airline services were gradually becoming established in the 1930s, and soon after the First World War the petrol engine, having proved itself for wartime use, heralded a new era for road transport, with buses and automobiles, and trucks for freight. The railways had already faced competition in cities from electric streetcars and trams, soon after the turn of the century.

Railways in several parts of the world looked towards new equipment and operating methods to help fight the competition. Around the turn of the century several railways introduced electric trains on suburban routes around big cities, and the first underground railways were built under cities. In the 1920s and 1930s the beginning of the diesel age was dawning on railways and diesel railcars—lightweight self-propelled coaches powered by diesel engines—were built to work some branch services. Some of these railcars were

After the First World War, steel began to replace wood in the construction of coaches. At first, steel panelling was used on existing wooden frames, but by the 1940s, all-steel coaches on standard length steel underframes, such as this LMS corridor composite (left), were in almost universal production in Britain, Europe and the USA.

rather like buses inside, with open saloon interiors and seats not quite so well sprung and padded as ordinary coaches. In Britain more routes were electrified, introducing main-line corridor electric trains, some with Pullman cars serving meals and light refreshments, to lines between London and the South Coast, often on journeys of no more than one hour.

In the second half of the 1930s the London and North Eastern Railway introduced new streamlined trains, which included new types of coach with a centre passageway type of layout, but with first-class cars having the seats partitioned into alcoves of four seats, one in each corner on each side of the passageway. Everyone had a corner seat!

In Europe the 1930s was a period of extremes, with the luxury first-class expresses on the one hand, all with supplementary fares, the ordinary first- and second-class expresses with accommodation no better than it had to be, and local trains still with wooden seats in

the third class and often with old six-wheeled coaches from the last century and sometimes still with oil or gas lamps. Even some of the express trains running long distances still had third-class carriages with wooden seats. In Britain second class had been abolished generally by 1923 and almost all third-class coaches had soft upholstered seats by the 1930s.

In America the first steps were being taken towards improving passenger cars, both in construction and passenger comfort, in the 1930s. Steel cars were then becoming standardized but they were heavy—over 60 tonne. During the 1930s the Budd Company began building car bodies in stainless steel, with parts welded together in such a way that much of the heavy independent underframe could be eliminated as the body structure was self-supporting. Other builders were also looking at lightweight metals, including aluminium, to reduce weight. Meanwhile some trains in America were fitted with air-conditioning to improve passenger comfort.

In the 1930s, streamlining became fashionable on both sides of the Atlantic. Steam locomotives were encased in bullet-like fairings, and rolling stock was given smooth sides and shrouded running gear. One suspects the objective was as much to gain publicity as to attain a few extra miles per hour; certainly, the 'streamliners' captured the public imagination. This was the futuristic observation car, complete with chrome-plated lettering, which brought up the rear of the LNER 'Coronation' express of 1937.

Coaches for Speed and Comfort

Until the 1920s railway carriages were often built in small batches. These were of individual sizes in such matters as the overall length of the body, internal compartments and saloons and windows, so that standard components could not be used. The running gear, such as wheels, buffers and couplings, had to conform to set standards, and coaches were also limited to a maximum height and width because of clearances under bridges, and also to length because of throw-over on curves in clearing platforms or even other trains passing on a curve. Coaches built up to the First World War often differed by a few inches even for the same basic type of coach. The Midland Railway in England was one of the first to standardize coach sizes; between 1895 and 1905 many Midland coaches were 14.6m or 16.4m (48ft or 54ft) long with standard compartments of 1.9m (6ft 6in) for third class and 2.4m (7ft 9in) for first class. Underframes could thus be used for several types of coach of the same length.

In the 1920s the London Midland and Scottish Railway (LMS) installed new machinery for making wooden-bodied coaches at Derby workshops so that each component could be mass produced. For the first time, parts such as sides, ends and roof were pre-assembled on a production line basis. Previously, carriages were built up piece by piece from the floor upwards.

By the end of the 1930s all four major railways in Britain had their own standard designs although there was no standardization between the companies.

After nationalization in 1948 British Railways introduced coaching stock designs in which as much as possible was standardized. (Third class in Britain and Europe became second class from 1956.) Window sizes were standardized and so, too, were doors. The new BR standard coaches built from 1951 were of all-steel construction with underframes to which the body was welded to form a strong box structure. At the different carriage building workshops components were jig-built, so that all the various parts would fit, regardless of which works was building the coaches. All the seats, windows and luggage racks were mass produced at one works and distributed to the others. In service if a window is broken there are only a small number of sizes to hold in stock as spares.

Since the Second World War most railway administrations have realized the advantages of standardizing designs to make construction easier and to reduce the stock of spare parts for maintenance and repair. In America common specifications were drawn up by the Association of American Railroads for the standard basic types of car. Length was standardized at 25.9m (85ft) over couplers when coupled, which gave a body length over the corners of about 25m (82ft 6in).

In Europe too the different railway administrations have gradually introduced standard coaches within their own systems, although the International Railway Union has established basic standards regarding size and equipment for coaches on international service at 26.4m (86ft 7in) long over buffers, 2.8m (9ft 3in) wide and 4.12m (13ft 5in) high.

During the 1960s and 1970s as new techniques were perfected to improve carriage construction and as new equipment was included for passenger comfort—air conditioning is now included in all new British Railways long-distance passenger stock and on many European coaches for principal expresses—new standard designs have been produced which differ in detail from the earlier types. In Britain it was also found that coach length could be increased since most inter-city routes with modernization had lost nearly all of the tight spots; latest standard coaches are now 22.96m (75ft 4in) over couplers, 3.81m (12ft 6in) high and 2.743m (9ft) wide. In America by contrast, Amtrak, the organization that today runs passenger services in America, has decided that its new coaches do not need to be quite so big as the older cars and its new Budd coaches of stainless steel and aluminium, with curved sides, while still at the standard 25.9m (85ft) length and 3.2m (10ft 6in) wide, are only 3.86m (12ft 8in) high.

Two distinct lines of development have emerged in modern coach design; in one the mechanical parts of the coach, that is bogies or trucks and wheels, together with the springs and suspension, have been updated and redesigned to withstand the new high speeds without derailment, and combined with new braking systems to stop safely and quickly. But the other envisages an entirely new type of coach body, designed in conjunction with new suspension systems, to run at much higher speeds round existing curves.

Almost universally, new coaches for high-speed services have full air-conditioning inside, and a high level of sound insulation, so that outside noises of train movement are hardly heard by passengers inside. It is in Britain that the most interesting developments are taking place; the Advanced Passenger Train will run at much higher speeds round curves than conventional trains and the coach bodies are designed to tilt inwards as the train

When it took over responsibility for most US inter-city passenger routes from the various individual railroads, Amtrak found itself with a motley collection of aged, run-down rolling stock, considerably inferior to the then current European standards. But over the past few years, it has progressively re-equipped its main services with new Budd-built stainless steel and aluminium-bodied 'Amfleet' cars which offer similar air-conditioned luxury to that found on principal European lines. Lower and lighter than traditional American passenger cars, a train of the new stock curves into Oakland on the Washington-Cincinnati 'Shenandoah' service.

The interior design of current European rolling stock for Inter-City and International services is second to none, surpassing airline standards. This is the interior of a French 'Grand-comfort' side-corridor coach, but vehicles to similar standards are in everyday use on the British, German and Swiss systems.

enters the curve. It is like a cyclist leaning into a curve as he goes round a bend. As the train reaches a curve, a sensing device will detect the side thrust and operate hydraulic tilting jacks which will lift one side of the coach so that it leans for a maximum of nine degrees towards the inside of the curve. As the train reaches straight track, the sensing device releases the tilt jacks and the coach body returns to the upright position. The tilting body is not required for safety reasons but to give passengers a more comfortable ride. Without body tilting, passengers would tend to be thrown sideways on a curve. The comfortable limit for passengers, even with tilting, is much less than the overturning or derailing speed of the train on a curve.

Another feature used on the APT and on many other new coaches in many parts of the

Situated at the very heart of Europe's railway system, the Swiss Federal Railways carry a high proportion of International traffic and provide much of the rolling stock. This is a standard Swiss 11-compartment second class coach to UIC standards for International traffic.

world is air springs. Instead of metal coil or leaf springs used on coach suspensions until now, high-speed coaches have air-cushions between bogie or truck frame and the car underbody. Air pressure is regulated by load so that the car body level remains constant, the air pressure being supplied by reservoirs through electrically operated valves worked by weighing devices.

Most modern passenger cars are now being built of lightweight materials with aluminium sections and panels, or lightweight steel. Lighter weight means higher speeds for the same amount of power, or the same speed for less power which helps to use energy more economically. Over the last two decades some railways have tried ultra lightweight trains using new principles. The Talgo type train, first seen in the 1940s, and developed in Spain, has low-slung coaches about half the length of conventional cars, but carried on an articulated coupling with only one axle below it. Each car, except those at the ends, thus has only two wheels and depends on its neighbour for support. Canadian Turbo trains, designed to run at 153km/h (95mph) or over, are also lightweight low-slung units articulated on single axle suspension units between cars. The car bodies tilt inwards on curves. Despite achieving weights only one-third those of a conventional train these lightweight prototypes have not developed widely.

For speeds up to 200km/h (125mph) modern conventional type passenger cars have proved quite satisfactory, and on new railways designed for speeds up to 290km/h (180mph), where curves are slight there is no need for body tilt.

The modern passenger car is now at an advanced stage of its development and the future will lie in bringing all types of car to these standards, whether for high-speed long-distance inter-city day or night travel, or short distance and commuter services.

Already, the improved suspension, bogie designs, insulation and air-conditioning developed for long-distance trains is being applied to the latest suburban and rapid-transit trains in Britain, America, France and Germany.

Wagons

The colliery wagonways of 1800 consisted simply of trains of wagons, hauled by horses, or running by gravity downhill, or cable-worked from a stationary steam winding engine, to carry coal from the mines to the rivers. From these early coal chauldrons developed the railway coal and mineral wagon. As railways became established as carriers of goods, other types of wagon, some covered with a wooden body and roof, were built for carrying different types of traffic.

The Victorian railway wagon in Britain changed little in size for more than 100 years, for until the 1950s the short four-wheeler with a body about 5m (16-17ft) long was still the standard with a capacity for coal wagons of 8 to 10 tonne. Covered vans for general or perishable goods often carried no more than 6 tonne. In the early years of railways, wagons often had 'dumb' buffers consisting of an extension of the main timber side frames to bump against the next wagon. Gradually sprung buffers were brought into use together with a standard three-link coupling. Wagons did not have brakes at all at first, but later they were fitted with handbrakes worked by a lever at the side. This was used both for holding them steady in sidings and to help in braking when a train was on the move going down a falling grade. Apart from the steam brake on the locomotive and the handbrake in the guard's van at the back of the train, wagon brakes were often applied to help keep train speed in check by the guard walking along the ground pinning down the brakes by pressing the handle down and putting a steel pin through a hole in the handle guidebar, as the train moved slowly forward. When the line levelled off the guard had to reverse the procedure by unpinning and lifting the brake handles, again while the train crept slowly forward. In Britain this system remained in use much longer than in Continental Europe or America, and still has not disappeared entirely. Train speeds were low, usually not more than 48km/h (30mph) at most.

As steel began to be available for railways towards the end of the last century it began to replace wood for wagons which could be made longer for special loads. Wagons of 9m (30ft) were built for carrying pipes and steel components, and some had drop centres for carrying bulky machinery, even traction engines or other road vehicles. Flat wagons carried other types of machinery that were not very high, or containers which could be loaded at a factory or depot, carried by road to a rail goods station and transferred to a flat wagon for the greater part of its journey by

rail. The guard's van, also known as a brake van, or a caboose in North America, was used by the train guard or conductor to keep watch during the journey and to apply the brake when necessary.

During the early years of the present century automatic vacuum brakes were fitted to a few goods vans that carried perishable traffic and ran at higher speeds, but not until the 1950s was a programme started to fit the majority of wagons with automatic brakes in Britain. In America and in Europe air brakes have been fitted to freight wagons for many years. Continuous power brakes, controlled by the driver right through the train, give far safer and better operation and allow trains to run at higher speeds.

During the last decade new wagon types have appeared on British Rail, longer, many on bogies or trucks, fitted with air brakes and with carrying capacities of around 75 tonne,

Nowadays the trend in freight traffic is towards bulk movement in trainloads, and the traditional 'mixed' freight of assorted wagons, such as the East German train (above), is becoming a rarity. Special wagons are usually provided for train load traffic; the quadruple-headed Union Pacific Railroad (US) train threading the Cajon Pass (right) is formed of a string of special flatcars, each designed to take two containers, while the British 'Merry Go Round' train (above) has special top-loading, bottom-discharge hopper wagons which automatically load and unload while the train is on the move.

with a total wagon weight, including load, of 100 tonne. Oil and chemicals are carried in 100 tonne tank wagons and many other bulk materials are carried in large bogie wagons or in long 45 tonne four-wheel wagons. Container traffic has gradually expanded, often on through journeys from North America to Britain or between Britain and Europe, and is carried on Freightliner container trains on BR at speeds of up to 120km/h (75mph).

In America freight cars have for many years been of high capacity, mounted on trucks and often today formed into long consists needing several diesel locomotives at the head end. In Europe, wagons are still largely four-wheeled but of higher capacity than the older British types and today about the same as the latest British wagons. Hopper wagons are used in many parts of the world; they are loaded from material dropped from overhead storage bunkers and the hopper wagons themselves are discharged from bottom doors into storage bunkers below. In Britain coal is moved between some collieries and power stations by shuttle hopper trains which load and unload while still moving, known as merry-go-round trains.

Disasters on the Railways

However good the organization of a railway, accidents and breakdowns somehow just seem to happen which bring trains to a stop. Fortunately, today, with high quality steel used in the working parts of trains and for rails, mechanical breakages causing accidents are rare, and with automatic signalling equipment used on many lines mistakes by signalmen and drivers are largely prevented. Yet sometimes automated equipment which stops signalmen from making mistakes breaks down itself. All that happens then is that signals go to red so that trains do not run into danger. But a fault in one small component must not be allowed to stop the entire train service and special rules allow signalmen to tell drivers to go slowly past signals at red in such circum-

'protect' the accident and summon help quickly. First they must put down detonators, or torpedoes as they are known in America, on the rails of other lines, about a mile from the accident to warn any approaching train of trouble by detonating with a loud and distinctive bang.

At the same time, as the crew are walking or running along the line, if they come to a telephone linked to a signalbox they must use it to warn the signalman of the accident and tell him to stop trains and summon help. There are often telephones at signals, and on lines with modern colour-light signalling the signals themselves and telephones are usually fairly close together. On some lines with continuous track circuiting the train crews have clips and

No railway accident caused more shock and horror among the general public than the Tay Bridge disaster of 1879. At the height of a fierce storm on the night of December 28, the centre 'high girders' of Sir Thomas Bouch's viaduct across the Tay estuary came crashing down into the foaming waters of the firth, taking with it to a watery grave a complete train and its passengers and crew. Despite an intensive search in appalling conditions (left) there were no survivors. A similar fate, but with less tragic results, befell the Severn Bridge near Chepstow in 1960, when in thick fog a loaded petrol barge hit and demolished one of the uprights of the bridge, toppling two spans into the river (below).

stances, until a normal section of line is reached.

Occasionally, perhaps because a telephone message is misunderstood a driver is given wrong information, or possibly the distance to a stop signal is misjudged or just through carelessness, a train might be derailed or even possibly hit another train. Sometimes a train might be involved in a derailment of another train. For example, perhaps part of a freight train derails and falls on to another track just as a train on that line is approaching. Fortunately big accidents are rare, but when they do occur passengers might be killed or injured. The first job is to stop other trains running into the debris and making the accident worse. The train crew, if they are not injured, must

wires on the locomotive to put across the rails of the other tracks to short-circuit the signalling controls and throw the signals to danger.

On fully track circuited lines the signalman in the signalling control centre, which may be many miles away, can see that something has gone wrong because the red 'track occupied' lights on his track diagram might suddenly light up on an adjoining track, when he knows there is no train present on that line. In that case the signalman himself will put the signals to danger just in case something is wrong until he has found out by telephone. It might be nothing serious. Very hot days can sometimes affect signalling equipment and cause short-circuits to track circuits. Broken rails will show up on a signalbox track diagram because the track circuits are interrupted, and so, too, will anything thrown on the line by vandals. Thus trains can be stopped before an accident is caused. But if an accident occurs the signalman telephones quickly for rescue services—fire engines, police and ambulances—to go to the scene. The breakdown gang, usually with a special train including a crane, will be sent from the nearest depot to the accident, at first to help in rescue work by carefully lifting large pieces of wreckage so that rescuers can reach people who might be trapped underneath and then to clear the line.

Today, even if accidents do occur, the results are not usually as bad as they would have been 20 or more years ago. Passenger cars today have all-metal bodies built as strong box structures. In an accident the ends might get damaged but generally the bodies do not get flattened like the old wooden bodies which sometimes broke up into splinters. Modern signalling has reduced the possibilities of a signalman making a mistake, and new types of cab signalling have made the chances of a driver missing a signal very much less. While there are more broken rails on many railways, because of increased and heavier traffic, the methods of finding cracked and broken rails are much better now. British Railways have a track testing train which can run at 65km/h (40mph) with detectors close to the rail which can pick up cracks in the rail. A paper tape in the train equipment with distances marked on it will record a suspected rail crack and it can be followed up by men on the line with hand detectors. Wheels, too, can be checked for cracks by special detector equipment. As railway speeds increase in many parts of the world scientists and engineers are improving safety equipment to prevent accidents and breakdowns.

Whatever the type of accident, the breakdown and rescue services will usually have instructions on the action they must take. The accident might be nothing more than a freight

tank wagon derailed, which would seem to be not very serious. But, if that tank wagon is carrying highly inflammable oil or chemicals, a very dangerous situation might occur if the breakdown gang does not carry out the right instructions. Perhaps there might be a tiny hole in the tank where it hit an adjacent wagon as it derailed. Some of the oil might be leaking, only a little perhaps, but a spark from nothing more than the brake block of a wagon on the breakdown train being positioned alongside could start a fire. If several tanks are carrying oil soon the whole train could be a blazing inferno with tank wagons exploding. Leaking chemicals can give off poisonous fumes so that rescue teams must wear breathing apparatus and people living nearby must be evacuated. This is why chemicals and fuel oil must be treated very carefully, both when loading and unloading normally, and also if tank wagons are involved in an accident.

Most railway accidents, however horrific, are caused by human error, often only a few seconds of negligence. Head-on collisions, now happily rare because of the development of sophisticated safety devices, can be particularly destructive; this was the scene (above) which confronted rescuers at Maroggia in Switzerland after an electrically-hauled freight collided with a passenger express. And it was simply a missed—or misunderstood—signal indication which led the driver of this British Railways Britannia Pacific to take a junction near Didcot at much too high a speed, turning both it and the following train on its side with disastrous results.

Early Signalling and Semaphore

When the first commercial railways were opened in the 1820s and early 1830s, nobody at first thought of providing signals to control trains because the need was not appreciated. The first passenger railways were based on a combination of the primitive colliery railway steam locomotives and track, with passenger accommodation taken from the road coach services. Colliery railways did not need signals because they were short lines and the driver could usually see if the line was clear, and speed was low, while horse-drawn road coaches could be steered to avoid other coaches or obstructions.

It was soon realized that some form of control was needed as trains could reach 48km/h (30mph) or more and were the fastest means of transport. The railways took the example of the newly-created Metropolitan Police Force in London and employed policemen to look after the security of the railway, to run stations and to control trains. Policemen signalled to trains by hand movements, one arm stretched out horizontally for clear,

As railways spread across Britain and Europe, it soon became obvious that some form of regulation of the speed and frequency of trains was necessary to avoid the increasing number of accidents and near-collisions. Many railway companies at first appointed a 'railway policeman'—the forerunner of today's signalman—at each major station and junction. By a simple series of hand signals—arm outstretched (right) for all clear, one arm raised (centre right) for caution, and both arms raised (far right) for stop—the policeman was able to regulate the flow of traffic through his station or junction.

one arm raised for caution and both arms raised for stop. These three basic handsignals were devised for the time interval operation of trains, with the aim of ensuring that trains could not run too closely behind each other. On most lines trains were not very frequent, but at certain junctions and stations it was possible for two trains to approach within a few minutes of each other. With the time interval system it was hoped that trains could be kept several minutes apart. After one train passed a station, if a second approached in the same direction within five minutes the policeman gave the danger signal to stop the second train. After five minutes a second train could proceed but under caution, and after ten minutes the policeman would give a second train a clear signal. Sand-timers, like today's egg-timers, were used because few people had watches. That did not mean that the first train was really ten minutes ahead, since it might have broken down and stopped only a mile or so down the line. The guard of the first train was then supposed to run back along the line to warn any following train to stop. Sometimes he did not always succeed and the second train would collide with the first and passengers would be killed and injured.

Hand signals were replaced by flag signals, or by oil lamps at night on some railways. Gradually a colour-code became established, red for danger (stop), green for caution, and white for clear. Because the policemen had other duties and might not always see an approaching train in time, other types of signal appeared, fixed on lineside posts. The signals were of a variety of shapes and sizes. Sometimes they were discs, sometimes large balls, sometimes rectangular boards. Some were hauled up and down the post by rope. When the signal was at the top of the post it might mean danger on some lines and clear on others. Some of the discs and boards were

As stations and junctions became busier and more complex, it became increasingly difficult for the policemen to retain full control over all movements. So fixed semaphore signals were provided, worked by the policeman from a crank at the base (left). The twin arms, one for each direction, were fitted between a slot in the post; outstretched horizontally they indicated danger—stop (the exact opposite of the policeman's horizontal arm signal), while inclined at 45 degrees they called for caution, and vertical, hidden in the slot, indicated 'clear'.

The Great Western Railway in Britain introduced the 'disc and crossbar' signal (below), the first to show both danger and clear indications. The disc was mounted at 90 degrees above a horizontal bar. The entire post could be rotated and thus either the bar could be presented to oncoming trains, indicating 'danger—stop' or, by simply rotating the post 90 degrees, the disc indicating 'clear'.

pivoted so that when face-on to a train they meant danger, and when edge-on (and invisible) they were clear. In America, a ball at the top of the post usually meant 'clear', hence the term 'highball' still used in American railroad parlance.

The Great Western Railway in Britain introduced one of the first types of signal to give both danger and clear indications. This was the disc and crossbar type. A long rectangular board face-on to the train signalled danger, but at right angles to it was a disc which when face-on meant clear.

In the early 1840s the London & Croydon Railway introduced semaphore signals with a pivoted arm giving different meanings by its position. The arm straight out horizontally meant 'danger', inclined down at 45 degrees meant 'caution', and vertical, hidden inside the slotted post, meant 'clear'. The semaphore signal originated from the naval telegraph between London and Portsmouth by which messages could be passed from hilltop to hilltop where the semaphores were erected. In railway practice the semaphore signal gradually became the accepted signal to control trains, not only in Britain but in many parts of the world. The time interval method of keeping trains apart persisted until the late 1880s in conjunction with semaphore signals.

Once the time interval system was replaced by the block system, semaphore signals only needed to show two indications, horizontal for danger and lowered at 45 degrees for clear. Soon after, green replaced white for clear in Britain because of the possible confusion with street and town lights. Distant signals, which could be passed while at caution, were later placed about 825m (900yd) before the stop signals to which they applied and gave the driver a warning of the indication shown by the stop signals so that he could slow down and stop in time. To distinguish them from

stop signals, distant signals had a vee notch cut out of the end of the arm. From 1925 distant signals were painted yellow and showed a yellow light at night for caution. From about the same time some signals were made to rise to 45 degrees upwards for clear in many parts of Britain, and both upper quadrant and lower quadrant signals survive today on some lines.

In America semaphore signals were also used but the three-position type has survived, since a caution indication is used as well as stop and clear to give advanced warning of the indication of the next signal ahead. Other countries, too, still use semaphore signals, particularly railways in Australia, New Zealand, Africa, India and South America built by British engineers. The indications are usually similar to those in Britain.

Today, despite modernization and widespread adoption of colour-light signalling, semaphore signals remain in use on almost every railway system in the world. In Britain, as in many other countries, the lower quadrant signal, adapted from the earlier slotted semaphore signal, has given way to the upper quadrant, which has the fail-safe advantage of returning to danger automatically if a wire or any part fails. This is a typical upper quadrant junction signal (left), with both the stop and the distant signal beneath it for the main route showing clear.

The Block System

When the first railways were built in Britain there was no real means of communication between stations, and trains ran at minimum time intervals behind each other. This system was very dangerous because if a train broke down there was no means of telling the station behind the train to stop the next train, other than by the guard running back and waving a flag or lamp, and, on some lines, setting off flares.

About the same time as the first railways were being built, the electric telegraph was being perfected and patented in Britain in 1837 by Charles Wheatstone and W. F. Cooke. Here was a method by which messages could be passed between stations and the Great Western Railway installed a trial section between Paddington and Slough. It was used for passing general messages about train running and for public messages, but no more. It was cumbersome, for it had five needles on each instrument and needed five wires between them. Above and below the needles were letters arranged in a diamond pattern so that when a needle deflected to right or left it pointed at a particular letter. Messages had to be spelt out letter by letter. Because of this and since many railwaymen at that time could not read, or use the telegraph, few railways used it. Even the Great Western did not use it very much. After several bad accidents one or two railways used the electric telegraph between the signalmen at each end of long tunnels, for example, so that they could send messages to each other to ensure that a second train was not allowed into the tunnel before the one in front had cleared the tunnel at the far end. Even that system, with the letter-by-letter messages, was complicated and caused accidents.

By the 1850s the telegraph had been simplified into instruments that could ring a single-stroke bell and an instrument in which a single telegraph needle could be made to point at two or three written indications on the face of the instrument, in some ways like one hand of a clock. The needle was operated magnetically by an electric current supplied by batteries and transmitted along the line from one signalbox to the next. This was a system far more suited to railway use. A code of bell signals became established, with specific meanings describing the class of train, when the train entered the block section, and when it left the block section. Instead of trains running vaguely at time intervals there could now be space intervals, precisely defined sections of line each of which could only be occupied by one train at a time. A block section, in very

The 'Block' section is the section of track between two signalboxes. When a train is ready to go, the signalman offers the train to the next signalbox by sending the 'Is line clear' bell signal. If the line is clear, the signalman in the next signalbox accepts the train by repeating the bell signal back to the first signalman, and moving his block indicator from "normal" to "line clear" so that the first signalman can then clear the signals controlling the entry to the block section for the train to depart.

As soon as the train starts and passes the signals controlling entry to the block section, the first signalman puts the signals back to danger and sends the 'train entering section' bell signal to the next signalbox. The signalman there acknowledges the signal, again by repeating it back, and moves his block indicator from 'line clear' to 'train on line'. These indications are repeated in the first signalbox, to remind the signalman there that there is a train in the block section and that if another train should approach, it must be stopped at his signals.

When the train reaches the next signalbox, the signalman there first puts his signals to 'danger' behind the train and then sends the 'train out of section bell' signal to the first signalman. When the first signalman has acknowledged this signal by repeating it back, the signalman in the second signalbox moves his block indicator from 'train on line' back to 'normal' and the section is once again clear, ready for the next train to be offered.

general terms, was the section of line between two signalboxes, and not more than one train was allowed in a block section on one line at one time. If a second train arrived at a signalbox and another train was already in the block section ahead the signalman had to stop the second train until he had received advice on the block telegraph instruments that the train ahead had cleared that particular block section. Even then some railways in Britain would not adopt the block system but it was made compulsory by Act of Parliament in 1889.

In other parts of the world the electric telegraph helped to control trains. In America Samuel Morse had invented the Morse telegraph code by which telegraph messages were sent by a series of dots and dashes to represent letters and the railways there used this form of telegraph to send messages about train running. On the long transcontinental lines, or anywhere where traffic was not very heavy, the timetable and train order system was used (and on some lines still is). Trains ran over the long single-line sections according to timetable except where extra trains were run or trains ran late. New passing places were arranged between trains in opposing directions by telegraph and the train crew instructed by written train order.

In America the block system was introduced on many lines but later than in Britain and with modern types of control. In Europe, too, the block system was gradually intro-

duced during the latter part of the last century. As the use of electricity became more common on railways, some lines added locking systems to the block instruments so that the block section had to be proved clear by trains operating treadles as they passed from one block section to the next, thus preventing signalmen from making a mistake by clearing the block instruments accidentally while a train was still in the block section.

Since the First World War electrical equipment has been added to normal block instruments so that signals cannot be set at clear unless the block section they control is proved clear. Moreover, new forms of block control by track circuits (see Interlocking and Safety Devices) meant that signals could be set to work automatically as trains passed from one signal section to the next. As trains cleared one section, signals further back could be set automatically to clear. This form of operation, known as track circuit block, is linked with modern centralized power signalling. In this case the block section runs from signal to signal rather than between each signalbox.

Today the block system in its various forms, controlled either by signalmen or stationmasters working in closely-spaced signalboxes or stations, or automatically by the trains themselves, is used throughout the world. The latest signalling schemes in Britain enable control of up to 160km (100 miles) of complicated, multi-track route from one power signalbox.

Early block telegraph instruments usually showed only two indications, rather than three as on modern equipment, and in pre-telephone days were often also used for sending messages, as was this Crookes block signalling instrument (above), originally installed on the Norfolk Railway in 1845.

Interlocking and Safety Devices

On the first railways there were few signals but there had to be points (called switches in America and some other countries) so that trains could cross from one line to another at stations or junctions, or to get in and out of sidings. The switches were usually operated by hand levers alongside. Early signals were also worked by hand levers on the post so that the railway policemen and pointsmen had to walk or run from points to other points and to the signals, moving the levers to allow a train into the station. Sometimes a pointsman might forget to change a set of points and although the signal was clear the train might be diverted on to the wrong line, possibly colliding with another train or becoming derailed. There was nothing to stop two signals being set at clear from different lines leading to the same line, again with the possibility of collision.

It took some years of railway operation before it was realized that it would be easier if signal and points levers were grouped together to save the men so much running about on the line. In 1856, a short distance from London Bridge station where the Brighton and Gravesend lines diverged, the first lever frame was installed where points and their related signals could be controlled from the one position. There was a simple form of locking so that each signal could only be set for a train to go through when the points to which it applied were set. There was no locking with the other signals or points. This came about four years later when an interlocked lever frame was installed at Kentish Town. Here signals were interlocked with other signals leading to the same line or where one line crossed another, so that before the signals for

British Railways signal engineers have always been at the forefront of new development, and these illustrations show the rapid development which took place in railway signalling practice in the latter half of the 19th century. The contemporary lithograph (left), dating from September 1866, shows one of the first 'signalboxes' on the South Eastern Railway outside London Bridge, where for the first time the levers working both points and their associated signals were assembled together, under cover, in a single lever frame.

one line could be set at clear, all the points on that line had to be correctly set, points that could lead to lines across had to be set for another direction if possible, and signals leading to lines across had to be at danger. Thus for the first time two lots of signals leading to the same line could not be clear together. Interlocking, as this was called, was gradually adopted from then on and was made compulsory by law in Britain from 1889.

In other countries interlocking between signals and points has been adopted gradually, certainly on lines with frequent and heavy traffic. On lines in remote parts of America, Australia and Africa, intermediate sidings and passing loops still have hand lever points and no signals, but operating rules mean that trains pass only slowly over the points, and if there are other trains it is up to the crews to control the trains so that they do not collide.

Towards the end of the last century electrical equipment was gradually introduced into railway signalling to provide additional safety. Treadles—long, thin hinged metal sections, placed along the inside edge of the rail so that the wheel flange of a locomotive or coach presses them down—were used to make electrical contacts connected to electric locks in signalboxes. These locks were connected to signal levers or to the block instruments. They could be used to prove that a train had passed a given point to release or lock signals or block instruments, depending on their location.

Track circuits, developed in the early years of the present century, were used for the same sort of thing. Track circuits now consist of sections of line of anything from a few yards to several miles in which the rails are electri-

cally insulated from each other and from the sections at each end. A low-voltage electric current is fed into the rails at one end of the insulated section and at the other is an electric switch called a relay. This is operated by an electromagnet. When no train is on the section the magnet is energized and the switches are in the raised position. When a train is on the track circuit its wheels short-circuit the current which does not reach the relay, the electromagnet is de-energized and the switches move to the lower position where they make different contacts. This switching action can be used to operate various equipment including lights on a signalbox track diagram, locks on other signals and points, locks on control equipment, or other relays.

The track circuit is today the basis of modern signalling in many parts of the world. Some lines are continuously track circuited so that the position of all trains can be seen on signalbox track diagrams. Track circuits can be used to control signals automatically.

In some parts of the world axle-counters are used instead of track circuits or simple treadles. Equipment on the line detects a set of wheels passing over it and operates a counter. If linked axle-counters are placed at each end of a block section and the one at the leaving end counts the same number of axles as the counter at the entry end, it shows that a train has passed into the section and all has come out at the far end. Thus axle-counters can form part of block section protection.

In today's all-electric signalling other types of relay are used for interlocking through electric circuits, instead of the mechanical locks of the old type of interlocking.

Automatic Warning Systems

Almost from the start of railways there were a number of attempts to repeat in the locomotive cab the indications shown by lineside signals so that drivers would not miss a danger signal. Nearly all relied on a lever on the track which could be raised or lowered in conjunction with the signal striking a matching lever on the locomotive as it passed. If the lever on the locomotive was struck by the track lever it could be made to do one of several things —sound the engine whistle, change a visual indicator, perhaps shaped like a signal arm, in the cab in front of the driver, or in later years to apply the locomotive brakes.

For more than 80 years engineers tried different forms of strikers from very primitive designs fitted to one or two locomotives operating from equipment at only a few signals in the 1850s and 1860s, to more extensive installations used by one or two railways in Britain around and after the turn of the century. Although they worked reasonably well, because they were fitted at distant as well as stop signals and thus every train engaged the equipment at every signal, breakages were frequent. So this form of mechanical contact system was abandoned on main lines.

Nevertheless it was taken up on the London underground railways and on a few other suburban railways for use as an emergency stop device if a train overran a stop signal at danger. The trip apparatus, as this form of train stop is known, is installed only at stop signals. When the signal is at danger an arm alongside the rail is raised above track level and engages a lever on the train alongside the train wheels, which is directly connected to the brakes. If a train goes past a danger signal the lever on the train is knocked back and the brakes are fully applied automatically. The driver has to get out of the cab to reset the trip arm before the train can proceed. Because trains do not normally run past signals at danger the apparatus is brought into use only on rare occasions although it is always available. Thus there is not the wear and consequent risk of breakage encountered when the system is used at every type of signal. Today the trip system is still the principal safety system on many urban electric railways.

Other forms of equipment were developed for main-line use to give warning signals in the locomotive cab. In France experiments started in the 1870s which led to the development of what is today known as the 'crocodile' ramp, and in 1906 the Great Western Railway (GWR) in England started trials with ramps. Both were for what was called

Although experiments were already under way, the disastrous double collision in fog at Harrow near London in 1952 hastened the development of the British Railways standard Automatic Warning System. Based on the induction principle, the equipment has a receiver, seen in this view (right) mounted on the frame of the locomotive's leading bogie, and two track magnets laid between the running rails. The first permanent magnet activates the equipment, while the second electromagnet, energised only when the signal is clear, cancels the warning and brake application, and gives a 'clear' indication.

automatic train control; the ramps consisted of metal strips between the rails, about 6-18m (20-60ft) long rising to about 90mm ($3\frac{1}{2}$in) above rail level and engaged a shoe on the locomotive. In the GWR system ramps were installed at distant signals. If a signal was at caution the ramp pushed up the shoe of a passing locomotive, which action sounded a horn in the engine cab and applied the brakes. The driver operated a cancelling handle and could then take control of the brakes. If the signal was clear the ramp had an electric

The advent of high speed trains has brought a requirement for systems to aid drivers, particularly in adverse weather conditions, by bringing into the cab information and details about signals, speed restrictions and other factors affecting the operation of the train. British rail now use passive transponders, mounted between the running rails (right). When interrogated by equipment on a passing train, they respond with a stream of pre-coded information about the state of the line ahead.

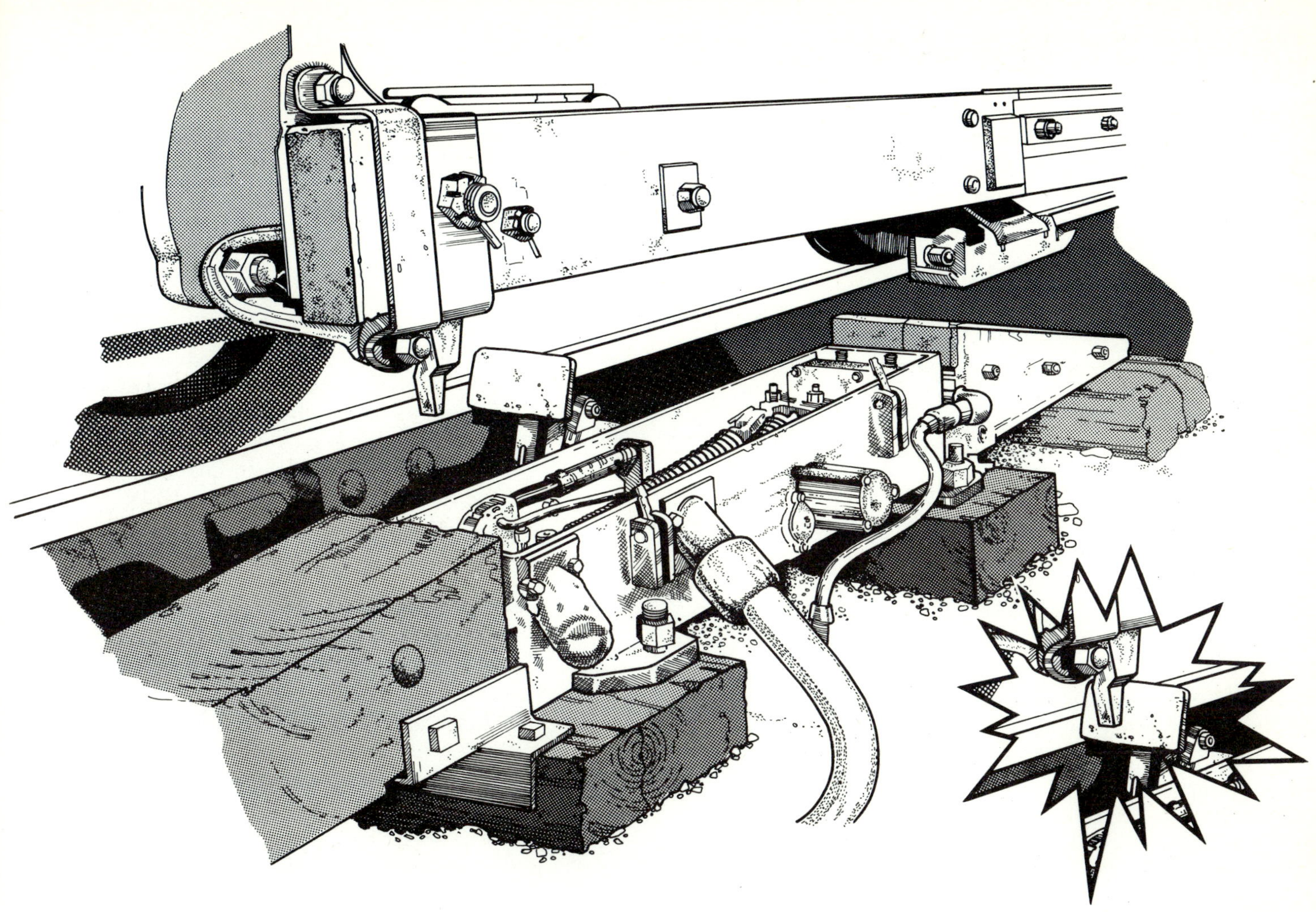

current flowing in it which passed through the shoe into the locomotive equipment. This in turn sounded a bell in the cab and stopped the brakes from being applied. This basically mechanical system was installed on most Great Western lines over the next 50 years and has only recently been superseded.

A later development was equipment which did the same thing but by induction, through permanent and electro-magnets on the track. In the British Railways standard automatic warning system (AWS), used at semaphore distant signals and at colour-light signals, a permanent magnet starts the sequence on the train to sound the warning horn and apply the brakes for caution, but if the signal is clear, or a colour-light at green, an electro-magnet, laid between the rails end-on to the permanent magnet, is energized and overrides the permanent magnet's effect by sounding a bell in the cab and preventing the brake application. Induction automatic warning systems are used in many countries.

More complicated are full cab signalling systems in which pulsed electrical codes transmitted along the rails on which the train runs, or along wires between the rails, can be picked up by the train receiver equipment (in much the same way as a magnetic impulse) which turns the different codes into signal indications in the cab. This type of equipment is very versatile, for it can also display on the driver's control desk the speed at which the train should be travelling and can check it against actual speed so that if the train is going too fast the equipment will apply the brakes to reduce speed, and it can tell the driver where the train is, in the form of distance travelled. The next development is full automatic driving control where the driver merely becomes a watchdog to see that the equipment is working correctly. Already some rapid transit and underground lines have automatically driven trains, including London's Victoria and Fleet lines.

Associated with the simpler types of automatic warning system is a control to prove that the driver is alive and well and in full command. This was originally called the deadman control, for the driver had to hold down a handle or pedal, usually part of the power controller, with his hands or feet. This system is still used on some railways, but in most countries a vigilance system is used connected to the AWS and designed so that the driver has to move a control every minute or so to acknowledge a vigilance warning, otherwise the brakes will be applied.

Although discarded by the mainline railways, the mechanical train stop (above) is the basis of safety on many underground and suburban rapid transit lines. Every stop signal on London's extensive Underground system is equipped with an electro-pneumatic trip arm. When the signal is clear, the arm lies horizontally, allowing trains to pass unhindered, but when the signal is at danger, the arm is raised, and will trip the brake valve and thus apply the brakes on any train attempting to pass. Because physical contact only occurs in unusual circumstances, wear on the mechanical parts is reduced.

Colour Light Signals

Although there were a few isolated examples of railway signals given by lights only using candles or oil lamps in mid-Victorian years, light signals did not become practicable until the early years of the present century. One of the problems was that light signals could not be seen by day.

The first signals to provide the indications by lights only for regular use were on underground lines, particularly the deep-level tube lines of London, built between 1890 and 1910. Although semaphore signals were used as starting signals in platforms, there was no room to put semaphore arms in tunnels, nor could they be seen in the darkness by an approaching train so that drivers depended entirely on seeing the signal light. The first tunnel signals thus had a lamp with a pivoted lantern housing with red and green glasses around it, worked by wire or rod from the station signalbox, to give the two indications red for danger and green for clear. Most of the signal lamps were oil lit, but one or two railways even in the 1890s tried electric lamps which were then gradually becoming sufficiently reliable for this sort of use. Oil lamps continued to be used by some underground railways, while others tried gas lamps, but between 1910 and 1920 most lines changed over gradually to electric-light bulbs, though still at that time with moving lantern glasses to

Spectacular view of colour-light signals (below).

give the colour indications but operated electrically or by compressed air valves. With this form of signal the one lamp was illuminated all the time.

Another type of light signal, gradually developed at this time, had a separate lamp for each colour indication with the coloured glass permanently in front of the lamps. Only the lamp for the particular colour wanted was illuminated. This type of signal had no moving mechanical parts and the lamps were switched on and off by other signalling equipment.

In the early years of the present century the electric lamp and glass lenses had been developed in America to a state that a colour-light signal indication could be seen in daylight, even in sunlight, at distances of up to 730m (800yd). By 1910 the daylight colour-light signal had been introduced on some American lines, but another 10 years were to pass before outdoor colour-light signals were seen in Britain, first on the Liverpool Overhead Railway in 1920. The signals showed two indications, red and green, with separate lamps and lenses for each colour. The Liverpool Overhead Railway was a purely suburban electric line with a frequent service but with speeds no higher than 48km/h (30mph). Two years later daylight colour-light signals were introduced to a British main line, the LNER Great Central route between Marylebone and Neasden, carrying trains at up to 96km/h (60mph). In 1926 the Southern Railway brought into use new colour-light signals between Holborn Viaduct and Elephant & Castle and, later in the year, at the major London terminals of Charing Cross and Cannon Street. These signals were part of complete resignalling, with power operation of points and signals. Moreover the signals themselves were the first, not only in Britain but also the world, to give four indications. In addition to red for 'danger, stop', yellow for 'caution, be ready to find next signal at danger' and green for 'clear', an extra caution indication given by two yellow lights one above the other denoted 'preliminary caution, be ready to find next signal at one yellow'. Thus a driver approaching a red signal would first have passed a double yellow signal, then a single yellow before seeing the red signal. Each signal thus showed the driver the state of the line for three signal sections ahead.

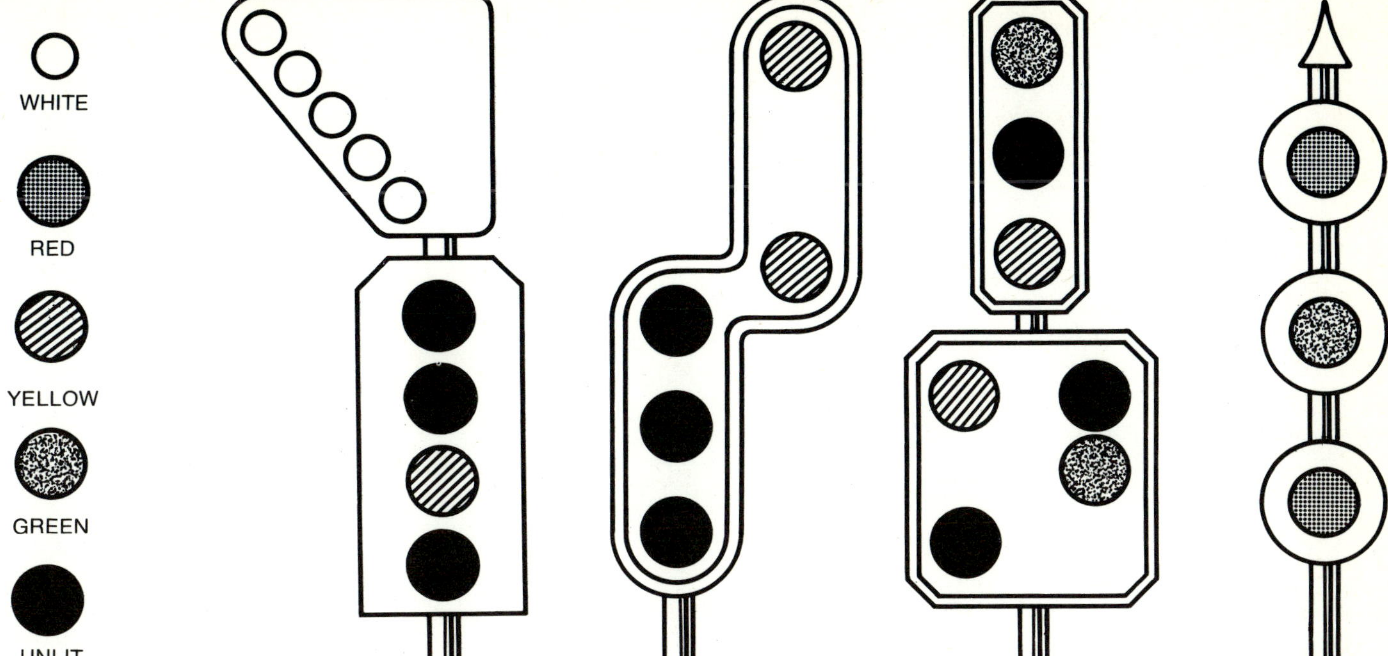

Britain (above) meaning line clear for left-hand divergence but next signal is at danger.

France (above) meaning line clear for divergence at points ahead at not more than 30 km/h.

Switzerland (above) meaning line clear for divergence at points ahead at 40 km/h; next signal ahead clear for exit from loop line at not more than 40 km/h.

USA (above) meaning clear at medium speed through interlocking area. (Points set for diversion at medium speed.)

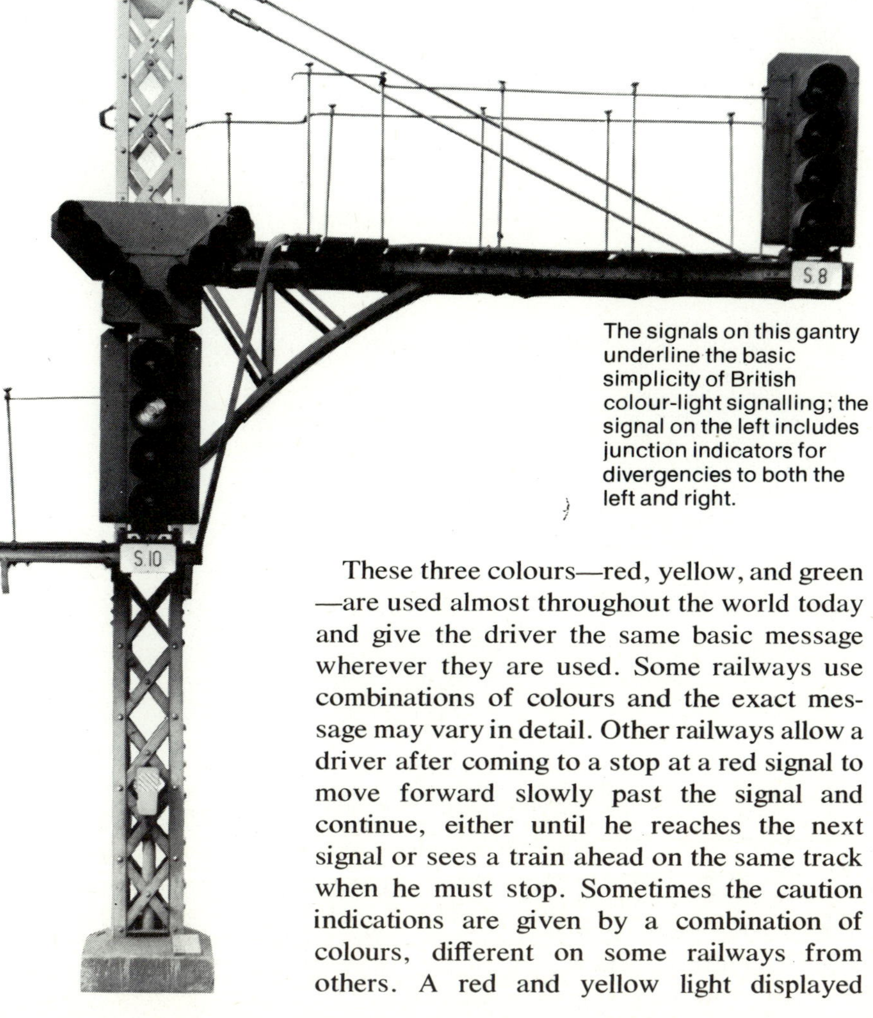

The signals on this gantry underline the basic simplicity of British colour-light signalling; the signal on the left includes junction indicators for divergencies to both the left and right.

These three colours—red, yellow, and green—are used almost throughout the world today and give the driver the same basic message wherever they are used. Some railways use combinations of colours and the exact message may vary in detail. Other railways allow a driver after coming to a stop at a red signal to move forward slowly past the signal and continue, either until he reaches the next signal or sees a train ahead on the same track when he must stop. Sometimes the caution indications are given by a combination of colours, different on some railways from others. A red and yellow light displayed together might mean proceed at caution but at low speed, green and yellow together might mean proceed at caution but at a higher speed. Sometimes different combinations of lights might indicate a specific speed. In America, yellow over green on a block signal, the 'approach medium' indication, means 'be prepared to pass next signal at medium speed', usually because the second signal is at red. This is broadly the same meaning as the British double yellow aspect. In Switzerland and Germany, green over yellow displayed at a signal approaching a station means proceed at low speed to take the diverging track at the points (switches) ahead.

In America and some other countries indications to slow down to take diverging tracks are given by the lower lights on multi-head signals. In Britain, junction indications are given by rows of white lights above the signal, angled in the direction the train is to take. In Britain and some other countries colour-light signals are of the multi-lens type with separate lamps for each colour. Searchlight type signals, with one lamp in each signal head and moving glass slides to give each colour, are also used in Britain and widely in America, Australia and other countries.

The Modern Power Box

After the development of the interlocking lever frame in the 1860s the signalbox became the control centre at each station or junction. Apart from the convenience of having all the signals and points at one location grouped for convenient operation by one or two men, signalboxes served to form boundaries between adjacent block sections. Each signalbox was equipped not only with large mechanical levers for signals and points but also the block telegraph instruments and bells by which the signalmen sent messages about trains entering and leaving each block section. Originally a limit of 228m (250yd) was imposed on the distance between a signalbox

The Southern Railway re-signalled the majority of its main line to Brighton in 1932, in readiness for the opening of its first main line electrification in the following year. Brighton station and its approaches was entirely re-signalled; this is the interior of the then new signalbox (below), showing the miniature levers for individual signal and point switch functions illuminated track diagram and peculiar clock-like rotary train describers.

few places where electricity was available, and although hand generators could be used they were not ideal except where no more than one or two points had to be worked. Thus power operation of points and signals did not develop generally until the 1920s, but even then levers were used to operate electric contacts and for mechanical interlocking.

In the 1930s in Britain the LNER built several power signalboxes in north-east England in which the signalling was all-electric, with colour-light signals, electrically-worked points, and signalboxes in which the controls were worked by small electric switches mounted together on a panel. They were

and points it controlled, later increased to 320m (350yd). So at stations and junctions with many sets of points several signalboxes were needed, block sections between them were short and drivers had to look for several sets of signals in a short distance. Although signalboxes were equipped with ordinary telegraph instruments for sending general messages using the Morse Code, and later telephones, trains were often delayed because a signalman at one signalbox was, perhaps, shunting a goods train from one line to another when an express train was due, because he had not been told that it was getting near to the next signalbox a few hundred yards away.

With several signalboxes controlling a section of line with each man looking after his own area, perhaps less than 730km (800yd) long, without close overall supervision, it was inevitable that train operation would sometimes be uncoordinated, especially when trains were late. When electricity was found to be suitable for operating points by electric motors around the turn of the century, it was realized that there need be no distance limit with electric points. At that time there were

In contrast to the SR boxes, the LNER opted for control-switch operation, where the movement of one switch both operated the points and cleared the signals for one complete route up to the next signal. The largest installation, at York (above, right) was not completed until after the Second World War, and when opened was the largest route relay interlocking system in the world, controlling over 33 miles of track on the approaches to York's 16 platforms.

arranged so that turning one switch operated the points and cleared the signals for each signal section. The equipment also checked that no trains were standing on the line concerned occupying the track circuits, and also that no other train had been signalled across or on to the same line. All the interlocking that did these checks was by electric relays. Thus the control of a large station or junction could be brought into one or two signalboxes each controlling a mile or more of line.

On plain line, that is track without points or junctions for more than a mile or so, signals, usually colour lights, could be arranged to work automatically from track circuits controlled by the trains themselves. Just before the Second World War another type of control panel had been evolved in which the switches to set signals and points, called route switches (or buttons), were placed on a track diagram in the signalbox in their geographical positions corresponding to the signal they controlled out on the line. Normally each signal had one button and by operating the buttons at one signal and at the next on the line on which the train was to go, all the points would be correctly set and the signal would clear if the line was free. In addition the route that had been cleared for a train was shown by white lights along the track concerned on the diagram. As the train moved along the line red lights were illuminated on the diagram instead of white, so that the signalman could see the position of the train even if he could not see the train itself out of the window. This type of signalbox control system has been installed widely in Britain in the last 20 years. To it has been added a display showing the description and number of the train, one display for each signal section. The description moves along the diagram automatically in step with the train by track circuit control, in conjunction with electronic display equipment or a computer. The displays themselves consist of small

Many centralised power signal boxes, such as that at Carlisle (left) employ sophisticated electronics to control signal and point functions up to 160km (100 miles) distant, with computers largely taking over many routine functions. Speed of operation and economy of manpower offered by this system has led to its widespread use throughout railway systems of mainland Europe; the panel at Aachen Hbf (above) is typical of installations currently in use on the German Federal Railway, and Europe.

cathode-ray tubes as on a television set.

During the last 20 years signalling and electrical equipment have become much smaller so that more equipment can be fitted in a given space. In addition developments in long-distance electronic controls mean that signals and points can be worked up to 160km (100 miles) away from a signalbox, with the controls, and the return indications to tell the signalman that the points and signals have changed for several signals and points carried over only two wires.

The latest British signalboxes control long lengths of line, some more than 160 route km (100 route miles). The large control rooms, usually air-conditioned, are like an office, with the signalling control panels arranged in a semi-circle so that the supervisor in charge can see from his central position all the trains under his command. Up to about six signalmen will work the panels, pressing the buttons to signal trains, telephoning to other signalboxes or answering calls from train crews telephoning from lineside telephones to report or for instructions. The track diagram has displays of white and red lights along the

In Europe and the USA large centralised marshalling yards use the 'hump' gravity sorting system (below) with automatic speed retarders.

tracks, red and green lights of signals and other lights to show places where shunting is in progress. Train movement can be planned for an hour or more ahead, for some trains will be under the control of one signalbox for an hour or more.

Signalling Systems of the World

Wherever railways are operated there must be some means of telling locomotive drivers when the line is clear to go, when he must slow down, and when he must stop. There are many different ways of doing this which depend on the normal speed of trains, whether the line is heavily used, what sort of traffic is carried and, to a lesser extent, what gauge the track is. Trains on narrow-gauge lines, for example, often run at low speeds, perhaps not more than 50km/h (30mph) at the most and, if trains are not very frequent, perhaps no more than 10 a day, lineside signals are not needed. Points are handworked by levers alongside them and there are no interlocking or other mechanical safety aids. There will probably be a general instruction that trains must not exceed a speed of 15km/h (10mph) when passing through points, and that drivers must keep speed low at stations and look out for hand signals from the station staff. In fact the station staff probably consists of one man who looks after train signalling, ticket issue, recording parcels for despatch, helps in the shunting of goods wagons, and acts as stationmaster. As there are no signals he will signal to train drivers by flags. Stations will probably

This distinctive German semaphore (above) is showing a 'clear' indication for the nearside track.

The Italian Railways use searchlight-type colour-light signals similar to those used in some parts of Britain and America.

have a double-track passing loop and possibly a siding, and normally drivers will be allowed to enter the station unchecked at low speed but must have a definite instruction, either verbally from the stationmaster or by a green flag, that they may proceed. This method of working, known as the timetable and train order system, is the simplest form of railway working and is used in many countries in remote areas as well as on branch lines in such places as Switzerland.

Railways with higher standards of safety equipment have lineside signals and some form of block working. It is in the detail that the various systems differ. Surprisingly, the signalling in many countries is similar. This is because when the railways in most parts of the world were being built in the last century, few countries had engineers with experience of railway construction and operation, so they came to Europe for advice and equipment. Also during the last century, many countries had colonies in other parts of the world which are today independent countries.

The countries which helped to build railways in other parts of the world or supplied equipment were Britain, France and Germany and thus the signalling systems round the world mostly followed one or other of the systems used in these countries. In Britain the semaphore signal was the standard type by about 1890. The signals showed which route a train was to take at junctions, but the driver had to remember the speed limit through the points. In Germany, semaphore signals are used but they point the other way to those in Britain, and the shape of the arm is different, for it has a rounded end. With the arm horizontal the signal means danger, stop. With the arm inclined up at 45 degrees it means clear. But if a second arm below the main arm is also inclined up at 45 degrees it means that points ahead are set for a divergence and the driver must slow down to a given speed. The signal does not tell the driver which track he is going to but only that the train must run at a low speed. In France signals are given by square or triangular boards, or by discs, which are face-on to a train to give the indication, or

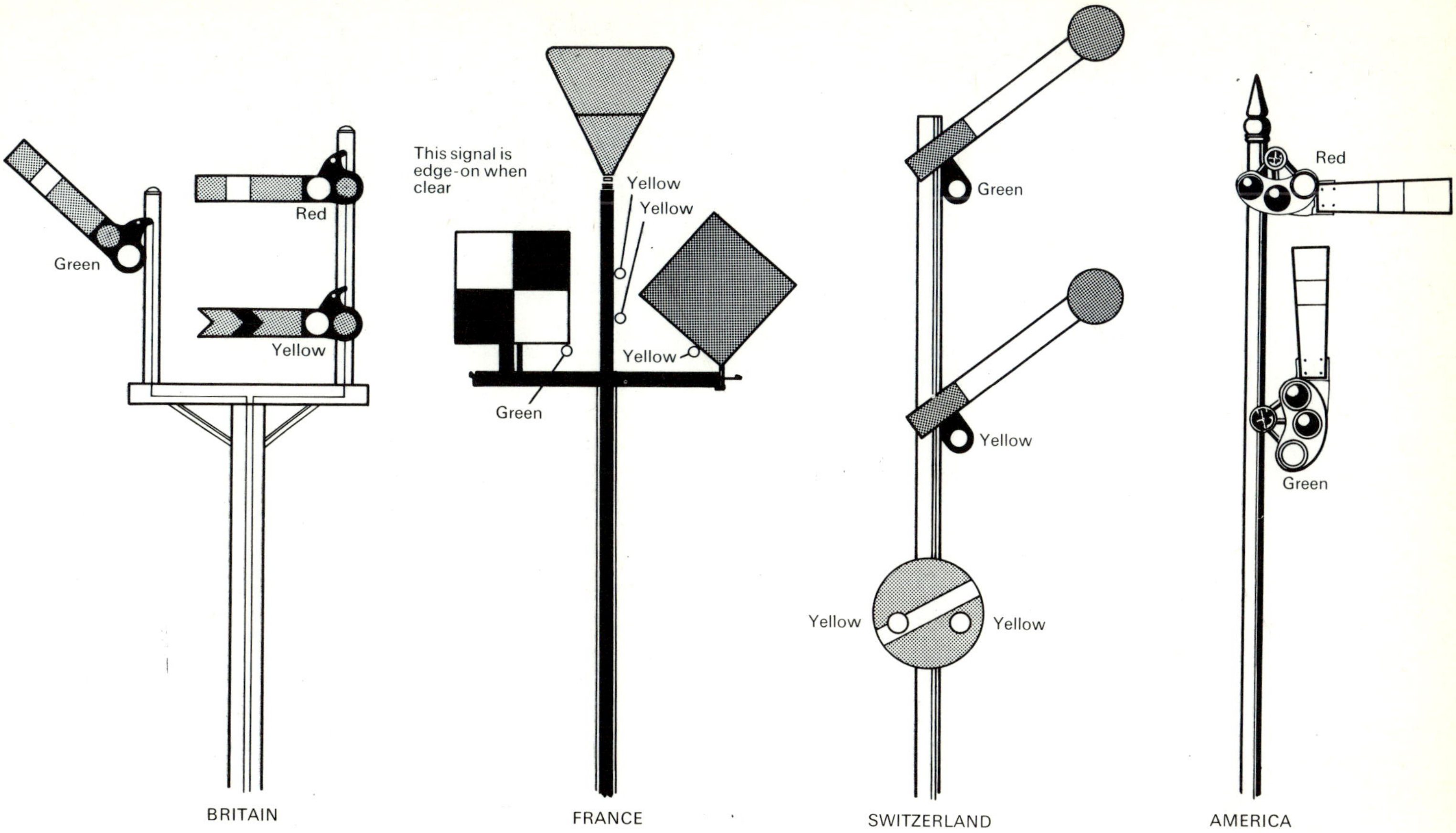

Green   Red   Yellow

BRITAIN

This signal is edge-on when clear

Yellow   Yellow   Yellow   Green

FRANCE

Green   Yellow   Yellow   Yellow

SWITZERLAND

Red   Green

AMERICA

edge-on when the signal is clear, or does not apply, rather like the early signals in Britain. The French stop signal is usually a square board with red and white squares on its face. A distant signal giving a caution indication is a square board painted yellow standing on one corner, and boards to indicate that points are set for a divergence are yellow-painted triangles. There are also other types of signal in France.

German signalling is found in many parts of central and eastern Europe, while British type signalling is used in South America (where British companies built the railways), India, Australia, and Africa. In America the signals give the driver an indication of the speed that the train must observe rather than the exact route it will take. The diagrams show a comparison of the indications given by mechanical signals in Britain, France, Germany and North America for a simple junction, clear for the divergence to the branch line but including a distant caution signal applying to the next signal ahead on the main line.

Colour-light signalling is being extended in most countries, and although standard indications are used, red—stop, yellow—caution, and green—clear, the detailed indications vary from three or four in Britain and France to combinations of lights giving up to 24 indications in North America. Some of the 'speed' signal indications look complicated. A driver on one of the railways with all these compli-

cated signals once said, 'If we see a green light we go, if it is yellow we slow down, and if it's red we stop!'

In other sections you have read about the block system, automatic signalling and other methods of train operation. In Switzerland some of the railways have gone one better by having automatic signalling on single lines. On two of the metre-gauge main lines across southern Switzerland automatic crossing movements can be made. One station signalling control panel takes in passing loops at several other stations. The signalman can signal several trains towards each other with several passing loops available and the signalling equipment automatically selects the best passing place for each train to cross another, and clears the signals at the right time without further action by the signalman.

The Union Pacific 4-4-2 in this 1909 vintage scene (above) is waiting at one of the distinctive, slender-posted, pneumatically operated, lower quadrant semaphore signals common in the USA at this period. The drawings (top) show the corresponding British, French, Swiss and American semaphore signal indications at a junction with the line clear for a divergence to the left.

107

Single Line Working

Many cross-country and branch railways were built with a single-line track, since, with passing places to allow two trains in opposing directions to cross, one track could handle all the traffic. Even today, 100 and more years later, many routes remain single-tracked, not only on cross-country and lightly-used main lines in Britain, but also certain main and cross-country lines in Europe, and some of the long-distance and trans-continental routes in North America, Southern Africa, Australia, New Zealand and in Asia. These routes are often nevertheless important communication links, even though the number of trains they carry may not be high. Some, for example, might have one or possibly two express passenger trains each way daily, a local stopping train and perhaps half a dozen or so freight services. With crossing places perhaps 20, 30 or even more miles apart train operation has to be carefully planned and organized if head-on collisions are to be avoided.

In Britain, without means of communication between stations in the early days, it was realized that there could be great danger of collision without a positive form of control. One method was to use a pilotman, that is a man specially appointed to ride on the locomotive of every train going through the single-line section between the passing stations. As there was only one man on duty for each section at one time it followed that he could only be in one place at one time. This system is still used today for emergency single-line working. From pilotman working it was realized that if a token of some sort, say a piece of wood engraved with the names of the

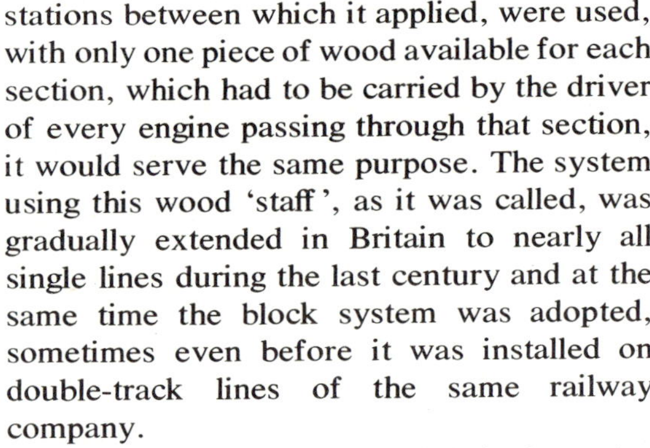

Most of Switzerland's metre gauge railways have long single-line sections, often carrying considerable volumes of traffic, such as the Rhaetian Railway block cement train (below) on the Tich Viaduct over the Albula Gorge in South East Switzerland.

stations between which it applied, were used, with only one piece of wood available for each section, which had to be carried by the driver of every engine passing through that section, it would serve the same purpose. The system using this wood 'staff', as it was called, was gradually extended in Britain to nearly all single lines during the last century and at the same time the block system was adopted, sometimes even before it was installed on double-track lines of the same railway company.

The staff system was inflexible in that trains had to run alternately, otherwise if two trains had to follow one another through the single line, the first one carried the staff and the second had to wait until the staff was brought back in some way.

From the staff-only system was developed staff and ticket operation, which allowed more than one train to go in the same direction, the drivers of all trains of a group except the last being given written tickets giving permission for them to go through the single line. The last train of a group carried the staff ready for a group of trains to run the other way. A signalman could only issue a ticket when he had the staff in his possession.

By the end of the last century the electric staff system had been developed in which special block instruments at each end of the single-line section were electrically connected so that only one of several staffs which they

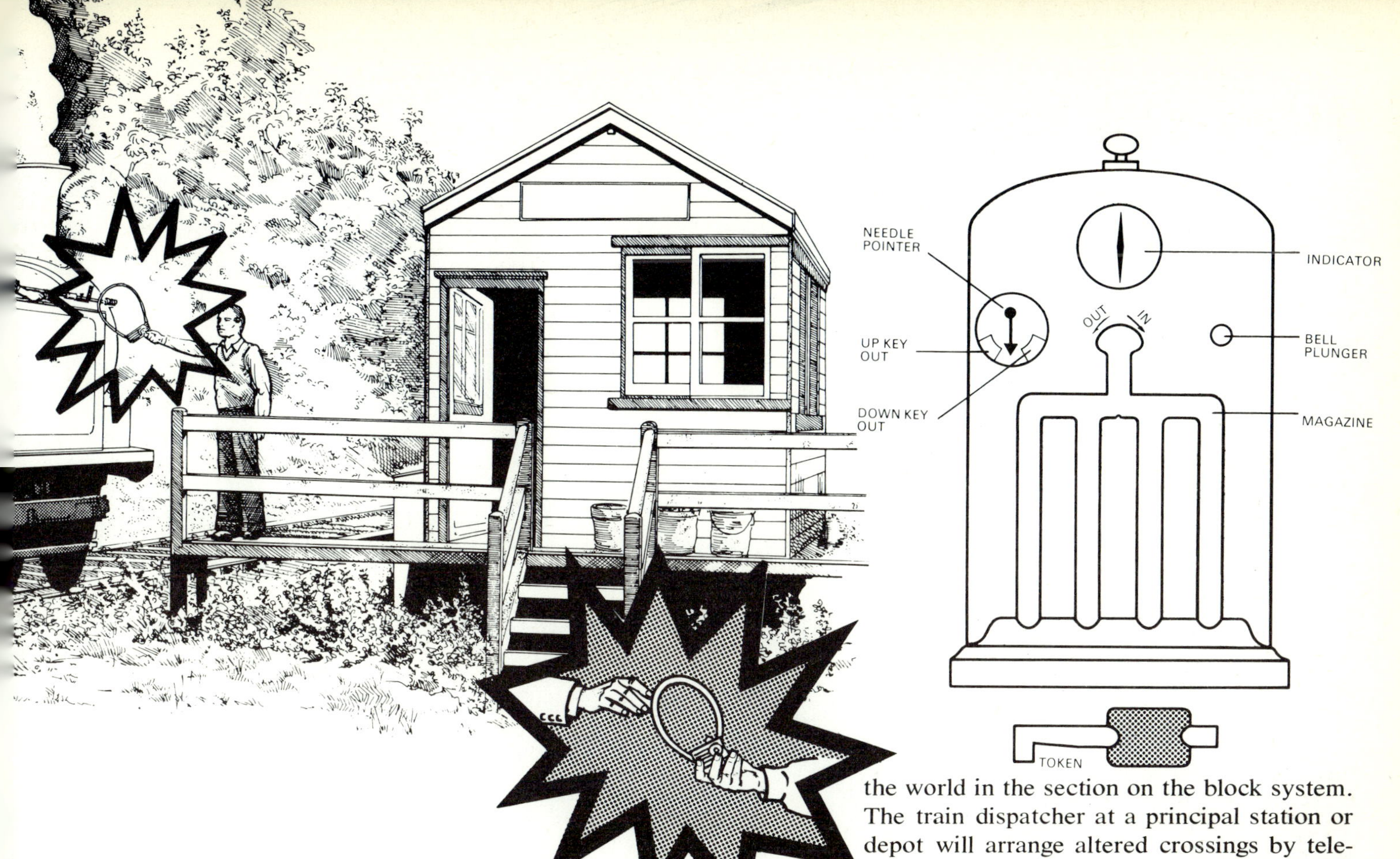

contained could be released at one time. This system was later modified to take steel keys about 23cm (9in) long, instead of long metal staffs. The key token system is used in many parts of the world today to control single lines. Only one key token can be removed from a pair of instruments at one time, so that while a driver has a key token with him no other train can have one for that section.

At every passing place the driver has to give up the token for the section he has just left and pick up another token for the section he is about to enter. Sometimes this exchange of tokens, which are carried in hoops, is done by hand and sometimes by token catchers fixed to the side of the locomotive and on the trackside.

Tokenless block is another form of single-line control system in which block instruments themselves are interlocked with signals governing entry to and exit from a single-line section, and the driver is not given any form of token. Once a train is signalled into the single-line section and passes over the entry-end track circuits or axle counters, the equipment is locked until that train arrives at the other end so that another train cannot be signalled into the section while the first is still there. This system is used in Britain on several single track main lines, and in parts of Europe.

You will already have read about the time-table and train order system used in parts of

The signalman (above) is handing the hoop containing the token (inset) to the driver of a train entering the single-line section he controls, and until the driver either surrenders the token to the signalman at the other end of the single line, or returns it to this signalman, the instruments will be locked in such a way that no other tokens can be removed from their magazines (above, right), and so no other train will be allowed onto the single line.

the world in the section on the block system. The train dispatcher at a principal station or depot will arrange altered crossings by tele-graph, or more likely today by telephone or telex, with the dispatcher at the next depot down the line, perhaps 80km (50 miles) or more away. The written instructions are given to the train crew, often as the train passes without stopping, to alter a scheduled crossing with a train in the opposing direction, perhaps because of late running or an extra train. It is then up to the crew to slow down at the new crossing point, which might not have signals, and run their train into the crossing loop ready to pass the other train. This system was formerly much used in the USA, and if mistakes were made and crossings were not correctly carried out the resulting head-on collisions were often referred to as 'cornfield meets' because they often happened miles from anywhere in Prairie country.

Today many single lines in several countries are controlled by CTC, Centralized Train Control. In this system single lines are usually fully signalled, but remotely from control centres up to 160km (100 miles) away. The dispatcher sits at a control desk with a diagram of the track under his control in front of him, with lights showing the position of trains. He has buttons or switches to control points and signals all along the line. CTC control rooms are just like the modern centralized power signalboxes in Britain, but CTC centres usually look after no more than one long single line with all its passing loops, and controlled with electric or electronic equipment. It is of course far safer and more flexible than the timetable and train order system.

Level Crossings

Although the Railway Age saw the construction of many bridges, there were also numerous flat, or level, crossings between the new railways and existing roads, especially in country districts or where trains ran infrequently.

From the very early days of railways in Britain, public roads crossing a railway on the level had to be protected by gates which swung alternately across the road (when a train was due until it passed) and the railway, to stop people and animals from walking on to the railway. Railways in Britain have always had to be fenced for the same reason. The drawn carts or people on horseback time did not always matter, but today, with busy road traffic, level-crossing gates across a road even for a few minutes can cause extensive traffic delays.

Sometimes level crossings with roads having little traffic did not have a signalbox alongside, but were under the control of a crossing keeper who kept the gates closed across the road and had to ask the signalman in the next signalbox by telephone for permission to open the gates to let a car across.

In many countries, because of the vast distances, railways are not fenced, except

need to have gates at public level crossings was required by law in an Act of Parliament passed in 1845, which also required that such level crossings had to have a man to work the gates, provided by the railway company. In later years this type of level crossing had a signalbox alongside and the signalman was the man who worked the gates, which were protected by the railway signals. The signals could only be set at clear when the gates were closed across the road. When the block system became established, in order not to delay trains, the signals had to be cleared usually when a train was accepted on the block instruments from the next signalbox. The gates had to be closed to road traffic for several minutes before the train actually passed. Sometimes a second train would come in the other direction as well, so that the gates might be closed across the road for 10 or even 20 minutes. When traffic consisted of horse-

Some level crossings are now equipped with full-width lifting barriers, often remotely controlled from modern power signal-boxes some miles away. The area is floodlit at night and the signalman can see the traffic using the crossing through dual closed-circuit television cameras (above, right of photograph) mounted at the top of a mast.

possibly in towns and cities, and many level crossings out in the country have no protection at all except a sign saying 'railroad crossing'. Drivers of road vehicles must approach the crossing with care, looking and listening for any trains that might be near the crossing. Trains in these countries usually have powerful headlights so that they can be seen at night in flat territory. Also most trains give whistle or horn signals which must be sounded as the train approaches the crossing. The 'two long-short-long' whistle code is used throughout North America for a train approaching a grade (level) crossing.

In Britain there are a few crossings over public roads which have no protection other than a warning sign but trains must reduce speed to 16km/h (10mph) or less or even stop first. Normally they are over crossings where both road and rail traffic is very light.

Because of the increased delays at busy

crossings, and the expense of keeping men mainly for level-crossing duties, British Railways looked at other methods from the 1950s. First, lifting barriers were tried at some crossings controlled by the signalman from a signalbox at the crossing in the normal way. But automatic methods and control from long distances were also becoming necessary. After looking at European level crossings BR adopted automatic half-barrier crossings. These crossings have barriers which when lowered protect only the entry part of the road to the crossing in each direction. Normally when no trains are near the barriers are raised. Alongside the crossing are light signals controlling road traffic, again normally out unless a train is approaching. When a train approaches the crossing, it operates a track circuit or treadle which sets off the barrier-lowering sequence. First, a yellow light shows to road traffic, just like ordinary traffic lights, then flashing red lights are displayed and road traffic, including pedestrians, must stop. A few seconds later the barriers drop down to bar the way and a few seconds later still the train passes. When the red lights are flashing no-one must go on to the crossing because a train is coming. After it has passed another train might be coming the other way which will be shown by a sign 'second train coming'. The crossing controls are arranged by a timing

In Britain, simple Continental-type lifting half barriers, automatically actuated by approaching trains (above), are replacing many of the once-ubiquitous but labour-intensive gated level crossings (below).

sequence so that the fastest train is not less than 37 seconds away when the yellow light comes on to stop road traffic.

On some busy roads full lifting barriers are installed but controlled by signalboxes often several miles away. The signalman can see the crossing by closed-circuit television and again light signals are provided to stop road traffic. These crossings are protected by colour light signals which cannot be cleared until the barriers are lowered, and the signalman can see on his television set that the crossing is free of obstruction.

The Development of the Brake

Braking is fundamental to all wheeled vehicles. Early railways followed road transport practice, using brake blocks pressed into contact with the wheels by screw and lever systems. At first brakes could only be applied on the locomotive and the guard's van, often called the brake van because its purpose was to supplement the braking power of the engine. By the 1850s some progress had been made in applying brakes on all vehicles of a train by linking them mechanically, but the most important step in this direction was the invention of the air brake in the United States by George Westinghouse in 1869.

In the first Westinghouse system air compressed by a steam-driven pump on the locomotive was stored in a reservoir. The driver could operate a valve which admitted air from the reservoir to a pipe running the length of the train, with flexible hose couplings between vehicles. In every vehicle the pipe communicated with brake cylinders. Air flowing into the cylinders moved pistons connected by rods and cranks with the brake blocks and pressed them against the wheels. A second position of the driver's handle cut off the air flow, but the pressure in the pipe held the brakes 'on' with the necessary degree of force. To release the brakes the handle was moved to a third position which let the air in the pipe escape.

The system described above is called a 'straight' air brake and is still used on locomotives. It has the drawback that a leak or break in the pipe could make the brake inoperative on vehicles in the train without the driver being aware of it. The straight air brake was therefore quickly followed by the automatic brake (1874) in which an escape of air applies the brakes without action by the driver. If part of a train breaks away, the brakes are applied on both halves. In this system air pressure is maintained continuously in the train pipe and the brake is applied by reducing the pressure. On each vehicle an auxiliary reservoir is connected to the pipe and also to the brake cylinders. When the pipe pressure is reduced by the driver an automatic valve lets air flow from the auxiliary reservoirs into the brake cylinders until the reservoir and brake pipe pressures are equal. The brake is released by the driver restoring air pressure in the pipe from the main reservoir on the locomotive.

In steam locomotives the air for braking is usually compressed by a steam pump. Electric and diesel locomotives have motor-driven compressors. Both pumping systems work automatically to maintain the required pressure.

In the automatic air brake the air itself

Although by the turn of the century universal both in America and on the European continent, the Westinghouse automatic air brake, shown here in diagramatic form (right), was only adapted as standard in Britain in the 1960s, and many older vehicles are still equipped with the less efficient but simpler vacuum brake.

The modern railway locomotive cab is far different from the early days of steam, when the trains were unbraked, and the only brakes on the locomotive were wooden blocks pressed into contact with the wheels by a simple lever system. This is the control console of a British Railways Class 87 25,000V ac electric locomotive (right). The Westinghouse air brake control is on the left, while the power controls are to the right. The dial display includes brake pipe and cylinder pressure gauges, while at the top left is the visual indicator of the Automatic Warning System, which is coupled to the brake controls.

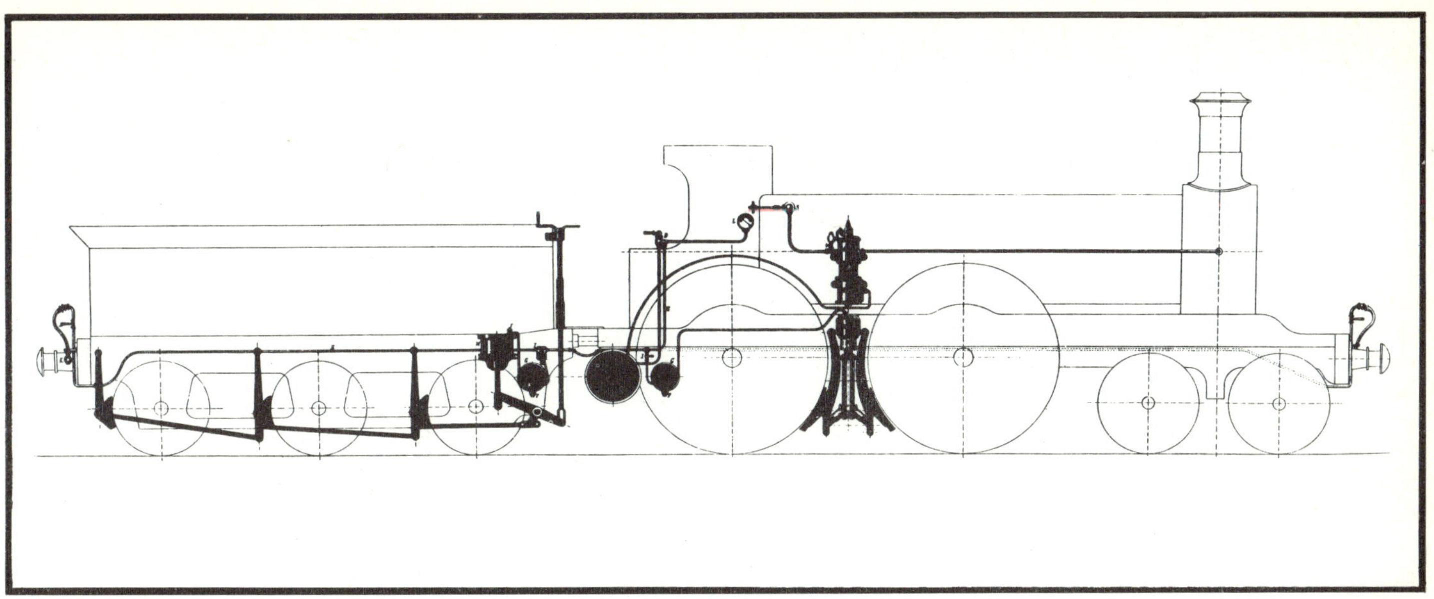

works the control valves on each vehicle and there is some delay before those at the rear of the train operate. To speed the action, particularly on suburban services with numerous stops, the electro-pneumatic brake was developed. The valves which admit air to the brake cylinders are then operated by electric currents controlled by contacts on the driver's brake handle and all valves throughout the train act together. This brake, however, is not 'fail-safe'. A fault in the electrical system could prevent the brakes being applied. Electro-pneumatic braking is therefore backed up by a conventional automatic arrangement.

An alternative to the air brake is the vacuum brake, in which the brakes are applied by normal atmospheric pressure. The brake cylinders are made with upper and lower portions and are interconnected throughout the train by a train pipe as before. Air is drawn out of the pipe until the pressure on both sides of the piston in each cylinder is below normal. This is the normal 'brakes off' condition. To apply the brake, air is admitted to the train pipe and enters the lower portion of the cylinders. It cannot reach the upper part, however, because of a one-way valve, and so the difference in pressure between each side of the piston causes it to move upwards and apply the brakes. The system is automatic because entry of air caused by a leak or break in the train pipe puts the brakes on.

Air is drawn from the train pipe by a motor-driven exhauster, or in steam locomotives by a device called an 'ejector' in which steam discharged through a series of nozzles draws air with it. The degree of vacuum is not high, usually about 533 to 635mm of mercury (21 to 25in) compared with a normal atmospheric pressure of about 762mm (30in).

Locomotives propelled by electric motors can be braked by reconnecting the motors to

act as generators and send current round a circuit containing resistance (rheostatic braking), the effort increasing as the resistance is reduced. On electric railways the current generated by the motors can be returned to the supply system (regenerative braking). Both systems become ineffective at low speeds, when air or vacuum braking is brought into action automatically to bring the train to a standstill.

In some trains designed for very high speeds a hydrokinetic brake is used to supplement friction braking. The brake consists of a bladed rotor revolving inside a casing containing a fluid, such as water/glycol mixture. The drag of the fluid creates a braking force, but at the same time its temperature rises (the kinetic energy of the train being converted into heat energy) and it must be pumped through radiators to cool it. High-speed trains with this form of braking in addition to friction brakes can be brought to a standstill from 200km/h (125mph) in just over 1.1km (under three-quarters of a mile). A conventional train running at 160km/h (100mph) requires 1.3km (0.8 miles) to stop.

In Britain, the switch from vacuum to air brakes coincided with the transition from steam to diesel and electric traction, thus creating even greater operating problems. Very few steam engines were equipped with air brakes, but almost all diesels are dual braked and capable of working with either type of stock. Some, like the Southern Region Class 33 diesel (above), can also work in multiple with diesel and electric multiple-units.

Railways in the Cinema

In their first cinematograph show on 28 December 1895 the French pioneers of cine photography, Louis and Auguste Lumière, included a scene of a train arriving at a country station. The railway must have attracted many early cine photographers whose aim was simply to produce the novelty of moving pictures. People and horse-drawn traffic were subjects which provided movement, but the train added the majesty of power. If the camera concentrated on its rods and cranks in close-up, fascinating moving patterns were produced. The observer at the lineside could appreciate them only momentarily as the train passed by, but the camera travelling with the locomotive kept them before his eyes. Much use was made of this device as the cinema grew out of the novelty stage and became a story-teller. The train was a part of everyday experience with an element of drama. In silent film days the thrill of speed could be conveyed by the whirling wheels and coupling rods of a locomotive, or tension could be created by showing wheels locked and skidding on the rails in a desperate effort to avoid collision.

In some parts of the world the railway was an episode in the national story. The Paramount film, *Union Pacific*, made in 1939, reconstructed the building of the trans-continental line which linked the Eastern and Western States of the USA to create a unified country. For a time the unity was shattered by the American Civil War, and some episodes of the conflict provided material for film makers over many years. One of these was the raid at Kennesaw, Georgia, in which a party of the Northern forces under Captain James Andrews seized the locomotive 'General' belonging to the Confederates and drove it for some 140km towards Chatanooga, pursued by the Confederate locomotive 'Texas' until

An immaculately turned out French Railways G class 4-6-0 gleams beneath the spotlights (below) at Stamboul Station during shooting of the Agatha Christie thriller 'Murder on the Orient Express'.

'General' ran out of fuel. This daring exploit was dramatised on film as early as 1911, and 16 years later the same theme was used in the comedy thriller *The General* with Buster Keaton, and in more recent years in the sound film *The Great Locomotive Chase*.

The foregoing films are fiction with a factual background. Perhaps the best-known purely fictional film with a railway setting is *La Bête Humaine*, a screen version made in 1939 of Zola's novel of the same name, but moved forward in time from the Franco-Prussian War to the years immediately before the Second World War.

Other producers have taken a more light-hearted view of railways. Among railway comedy films the titles *Oh! Mr Porter* and *The Titfield Thunderbolt* stand out like peaks. The former, starring the British comedian Will Hay, was made in 1937 and its setting is an imaginary railway in Northern Ireland. The story tells how a new station-master at 'Buggleskelly' decides to stimulate business at this somewhat run-down and seedy spot by running an excursion train. All the tickets are

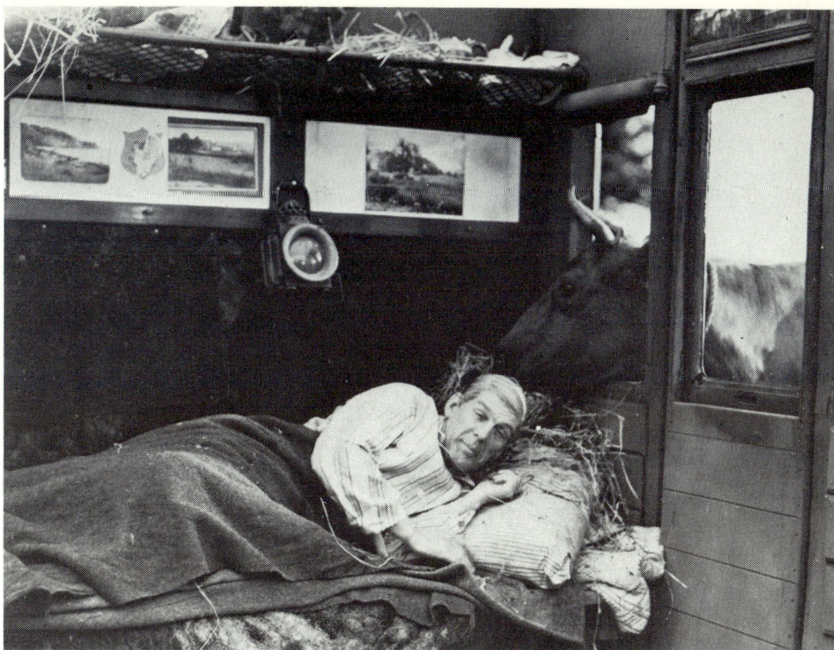

bought by one man for a football team which is in fact a gang of gunrunners. A succession of hilarious and exciting incidents leads at length to their capture, but it all proves too much for the excursion train locomotive, 'Gladstone', which blows up as a climax after the gunrunners have been caught.

The years after the Second World War saw some railways in decline and much controversy over the closing of unprofitable lines together with efforts to preserve them, partly for use and partly for the pleasure of steam railway enthusiasts. A successful preservation scheme in Wales which has turned the Talyllyn Railway into a tourist attraction suggested the plot of *The Titfield Thunderbolt*, made in England in 1952.

Radio and television have brought some books of earlier years back into favour. Among them is *The Railway Children* by Edith Nesbit, a story of the years before the First World War which became popular as a radio serial when broadcast by the BBC after the war of 1939-45. It became a highly successful film in 1969 and is probably better

known today as a film than as a book. The railway preservation movement, now worldwide, is a boon to film makers seeking steam-hauled trains for their stories. In *The Daring Young Men in their Flying Machines* an old Scottish locomotive preserved by British Railways does duty as a French locomotive of the early years of the century. The requirements of film companies have become a valuable source of extra revenue for the operators of preserved lines, who have become adept at disguising their locomotives to harmonise with different periods and parts of the world. International expresses, somewhat overshadowed now by air travel, retain their former glamour in many films and in filmed versions of novels. Often they are settings for espionage and crime, as in *Rome Express,* made in England in 1933, and in the filmed version of Agatha Christie's detective novel, *Murder on the Orient Express,* of recent years.

The Permanent Way

Tracks of various kinds to guide vehicles and make their movement easier date back many centuries before the invention of the steam locomotive. If one accepts the use of stone blocks placed end to end to form a smooth path for wagon wheels, there is a case for saying that railways were known in Biblical times. The true ancestors of the railway as known today, however, were lines laid with wooden rails in mines, along which trucks were pushed by hand. They date at least from the 16th century, when they were found in the copper, tin and lead mines of central Europe.

It appears that flanged wheels were used at this early period, but in some of the mine railways the wheels were plain. In this case the rails were laid close together and the wagon was guided by a pin on the underframe which projected downwards into the space between them. Sometimes a wheel at the lower end of this vertical pin, or axle, made rolling contact with the insides of the rails so that the wagon was guided without friction. An Englishman who visited the gold mines at Kremnitz, Lower Hungary, in 1669, was impressed by the ease with which heavy loads could be moved. 'By this means,' he wrote, 'a little Boy will run full speed with three or four hundred pound weight of Ore or Earth before him, wherever you command him, without

By the beginning of the 19th century, cast iron was starting to replace timber for running rails on most wagonways. This wagonway at Belvoir Castle (right) was laid down about 1815, and the horse drawn wagon is running on typical short fish-belly rails mounted on stone blocks, at first a popular alternative to the traditional timber transverse sleeper. As can be seen in this striking view of the Canadian Pacific Railway under construction through desolate country near Moose Jaw, Saskatchewan in 1880 (below) many early lines were quite literally merely laid direct on levelled ground, with the flat-bottomed rails spiked directly to rough wooden sleepers.

any light, through those dismal dark passages of the Mine; and it was very new to me to hear the rattling they make in the Mine . . .'

Wooden railways lasted for some three centuries and by the end of their era were used in various mining and quarrying industries for transporting materials in the open as well as underground. Rails were made of lengths of timber up to 150mm (6in) square secured to transverse sleepers at intervals of about 600mm (2ft). In mine workings wagons were pushed by hand because of restricted space, but when lines were laid on the surface the horse became the normal motive power. The use of flanged wheels for guidance enabled rails to be laid farther apart and improved the stability of the vehicles. Iron rails came into use towards the end of the 18th century. At first they were rectangular in section like the wooden rails they replaced but this simple form was soon varied to make more effective and economical use of the metal.

An alternative to the rail for flanged wheels was a rail of L section. The vehicle wheels were then flangeless and rolled along the bottom of the 'L', the 'upright' providing guidance. Railways of this type were called 'plateways'. They survived into the earliest days of steam traction but were then soon abandoned.

Early iron rails were cast, and their brittleness was a problem when they had to carry the weight of steam locomotives. In 1820 John Birkinshaw of Durham, England, developed a process for rolling wrought-iron rails in lengths of up to 6.1m (20ft). Most of the Stockton and Darlington Railway, opened in 1825 and the first public railway in the world to use steam traction from its inception, was laid with Birkinshaw rails weighing approximately 14kg per metre (28lb per yard).

The transverse sleepers which carry the rails continued to be of timber after the introduction of iron rails, but there was a period lasting into the early years of the steam railway when some engineers favoured stone blocks under each rail instead. They were roughly square and about 200mm (8in) thick. Blocks of this kind were used on the Surrey Iron Railway in England, a plateway built in 1803 to carry limestone from the North Downs to the Thames. Stone-block sleepers were also used at first on the London and Greenwich railway, opened in 1836, and on the London and Birmingham, opened in 1838. The blocks on the London and Birmingham line were 600mm (2ft) square and 300mm (1ft) deep. Almost exactly one hundred years after the opening, a number of them were discovered during road-widening works at Watford, where they had been buried in a bank to strengthen it. It is believed that the first official use of the words 'permanent way' occurred in a London and Birmingham report of 1837 in order to make a distinction between the temporary contractor's track and the rails on which the trains would run when construction of the line was finished.

The iron or steel rail on transverse sleepers soon became the worldwide standard for railways, but there was an exception for a short time in Great Britain, the birthplace of the steam railway. The engineer Isambard Kingdom Brunel not only chose the broad gauge of 2.146m (7ft 0½in) for the Great Western Railway but laid the rails on longitudinal timbers 4.75m (15ft 7in) long. These were braced by

transverse wooden ties at a wider spacing than ordinary sleepers, and the ties were spiked to 254mm (10in) dia piles driven vertically downwards into the roadbed. The rails themselves were the so-called 'bridge' rail, of inverted U section with flanges for attachment to the longitudinal timbers.

In 1855 Henry Bessemer patented his 'acid' converter for making mild steel and the end of the wrought-iron rail was foreshadowed. The first steel rails were laid in England at Derby in 1857.

Between the wooden and the iron rail there was an intermediate stage in which wooden rails were reinforced with iron plates. By the time of the first steam locomotives iron rail was used exclusively, rolled in a variety of cross and longitudinal sections devised to combine strength with economy of material.

In the early 1830s a British engineer, Joseph Locke, developed a 'dumb-bell' rail, so-called because in cross-section it consisted of symmetrical upper and lower portions (called the upper and lower 'tables') separated by a narrow vertical portion like the bar of a dumb-bell. The rails rested in chairs screwed to the sleepers and were secured in the chairs by wooden keys. It had been intended that when the upper table of the rail became worn the whole rail should be turned over, the lower table becoming the upper. In practice, however, it was found that the lower table became dented where it rested in the chair by the impact of passing trains and was unsuitable as a running surface. The idea of reversal was abandoned, and in due course the design evolved into what is now known as the 'bull-head' rail, no longer symmetrical like Locke's dumb-bell but with the top portion (the rail head) deeper than the bottom (the foot).

The bull-head rail was for many years the standard in Great Britain, although not widely used elsewhere. Head and foot of the bull-head rail are of the same width. The narrow

Apart from Britain, where a considerable amount of bull-head rail is still used, flat bottom rail, spiked, screwed or clipped to baseplates, is virtually universal throughout the world. CP Rail's 'Canadian' Express (above), threading the suburbs of Montreal, is riding heavy section flat bottom rail with staggered rail joints, a feature essentially peculiar to the North American continent. In Britain and most of Europe, new flat- bottom track has welded rail joints, forming continuously welded rail (cwr) in lengths of well over a kilometre.

upright part between them is called the 'web'. Like the original dumb-bell rail, the bull-head rail rests in a chair, generally of cast iron, and is secured by a wooden or spring steel key driven between the outer jaw of the chair and the rail. As well as supporting the rail, the chair spreads the load of passing trains over a larger area of the sleeper than if the narrow foot rested directly upon it.

The alternative and now generally used type of rail—the flat-bottom rail—was introduced only a year after the bull-head and was designed by Charles Vignoles, another famous railway builder of the 1830s.

In the Vignoles rail the head was similar to that of Locke's dumb-bell but the foot was flat and wide enough to be spiked directly to the sleepers. In modern versions, however, there is often a baseplate between rail and sleeper to spread the load, and the rails are held down by various forms of spring clip designed to allow easy removal when necessary. Some types of fastening hold rail and baseplate together to the sleeper. In others the baseplates are separately secured to the sleepers, the removable spring clips holding the rails to the baseplates.

Charles Vignoles was associated with railway building in Sweden, Mexico, Brazil, France, Switzerland, Spain, Poland and Ireland. Thus his type of rail spread throughout the world, and was eventually adopted in his own country, although not until the late 1940s.

In both bull-head and flat-bottom track the ends of rails are joined by fish-plates. These are flat metal bars fitted in pairs on the outside and inside of the rails at the joint. The fishplates and the rail ends are drilled for the fishbolts, on which nuts are tightened to clamp both fishplates firmly against the rail webs. The joints normally occur between sleepers and are called 'suspended joints', but it is common practice to reduce the sleeper spacing as the ends of the rails are approached. A gap is left between the ends of rails to allow for expansion.

Rails are produced at the rolling mills in various lengths, the limits being set by considerations of transport to site. In Britain a length of 18.29m (60ft) is now standard but in Germany they may be as much as 30m (98ft 5in) long. After being laid in the track, the individual lengths of rail are often welded together to form continuous welded rail (cwr) over long distances. Rails are classified according to their weight per unit length, eg 55.79kg/m (113lb/yd) for the current standard flat-bottom rail used on British Railways.

One of the familiar railway sounds of the past was the click of wheels passing over rail joints. Today it is becoming less often heard because of the growing practice of welding rails together. This is not done simply to give a smoother and quieter ride. Rail joints are a weak link in the permanent way, particularly under high-speed traffic, and it is estimated that as much as a third of all rail failures occur close to joints.

Rails are often first welded together in trackside depots in maximum lengths for convenient transport, and assembled with concrete sleepers in complete pre-fabricated sections of track. The sections are then conveyed to site for laying, after which they are welded together over as great a distance as practicable. Points and crossings may make a break in continuity necessary, and here the usual type of butt or square-ended joint may be replaced by a special expansion joint in which the ends of adjacent rail sections are tapered off so that they overlap, and each rail can expand in high temperature conditions without the gap being closed. Expansion is not uniform over the whole length of rail which has been welded but occurs chiefly towards the ends. Its effects are better resisted by modern concrete sleepers and track fastenings than by older equipment.

Sections of rail have to be isolated electrically from their neighbours at intervals to form the track circuits through which signalling is controlled. Various types of jointless track circuit have been developed for use in welded track but in some conditions these are not acceptable on electrified lines and insulated rail joints have to be used, a small block of insulating material being inserted between the rail ends.

Railway track is laid on a foundation of ballast which is shaped to distribute the load imposed on the sleepers over a wider area of the soil below. If the soil is soft clay there is a tendency for the movement of the sleepers under traffic to 'pump' the clay up into the ballast. To prevent this happening a layer, or 'blanket', of other material such as sand or crushed ashes—sometimes even plastic sheeting—is laid on the soil before the ballast is put down. In all cases the soil, known as the 'formation', has to be shaped to drain water away to the sides.

Much work is involved in keeping the permanent way in good shape, and under conditions of intensive traffic at ever higher speeds it becomes increasingly difficult to find time for maintenance without interrupting the train service. Railways are therefore turning to road-building practice and experimenting with track laid directly on a continuous foundation of reinforced concrete. It has been found that this system reduces pressure on the ground, so that there is less settlement under load and

The concrete and asphalt track under test (above) has the advantage that it can be subjected to traffic loading within a few hours of laying, while the solid reinforced concrete trackbed (inset right) has the advantage of absolute rigidity and thus constant almost permanent alignment, coupled with exceptional durability, and is thus much favoured for tunnel locations. Despite these developments, however, and the widespread use of flat-bottomed continuously welded rail (cwr) on most high-speed lines, much bull head rail supported in cast-iron chairs remains in use on lesser-used, low speed lines in Britain (inset above).

track stability is improved. If the concrete is laid to replace existing track, the old ballast may be used as a foundation. On new alignments the ground is prepared by methods similar to those used in road building.

In the course of experiments in several countries supported by the International Union of Railways, a road-making machine called a slip form paver has been adapted for railway use. It is incorporated in a concrete-laying train of five units—a concrete elevator and feeder, two travelling gantries, the slip form paver, and a hole borer. Concrete is prepared off-site and conveyed to the train in dump trucks. The trucks mount ramps on the elevator and feeder unit and transfer their load into a hopper. Meanwhile, on the lower floor of the gantry units sections of reinforcement material are being welded together.

In the paver unit at the rear of the train the reinforcement is raised into a position where the concrete arriving on the conveyors can be formed around it, and the complete reinforced slab is deposited on the ground as the train moves forward.

The train carries sufficient reinforcement material for 200m (656ft) of slab to be laid. When this is used up the feeder and first gantry unit can be released to travel to a point where a pallet with further reinforcement can be picked up and carried back to the train. The hole-boring machine is a separate unit which follows the train and forms a pattern of holes in the wet concrete for the rail fastenings. Up to 39.6m (130ft) of slab can be laid in an hour.

The train is propelled by hydraulic power from a diesel-driven pump. It has power steering controlled automatically by guide wires stretched along the line of route. Feeder arms connected to micro-switches follow the wires and detect any divergence from course or level, sending correcting signals to the hydraulic rams of the steering and levelling systems. The concrete, shaped to allow drainage towards a centre channel, is laid with a surface accuracy of 1mm in 10m.

Among the countries where sections of paved concrete track are in use are France, Great Britain and New Zealand. In Britain, experiments are also under way on paved high speed turnouts.

Track and Loading Gauges

Early vehicles running on rails were propelled by hand and mostly used in mines underground. When railways were built above ground to distribute the coal and minerals that had been mined the wagons were drawn by horses and the distance, or gauge, between the rails was approximately the same as the width of road vehicles. There were many minor variations, and it was by chance that the Willington Colliery wagonway, where the British engineer, George Stephenson, gained his early rail transport experience, had been laid to a gauge of 1.435m (4ft 8½in). This eventually gained such widespread acceptance that it has become known as the standard guage.

Even in Great Britain, however, where the steam railway originated, there was somewhat haphazard development at first. The best known breakaway is the 2.146m (7ft 0½in) chosen by Brunel for the Great Western Railway, but other engineers, without going as far as Brunel, thought that widening the standard gauge by a few inches would enable more powerful engines to be built, which would be easier to maintain because their working parts would be more accessible.

Some of the pioneers of railway building in Europe had their say on the gauge question in 1845 when they appeared before a Parliamentary Commission in England. Charles Vignoles expressed a preference for 1.83m (6ft), although he did not have the opportunity to put it into practice. Joseph Locke was a stout supporter of the standard gauge, which he had recently introduced into France, but stressed that the most important consideration was uniformity of gauge within a country. He recommended conversion of the Great Western Railway to this end, but that company's broad gauge was not finally abolished until 1892. Brunel defended his choice of the broad gauge with vigour. Despite the inconvenience of transhipment where broad and standard gauges met, he maintained that uniformity would not be to the public advantage because he believed that 'a great deal of the progress that has been made in railways has arisen from the fair emulation which exists between the promoters either of two gauges or of other varieties, and that the system of generalizing, whether the gauge or anything else, would do harm rather than good'. However, the Com-

Many differing loading gauges are to be found, even on standard gauge track. Britain's loading gauge, with many tunnels and cramped city-centre track layouts, is among the most restrictive, whilst in contrast, the American loading gauge is very generous, allowing the construction of such massive motive power units as this Union Pacific Railroad 'Big Boy' 4-8-8-4 (below).

mission recommended the adoption of the 1.435m (4ft 8½in) gauge as standard in Great Britain.

Eleven principal gauges are still used in different parts of the world, from 1.676m (5ft 6in) to 0.610m (2ft). At some places where different gauges meet provision is made for through running by changing the wheelsets of vehicles. A recent development in Spain, where there is a change of gauge at the French frontier (from the Spanish 1.676m to the French 1.435m) is the building of freight vehicles with wheels that can slide along the axles to fit either gauge. Each wheel is mounted on a sleeve. When the vehicle enters the changeover section guide blocks at each end of the axle engage with slides at the trackside and are moved outwards to unlock the sleeves. Beyond this point the track widens (or narrows) to the new gauge, shifting the wheels as it does so, and at the end of the section the wheels are again locked in their new positions.

The claim to be the world's smallest public railway is made by the Romney, Hythe & Dymchurch Railway in England, with a gauge of only 381mm (15in). Smaller private miniature railways use 261mm (10¼in) and 185mm (7¼in) gauge tracks.

Loading gauge refers to the permissible overall dimensions of vehicles on a railway and is governed by the clearance necessary for passing through bridges and tunnels. Early steam railways in England had restricted loading gauges because the engineers did not foresee the size of locomotives and rolling stock that would be required in the future. On British Railways it is still only 3.86m (12ft 8in) in height above rail level and a maximum width of 2.69m (9ft 3in). This compares with the recommended standard for the mainland of Europe of 4.28m (14ft 0½in) by 3.15m (10ft 4in). Some lines of sub-standard track gauges in countries where there are many miles of open country with no bridges or tunnels have quite generous loading gauges. On the 1.067m (3ft 6in) gauge South African system, for example, the dimensions are 3.96m (13ft) by 3.05m (10ft), enabling locomotives to be built with massive boilers, and passenger stock to be much more roomy than would seem possible judging by the close spacing of the rails.

Whilst it is possible to work rolling stock of differing loading gauges over the same line provided the track gauge is the same, it is clearly not possible to run trains of differing track gauge unless complicated special multi-gauge tracks are provided. Several European countries, as well as Africa and Australia, nevertheless have mixed gauge sections on their railway systems; this is the mixed-gauge motive power depot at Regva in Portugal with a narrow-gauge locomotive in the foreground on the same set of tracks as the broad gauge locomotive on the multi-gauge turntable in the background. Note that some sections of line have completely separate running rails for broad- and narrow-gauge vehicles, while others, such as the track in the right foreground, have one running rail common to both gauges.

How an Electric Locomotive Works

Electric motors in industry take various forms, but the motors which drive an electric locomotive are nearly always of the same basic type. Current flows through the windings of electromagnets to create a magnetic field, and then through coils carried by a drum, or armature, which is pivoted in the field. The resultant force on the current-carrying coils of the armature makes the armature revolve.

Current is supplied to the armature through carbon brushes bearing on the copper segments of a commutator on the armature shaft. As the commutator revolves, and its segments pass under the brushes, the direction of current in the armature coils is repeatedly reversed so that the force acting on them keeps the armature revolving in the required direction. This process of current reversal is called 'commutation' and is the most critical aspect of motor design.

The motors of a modern electric locomotive are carried in the bogies alongside the axles they drive, a pinion on the armature shaft meshing with a large gearwheel on the axle. A typical modern 3,728kW (5,000hp) locomotive has four axles each driven by a motor of 932kW (1,250hp) weighing 3,048kg (3 tons).

Where the supply to the trains is at 750 volts or less, current may be fed to them through a 'live' rail laid alongside or between the running rails and collected by sliding shoes attached to shoebeams on the bogies. Voltages used on main lines are usually 1,500 or 3,000V direct current (dc) or in the region of 15,000 or 25,000V alternating current (ac). From 1,500V upwards the power is supplied from an overhead contact wire suspended above the tracks. It is picked up by a collector mounted on a light, jointed framework called a pantograph, and held in contact with the wire by springs acting on the pantograph frame.

From the collector the supply passes to a circuit-breaker, often mounted on the locomotive roof close to the pantograph. This is a switch capable of breaking very high currents, which opens automatically in the event of an electrical fault in the locomotive.

The interior of the locomotive body between the end cabs is occupied by the switchgear and other apparatus which controls the locomotive, and by various machines and other equipment providing auxiliary services such as current for battery charging and compressed air for braking. Control systems take two basic forms according to whether the supply is ac, as is commonly used in industry and the home, or dc, of which the most familiar example is the current from a motorcar battery. In either case the control system has two fundamental functions: (1) to increase the voltage applied to the motors gradually to their full operating value while the train is accelerating; (2) to regulate speed (which is related to voltage).

In a dc locomotive the supply voltage is divided between the motors (eg 4 motors operating in pairs at 750V each on a 1,500V system). At starting it must be much lower than this to avoid a dangerous inrush of current, and so it is reduced by means of resistances which are cut out in steps as the locomotive accelerates. Resistances, like the elements of an electric fire, become hot when current flows through them and so must only be left in circuit for short periods. To provide low voltages for slow running, therefore, the control system allows the motors to be interconnected in various ways so that each receives a certain proportion of its normal operating voltage. After full voltage has been applied, higher speeds can be attained by weakening the magnetic fields.

On ac railways the contact wire voltage is reduced from several thousand volts to several hundred by means of a transformer inside the locomotive. The motors can be supplied

Roof mounted equipment on a BR Class 87 locomotive (below). Power for the locomotive is taken from the 25kV 50 Hz overhead supply by a 'cross arm' pantograph.

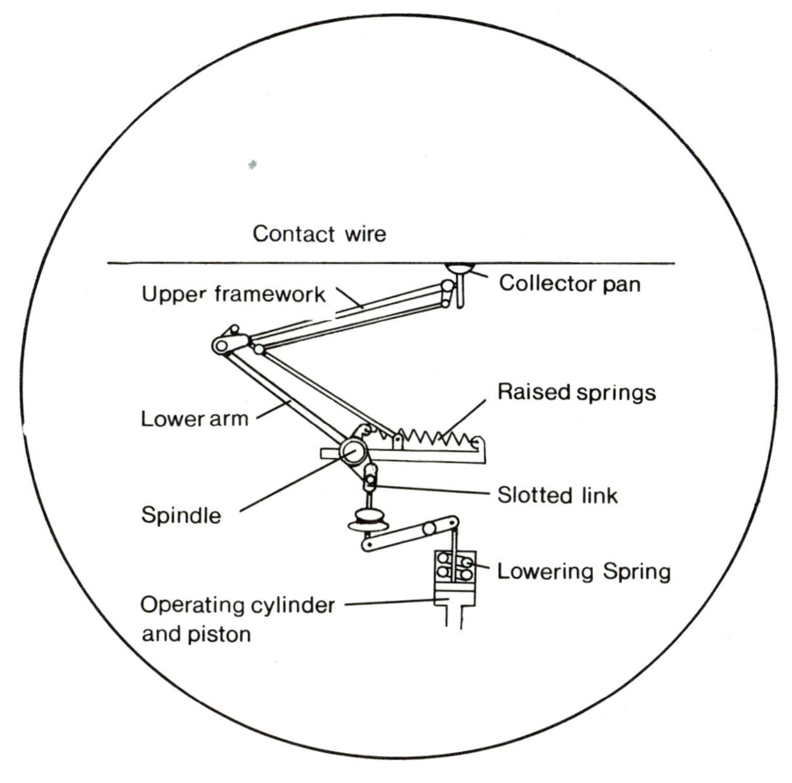

with a large number of different voltages within the range for which they are designed by connecting them to different points on the transformer through a motor-operated switch called a tap-changer. No waste of energy is involved in this system and the locomotive can run continuously with the tap-changer in any position. In many ac locomotives today the current tapped off from the transformer is converted into dc by semi-conductor rectifiers before being fed to the motors.

In both control systems described, the voltage is varied in steps during acceleration, and these must be small to avoid sudden changes in tractive effort which could cause the wheels to slip when starting heavy loads. Ideally, the control would be continuous, and today this can be achieved both in ac and dc locomotives by means of electronic circuits using thyristors. A locomotive with thyristor control may be driven by the driver moving his controller handle in the same way as if he was operating ordinary switchgear. Often, however, the driver simply sets dials to a desired speed, or a tractive effort appropriate to his load when starting his train. He can then concentrate on observing the signals and the track ahead while the locomotive automatically 'obeys' the instructions it has been given.

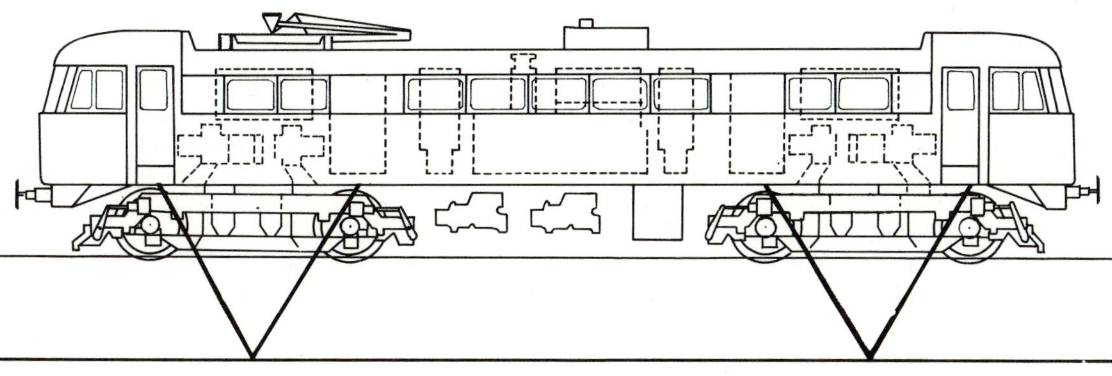

Diagram and details (above left) of a pantograph for 25kV ac systems.

(left) Diagram of British Railways electric locomotive using the 25kV ac system.
1 Transformer
2 Tapchanger
3 Rectifier unit
4 Control gear
5 Traction motor
6 Smoothing reactor
7 Traction equipment blower
8 Brake resistor
9 Compressors and exhausters (other side)
10 Battery charger and battery (other side)

A cut-away illustration (left) of an axle-hung, nose-suspended traction motor.

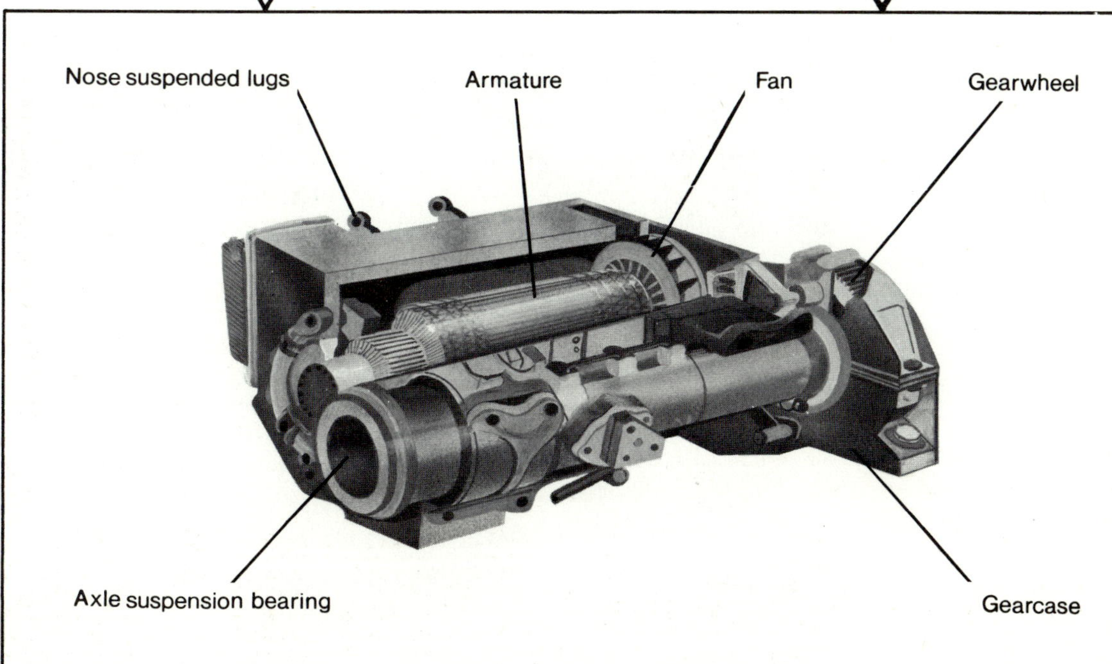

Transmitting the Current

The two main methods used to carry electricity from the generating station to the locomotive involve the use of either overhead wires or trackside conductor rails.

The former system requires supports for the insulated overhead 'contact' wire all along the route, and at junctions and other busy locations quite substantial structures, or gantries, are required. Bridges and tunnels have to be built or modified to allow sufficient clearance for the overhead equipment to be erected safely above carriage rooftop height, and on many existing lines this means that bridges have to be raised, or the tracks beneath them lowered, to give adequate clearance. Power is collected from the copper overhead wire either by a bow collector or, nowadays, a pantograph. Both are sprung to absorb minor fluctuations in the height of the contact wire, and the contact wire itself is hung so as to zig-zag horizontally back and forth across the top of the collector so that a groove is not worn in the top of the collector, or 'pan'.

Conductor rails take the form of an additional rail or rails of high-conductivity iron laid on insulated supports alongside or between the running rails and carrying the electric current. This is collected by shoes or brushes mounted on insulated brackets carried on the bogies of locomotives or trains rubbing along the top, side or even, in some cases, bottom of the conductor rail.

Most electrification systems, whether using overhead or conductor rail transmission, employ a positive feed through the insulated equipment and an earthed return through the running rails, but there are some systems in use which use an insulated return, requiring a second overhead wire or conductor rail.

The actual method of current transmission employed on any one system does not affect the concept of electric traction, although, unless they are specially equipped for multi-system collection, locomotives and trains can obviously only be used on the type of system for which they are equipped. And the voltage adopted does not necessarily dictate which system should be used, although in practice conductor rail systems tend to be used for low-voltage installations, perhaps in confined locations such as underground or suburban railway systems, while overhead systems tend to be equipped at higher voltages, so as to reduce the ampere load on the contact wire. This allows a reduction in the diameter of the heavy and expensive contact wire and, in turn, in the weight and complexity of the overhead structures needed to support it. Higher voltages can also be transmitted over longer distances, so that the number of sub-stations can be reduced, although as voltages increase so do the problems of insulation.

Almost without exception, the early electrification schemes employed direct current (dc) systems, and even where they took their supplies from alternating current (ac) generating stations, converters or rectifiers were used to 'convert' the current to dc characteristics, mainly because dc motors and control systems are much simpler to operate and maintain.

However, with the advent of nation-wide high-voltage ac grid electricity transmission systems after the Second World War, it became clear that the use of high-voltage ac, taken direct from the national grid, would enable substantial savings in lineside fixed equipment, provided the locomotives used could in some way be equipped as mini sub-stations, taking current from the overhead at 25,000V 50 cycles ac but transforming and rectifying it to a much lower voltage suitable for the dc control circuits and traction motors. The idea was first tried in Hungary in 1932 and, later, in Germany in 1936, but technical difficulties were such that it was not until after the Second World War that the SNCF (French Railways) were able to open a successful experimental section of line in northern France, quickly followed by widespread adoption for new schemes in the north-east in preference to the existing 1,500V dc system in use south of Paris.

In Britain, too, a pre-war Government Report which had recommended the adoption

Just how much lighter modern overhead structures for high voltage ac electrification can be is seen in this dramatic view (below) of a BR 25,000V ac electric locomotive approaching at speed on the Euston-Glasgow West Coast route. The lightweight contact wire needs only a simple catenary wire to support it, and these in turn can be carried by insulators mounted on lightweight structures of tubular or angle construction.

The weight and complexity of the overhead structures necessary for medium voltage dc overhead electrification is amply illustrated by this view (left) of a freight train at Penistone on British Rail's only surviving 1500V dc electrification, between Manchester and Sheffield. In contrast, the 750V dc conductor rail system, used for many suburban, rapid transit and underground lines, is neat and simple, even when applied to complicated junctions such as those at the approaches to Waterloo Station (below left).

of the 1,500V dc overhead system as a future standard was overturned in favour of high-voltage ac, and all the electrification schemes carried out in Britain over the past 20 years, apart from extensions to the existing Southern Region conductor rail system, have been at 25,000V ac; two of the existing 1,500V dc systems have since been converted to high-voltage ac, leaving the Manchester-Sheffield line as the only remaining example of 1,500V dc electrification in Britain. Although additional equipment is needed on each loco-motive—at first, mercury arc rectifiers and, later, semi-conductor rectifiers—25,000V ac electrification shows considerable economies in fixed installations compared to dc systems; sub-stations can be spaced five or six times further apart, and substantial savings can be made in the weight and complexity of the overhead equipment.

But electrification systems are the one area of railways in which there is almost no stan-dard; even within Europe there are many different systems in general use, often within the same country. Britain and France both have 25,000V ac and 1,500V dc overhead installations, as well as extensive suburban networks employing various conductor rail systems at voltages ranging from 600V to 1,200V dc, while Austria, Germany, Norway, Sweden and Switzerland all use 15,000V ac single-phase $16\frac{2}{3}$ cycles overhead systems.

Luxembourg, Bulgaria, Hungary, Portugal, Romania and Turkey, like Britain and France, have adopted 25,000V ac as their standard, but Belgium, Italy, Poland and Russia all have extensive 3,000V dc systems, and the Danish, Netherlands and Spanish railways are equip-ped at 1,500V dc!

The extensive electrified network of South African Railways uses a 3,000V dc supply, while the suburban lines around Melbourne and Sydney in Australia, and Wellington in New Zealand are all equipped at 1,500V dc. And in South America, the Argentine State Railways are electrified at 800V dc, using conductor rail, while Brazil uses 3,000V dc overhead.

Railways go Electric

Apart from Siemens' short experimental line at the Berlin Exhibition in 1879, the first public electric railway in the world was Magnus Volk's narrow-gauge line which runs along the seafront at Brighton in southern England, opened on August 3, 1883. Originally a 610mm (2ft) gauge line, with the trains taking current from the running rails, it was successfully extended early in the following year and relaid to 826mm (2ft 8½in) gauge, this time with an insulated third rail laid between the running rails to carry the 50V dc power supply to the trains. This system, still in use today, was almost certainly the first to use the now-commonplace conductor rail.

Despite its diminutive size, the success of Volk's railway did not pass entirely unnoticed, and among those watching developments were the directors of the City and South London Railway, originally promoted in 1884 as a cable-operated tube line under the Thames, and the directors of the Liverpool Overhead Railway, proposed in 1882 as a steam line. Both companies decided to use 500V dc electric traction, supplied to the trains through a third rail mounted between the running rails. The first trial trains on the City and South London, using small four-wheeled locomotives, ran in the completed section of tunnel in 1889, but it was 1890 before the line was opened to the public, the first electric tube railway in the world. The centre third rail on this line, unlike most of its successors, was not raised above the level of the running rails—indeed, it was a little lower—so at points and crossings special wood ramps had to be provided to prevent the collector gear from fouling the running rails and causing short-circuits.

Meanwhile, construction work was under

Encouraged by the success of his seafront electric line, Magnus Volk embarked on a rather more eccentric proposal for an over-sea line on the South Coast of England (below). It consisted of a movable section of pier, mounted on four long tubular legs, each of which had a bogie which in turn ran on a submerged track. Nicknamed 'Daddy Longlegs' the car made a successful inaugural trip at low tide on 29 November 1896.

way on the Liverpool Overhead Railway (LOR), and the majority of the line was opened for traffic in 1893; again the traction supply was 500V dc, reaching trains through a raised centre third rail, although this was switched to the now more conventional position outside the running rails in 1905. The LOR was the first electric railway to employ electric trains rather than locomotives; the first trains consisted of two motor coaches, arranged back to back, with drivers' control positions at the outer ends. Both these and the City and South London trains were equipped with Westinghouse air brakes, and this more powerful brake has been fitted, with minor modifications, to almost all electric locomotives and trains built since, even in Britain, where otherwise the vacuum brake was in almost universal use.

Meanwhile, the arrival of electric traction had not passed unnoticed elsewhere; in Sweden, two narrow-gauge lines near Stockholm were electrified on the then novel 1,500V dc system in 1895, while in the United States the Baltimore and Ohio Railroad electrified its 'Belt' line in August 1895, originally with overhead equipment but from 1902 with third rail. And the Chicago Elevated Railway was electrified in 1895, whilst New York's famous elevated railway (the El) was converted to electric traction early in the present century. Despite the undoubted success of the pioneer schemes, which had amply demonstrated the superiority of electric traction over steam,

especially for suburban work, many of the main-line railway companies remained totally unimpressed, preferring to keep steam engines, with their cheap, abundant fuel and low labour costs, rather than invest in expensive new electrification schemes.

But for some at least there was soon to be a rude awakening from this apathy; in 1891, almost unnoticed by the railway companies, the first electrically-powered trams had taken to the streets of Leeds in Yorkshire, and it was not long before the authorities in London, Liverpool, Manchester and Newcastle followed suit. Cleaner, faster and more convenient than many of the steam-worked suburban lines with which they competed, the electric trams soon began to attract passengers away from the suburban lines in their droves, and the railway companies began to realize that the tide could only be turned by the provision of an equally attractive electric railway service.

The North Eastern Railway, suffering from competition in Newcastle, introduced electric trains on its North Tyneside group of lines, radiating eastwards from Central Station, in March 1904, and early the following month the Lancashire and Yorkshire, which was encountering similar troubles in Liverpool, switched to electric traction on its Liverpool-Southport line. As the little Mersey Railway, which provided a service from Liverpool under the River Mersey to Birkenhead and the Wirral, had already converted its entire line from

The first public demonstrations of the practicality of electric traction were Ernst von Siemens' short demonstration line at the Berlin Trades Exhibition in 1879 (above right), and Magnus Volk's narrow gauge line, built along Brighton sea front in 1883 (above left) and generally accepted to be the world's first public electric railway. Both Siemens and Volk used low voltage direct current supplies for traction purposes, and although voltages quickly increased to 600 volts to deal with greater loads, it was some years before higher voltage alternating current was considered as an alternative method of transmission. Even today most purely urban lines operate on medium voltage direct current systems.

steam to electric in 1903, Liverpool, with the Overhead Railway as well, was suddenly in the van of railway electrification. Both the North Eastern and the Lancashire and Yorkshire systems employed an outside third conductor rail with earthed return, the former at 600V dc and the latter at 630V dc, but the Mersey Railway had opted for a 650V dc insulated return system, with the fourth rail laid between the running rails.

In London, although the newly electrified underground and tube lines were beginning to thrust out of the capital into the suburbs, the main-line companies remained complacent, and it took the loss of over half of its traffic to the new LCC trams on its South London line from Victoria to London Bridge between 1902 and 1909 to jolt the London, Brighton and South Coast Railway into action. Already shaken by a proposal to build an entirely new rival high-speed all-electric line from London to Brighton in 1900, the LBSCR had hurriedly obtained parliamentary powers to electrify its entire network on the then little-tried 6,600V ac overhead system in 1903, and in 1906 it began to examine the possibility of electrifying its suburban lines on this technically superior but vastly more expensive system. Encouraged no doubt by the Midland Railway's decision to electrify its short Lancaster-Morecambe-Heysham section on the same system—it was opened in April 1908—the LBSCR pressed ahead and the first public trains on the 'Elevated Electric', as it became known, ran on December 1, 1909.

Other companies, too, began to think seriously about electrification of their suburban lines in the face of this threat, and by the outbreak of the First World War the London and South Western and London and North Western Railways had both announced schemes for electrifying their suburban services into London, while the Lancashire and Yorkshire had decided to extend its experimental Bury-Holcombe Brook scheme into Manchester. All three used conductor rail and all were completed in 1916; the LSWR electrification was destined to be the forerunner of the huge Southern Electric third rail system, built up by the Southern Railway in the inter-war years, while the Manchester-Bury line has gained fame of a different sort as the only line in the country to use a protected side-contact conductor rail rather than the usual unprotected top-contact variety.

During the first decade of the present century electric traction began to appear in nearly all the major European countries; France saw its first electric trains in 1900, Italy in 1901, Germany and Czechoslovakia in 1903, Switzerland in 1906 and the Netherlands in 1908. The first railway to be electrified in Japan was converted as early as 1906, and Argentina got its first electric trains in 1909, and Brazil a year later.

Many of these first schemes originated as suburban electrifications, but in Switzerland, the Netherlands, Germany and Italy in particular they proved to be the forerunners of considerable systems, as did those in Austria

and Norway (first electrified 1911) and Sweden (1915). Britain, too, had a foretaste of main-line electrification with the opening in 1916 of the North Eastern Railway's 18-mile-long Shildon-Newport line, an important mineral route in the Middlesbrough area. Equipped at 1,500V dc overhead, the NER saw it as a testing ground for the proposed electrification of its East Coast route main line. But post-war developments put paid to that idea, and the Shildon line itself reverted to steam traction in 1935.

Despite massive enthusiasm in the early years of the present century, and the almost total recognition that electric locomotives and trains are the most powerful and efficient forms of railway traction, today electric trains still run over only a minority of the world's railways, and some countries have no electric railways at all.

It is because electric locomotives and trains do not have to carry their own power source,

The first line in Britain to switch entirely from steam to electric traction was the tiny Mersey Railway running through the Mersey Tunnel from Liverpool to Birkenhead. Like London's Underground, the system used third and fourth rail electrification, while the rolling stock owed much to current American practice (below), featuring clerestory roofs, large side windows with end doors, automatic couplers and diamond-frame bogies.

When the Manchester-Bury line was electrified in 1916, it was notable both for the high voltage employed—1200V dc—and for the unique protected side-contact third rail method of current collection. Less prone to icing and other interference than the usual unprotected top-contact third rail systems, the line was re-equipped with new stock in 1959 (left) and today remains in use as the only line of its type in the world.

Electric traction, particularly for suburban work, began to flourish in both Britain and America in the early 1900s. In Newcastle, to combat increasing competition from the new electric street tramcars, the North Eastern Railway introduced third rail electric trains (top left) in summer 1904. Similar competition from London County Council electric tramcars forced the LBSCR to electrify its South London line from Victoria to London Bridge in 1909. The original trains (below left) were equipped for 6,600V ac overhead operation but the line was later converted to the standard Southern Railway 750V dc conductor rail system.

and the fuel to feed it, as do steam and diesel locomotives, that they are so economical, reliable and easy to maintain. Instead, an electric railway relies for its traction on a remote, fixed generating station, the power reaching the locomotives and train through a transmission system which might take the form of either a conductor rail or an overhead wire. But the high first cost of the fixed equipment has restricted electrification of the world's railways. Only where there are obvious environmental advantages—as on underground railways—or where the general level of traffic is very high can electrification be justified; and even those railways which have adopted electric traction usually convert only sections of line at a time so as to spread the cost.

Electric traction is no new idea—the theory of electric traction is almost as old as that of the steam engine. It was as long ago as 1839, when the steam engine was still in its infancy, that the first successful electric locomotive was built and demonstrated by Robert Davidson. It was powered by a 40-cell iron/zinc battery and was reported to have achieved a speed of 6.43km/h (4mph) on a line near Edinburgh in Scotland. This diminutive machine was ahead of its time, requiring its own heavy batteries as a power source because large-scale electricity supplies and transmission systems were still in the future. In contrast, coal was cheap and readily available, and it is not therefore surprising that electrification did not surface again as a serious proposal for another 40 years.

By this time reliable electric traction equipment could be made and, even more impor-

tantly, large-scale power supplies were becoming available, at least in Europe and the United States. Since then electrification has slowly superseded steam and, later, diesel traction on some lines until today about 150,000km (95,000 miles) of route, or about 12 per cent of the world's railways, are electrified in some way. Development has been swifter in recent years, with the establishment of national high-voltage grid systems enabling electricity supplies to be taken direct at suitable locations. The world energy crisis, too, has made electric traction more attractive in financial terms than the oil-hungry diesel, and even a steam engine is estimated to burn between three and four times as much coal as a power station takes to produce electricity to do the same work—and power stations can use a much lower-grade fuel. For the same reason, nuclear fuel is more likely to be used in the future in fixed generating stations to power orthodox electric trains than to take to the rails in the form of a nuclear locomotive.

In some countries, where hydro-electric power is readily available and cheap, a much higher proportion of the railway system is electrified; in Switzerland, for example, the Federal Railway system is almost totally electrically worked, and hydro-electric power is used by the electric trains of both the Norwegian and, to a lesser extent, Swedish Railways systems. Even in countries which do not enjoy cheap electricity supplies, the rising costs of alternative fuels and the environmental attractions of electrification are forcing railway administrations to look anew at electric traction, despite the heavy initial capital outlay.

In America, both Chicago and New York had extensive elevated railway systems—the 'El'—which were converted to electric traction. As can be seen from these vews of the elevated tracks at 110th Street (top) and the twin structures on the Bowery line (above), the overhead structures allowed unimpeded movement for pedestrians and other traffic at ground level. However, they were noisy, obtrusive and, being carried entirely on steel girders, were very costly to maintain. Nowadays, most urban railways run underground, and few 'overhead' lines remain.

Higher Voltage and More Routes

The First World War and its aftermath brought electrification virtually to a halt throughout the world, for the main combatants were also the principal suppliers of equipment. Outside Britain, when work resumed, the early preference for low-voltage dc conductor rail systems gave way to increasing use of higher-voltage dc overhead systems, and single-phase high-voltage ac. In the inter-war period, Algeria (1932), Australia (1919), Belgium (1935), Chile (1924), Denmark (1934), India (1925), Jugoslavia (1935), New Zealand (1923), Poland (1927), South Africa (1926) and the USSR (1929) all saw their first electric railways; all used the overhead system of electrification and with the exception of Poland, which at first used 600V dc, all used either 1,500V or 3,000V dc.

In contrast, the railway administrations of Britain in general turned against further electrification. The newly-formed LNER scrapped the North Eastern's plans for main-line electrification, and the Great Western twice rejected proposals for the electrification of its West of England main lines. Indeed, apart from the Southern Railway, the only entirely new scheme to be completed in Britain before the Second World War was the electrification of the Manchester-Altrincham line, worked jointly by the LMS and LNER, at 1,500V dc in 1931, although there were extensions to the LNER Tyneside electrified lines in 1938, LMS extensions of the Mersey Railway scheme to cover its own tracks into the Wirral in the same year, and continued expansion of the

This was the striking headboard (above) on the electric train to pioneer the 25,000V Manchester-Crewe line.

Principal Electric Railways of the World

Country	Approx route length electrified (km)	Voltage	Conductor system
Algeria	300	3,000 dc	Overhead
Argentina	130	550/800 dc	Third Rail
Australia	860	1,500 dc	Overhead
Austria	2,500	15,000 ac	Overhead
Belgium	1,280	3,000 dc	Overhead
Brazil	2,300	1,500 and 3,000 dc	Overhead
Bulgaria	1,150	25,000 ac	Overhead
Canada	43	2,700 dc	Overhead
Chile	880	3,000 dc	Overhead
China	680	25,000 ac	Overhead
Costa Rica	125	15,000 ac	Overhead
Cuba	145	1,200 dc	Overhead
Czechoslovakia	2,050	1,500 and 3,000 dc	Overhead
		25,000 ac	Overhead
Denmark	100	1,500 dc	Overhead
Egypt	26	1,500 dc	Overhead
France	9,600	600-850 dc	Third Rail
		1,500 dc	Overhead
		25,000 ac	Overhead
Germany (East)	1,400	800 dc	Third Rail
		15,000 ac	Overhead
		25,000 ac	Overhead
Germany (West)	10,330	1,200 dc	Third Rail
		1,200 dc	Overhead
		15,000 dc	Overhead
Hungary	1,100	1,000 dc	Overhead
		25,000 ac	Overhead
India	4,200	1,500 dc	Overhead
		25,000 ac	Overhead
Indonesia	77	1,500 dc	Overhead
Italy	9,500	3,000 dc	Overhead
Japan	12,800	600-750 dc	Third Rail
		1,500 dc	Overhead
		20,000 ac	Overhead
Jugoslavia	2,300	3,000 dc	Overhead
		25,000 ac	Overhead
Luxembourg	140	3,000 dc	Overhead
		25,000 ac	Overhead
Morocco	710	3,000 dc	Overhead
Netherlands	1,710	1,500 dc	Overhead
New Zealand	100	1,500 dc	Overhead
Norway	2,450	15,000 ac	Overhead
Pakistan	153	25,000 ac	Overhead
Poland	4,700	600-800 dc	Overhead
		3,000 dc	Overhead
Portugal	430	1,500 dc	Overhead
		25,000 ac	Overhead
Romania	490	1,500 dc	Overhead
		25,000 ac	Overhead
South Africa	4,640	3,000 dc	Overhead
Spain	3,850	600, 1,200, 1,300, 1,500 1,650, 1,300 dc	Overhead
Sweden	7,530	1,350, 1,500 dc	Overhead
		15,000 ac	Overhead
Switzerland	5,040	830, 900, 1,000, 1,200 1,500, 1,700, 2,000, 2,200 dc	Overhead
		11,500, 15,000 ac	Overhead
Turkey	200	25,000 ac	Overhead
United Kingdom	3,500	600 dc	Third and Fourth Rail
		630, 650, 660, 750 dc	Third Rail
		1,200 dc	Side Contact Third Rail
		1,500 dc	Overhead
		6,250/25,000 ac	Overhead
United States	2,000	650, 700 dc	Third Rail
		600, 1,500, 3,000 dc	Overhead
		11,000, 50,000 ac	Overhead
USSR	36,100	1,500, 3,000 dc	Overhead
		25,000 ac	Overhead
Zaîre	860	25,000 ac	Overhead

Many American electric locomotives of the 1940's were similar in outline to the semi-streamlined US diesels of the same period with high cabs and a pronounced bonnet, as in these two Virginian railway electric locomotives (above) wheeling coal empties up the lush New River Valley near Narrows.

London Underground and tube railways.

Alone among the new 'Big Four', the Southern Railway decided to press ahead with suburban electrification, and between 1925 and 1931 electrified its entire complex of suburban lines in South London, including the conversion of the ex-London, Brighton and South Coast Railway 6,600V ac overhead lines to the now-standard 660V dc conductor rail system. And with the complex approaches to London thus equipped, it set about electrifying its main lines to Brighton (1933), Eastbourne and Hastings (1935), Portsmouth (1937) and Reading (1938) as well as many other lines in a programme that was only brought to a halt by the outbreak of war in 1939.

The Southern's predecessor, the London and South Western, had been an early advocate of multiple-unit operation when it electrified its lines in 1915. By means of control cables and circuits connected throughout the train, as many motored units as operating conditions and platform lengths would allow could be controlled by the driver from the one controller at the head of the train, and this arrangement was very attractive in terms of flexibility of formation and quick-turn-around at termini. The Southern therefore adopted multiple-unit operation even for its main-line schemes, and, apart from certain special services, all 1,630km of the present system are worked by multiple units.

The Second World War brought progress once more to a halt, but ironically the level of damage and destruction in Europe was such that a new impetus was given to electrification in the immediate post-war years. Most based their extensions on their existing systems, but both Britain and France decided to abandon their previous 1,500V dc standard in favour of high-voltage ac at the industrial frequency of 25,000V at 50 cycles per second, and this is now regarded as the world standard, having been adopted for most entirely new schemes with no prior commitment to earlier systems. Apart from extensions to the Southern Region dc conductor rail system, all the lines electrified in Britain since 1956 have been equipped at, or converted to, 25,000V ac. It has been adopted in Bulgaria, China, Eastern Germany, Hungary, India, Luxembourg, Pakistan, Portugal, Romania, Turkey and Zaïre, both for suburban and main-line applications.

It has proved the only system capable of meeting the present demands for both heavy freight movement of up to 2,000 tons and high-speed passenger operations up to 240km/h (150mph). In America the demand for ultra-heavy freight haulage led to the adoption of no less than 50,000V ac at 60 cycles per second for the 125km (77.6 miles) Black Mesa and Lake Powell Railroad, opened in 1973, and this voltage is proposed as the future standard for North America.

Electrification Today

More electric railways are now under construction or being planned than ever before. This is because the realization that diesels, whilst initially cheaper, are expensive to maintain has coincided with the world energy crisis. Increased fuel prices since 1973 have made electrification more attractive not only when compared with the diesel rail option, but, much more importantly, when compared with the road alternative, particularly for urban rapid transit. Moreover, latest estimates show that present consumption of oil-based fuels may outstrip supply from known reserves by the late 1990s, and that fuel prices will therefore increase dramatically. And throughout both Europe and America people concerned with the environment have become increasingly critical of car and coach commuting, pressing instead for the adoption of virtually pollution-free electric rapid transit rail systems.

In Britain, extensions are under way to existing urban electrified lines in London, Liverpool and Glasgow, whilst both Birmingham and Manchester have plans for new rapid-transit type underground railways to link existing lines. And in Newcastle, a light rapid transit Metro system is under construction beneath the city centre and will eventually link the old North Eastern Railway North

Despite the ravages of two World Wars, the German Federal Railways have extended their 16,000V ac electrification so that it covers most of the main lines, as well as the suburban lines around Hamburg, Frankfurt and Munich. Curving across the lengthy Altenbeken Viaduct (right) with a long Hamm-Kassel freight is a DB Class 150 Co-Co, one of the standard work-horses of the system.

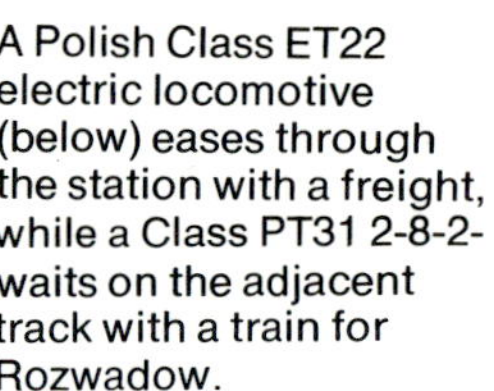

A Polish Class ET22 electric locomotive (below) eases through the station with a freight, while a Class PT31 2-8-2- waits on the adjacent track with a train for Rozwadow.

and South Tyneside lines, somewhat short-sightedly de-electrified by British Railways in 1963. Throughout Europe and North and South America, as well as in Australia, India, Japan, and Hong Kong, existing urban lines are being refurbished and extended, or entirely new lines built. And there are proposals for new rapid transit lines in Egypt, Iran, Israel, Singapore and New Zealand. Proposed conductor systems vary widely, from low-voltage dc with conductor rails to 25,000V ac overhead, the choice often being dictated by the desire for compatibility with existing equipment. In most cases, however, the rolling stock will be similar, with air-conditioned lightweight trains with automatic sliding doors and high-capacity seating layouts. Several installations, such as the Victoria and Fleet Lines of London Transport, and the San Francisco Bay Area Rapid Transit (BART) system, have sophisticated automatic control systems for starting, signalling and stopping, with one-man supervision.

Main-line electrification, too, has been spurred by the energy crisis and the rapidly rising costs of diesel operation. All the major European railway administrations have long-term plans to extend electrification, and most have schemes under way at present. On mainland Europe the spread of electrification in each country has meant that at many points differing systems have met; usually a change of locomotive is necessary, but the French have led the way with dual-voltage locomotives that can work on both their 1,500V dc and 25,000V ac lines, and some remarkable quadri-current 4,500hp C-C locomotives for international services which can in addition work over the 3,000V dc lines in Belgium and the 15,000V ac systems of the German and Swiss Railways. In Britain, multiple-units working from 750V dc conductor rail in underground sections and from 25,000V ac on surface sections have been introduced on the ex-Great Northern line from King's Cross.

The Soviet Railway system, still being extended, is already by far the largest electrified railway in the world, with 37,000km (22,992 miles) of line equipped. As might be expected, it has both the longest electrified line, from Moscow to Irkutsk, 5,213km (3,240 miles), and the world's most powerful electric locomotives, 184 tonne 25,000V ac Bo-Bos developing 45,088kg (99,400lb) tractive effort.

Apart from urban schemes, electrification in the United States has tended to lag behind Europe, partly because of scarce financial resources and uncertainty over the future of many of the railways, and partly because of the large numbers of diesel electric locomotives already available. But at the end of 1976 Amtrak took the unusual step of leasing two European electric locomotives—one from Sweden and one from France—as well as a pair of the Japanese Shinkansen 'Bullet' trains, for comparative tests on the high-speed north east corridor section of line between Washington and Boston, and it seems almost certain that there will be renewed interest in electrification—at least of the heavily used routes—in the USA over the next few years.

In Britain, France, Germany and Italy electrically-worked trains are regularly scheduled at speeds in excess of 150km/h (93mph) and all four countries are working towards the development of trains and overhead equipment suitable for speeds up to 240km/h (150mph).

These Class 313 units (left) which have high-capacity seating, and air-operated doors, are the first of a new generation of suburban stock for all British Rail electrified lines, both ac and dc.

The French Railways post-war decision to switch from its existing 1,500 V dc to high voltage ac for future electrification schemes means that through trains often have to work over both systems. One of the quadri-voltage locomotives (above) heads an SNCF express over a section of line equipped at 25,000V ac.

Breathtaking views are all part of the day's work on many Swiss mountain railways. A Rigi Railway motor coach and trailer (left) together with a wagon for skis, approaches Rigi-Kulm.

High Speed Trains

Speed has been an important element of railway development from the very earliest days; it was the comparative speed of the first railways that robbed the canals of their traffic and drove them to ruin, and it was speed, allied with comfort, that fuelled the competitive spirit among the 19th-century railways of Britain and the USA.

Britain has always led the way in the development of high-speed running; at the end of the 19th century, with fierce rivalry for traffic, new, powerful locomotives and track-work second to none, the incentives to push the upper known limits of speed on rail ever higher were very great. The Railway Races between the East Coast and West Coast companies, to Edinburgh and Glasgow in 1888, and to Aberdeen in 1895, really showed just how much time could be saved on existing schedules with smart timetabling, slick station working and, above all, spirited driving. By 1904 the Great Western Railway was claiming to have topped 160km/h (100mph) with its 'City of Truro' locomotive, and higher speeds were becoming commonplace. In the 1930s both the LMS and LNER introduced high-speed 'fliers', with special rolling stock hauled by streamlined locomotives, as did the French and certain American railroads.

The Second World War brought reductions in maintenance and lengthening of schedules, but in the 1950s the British, French, German and Italian railways all began to develop high-speed trains. But whereas on the European continent the development was centred around the 'Trans Europe Express' network of special, restricted capacity first-class only trains on which supplementary fares were payable, in Britain the policy was to develop the speed of the basic service, with all the major inter-city trains on any given line speeded up in unison. Thus, when 160km/h (100mph) running was first introduced on British Railways in 1964 on the East Coast route, all the main expresses, powered by the powerful English Electric 'Deltic' locomotives, were re-scheduled to take maximum advantage of the new upper limit. And when the West Coast main-line electrification from London to Birmingham, Manchester and Liverpool was opened throughout in 1966, the main service, with hourly trains to each destination, was designed to allow for continuous 160km/h (100mph) running.

It is firm British Rail policy that investment in modernization should not be restricted to a few crack trains, but should provide improvements in speed and comfort for all passengers, and this principle is embodied in the design of both its High Speed Train (HST) and the Advanced Passenger Train (APT).

High Speed Trains, now in service on both the Eastern and Western Regions of British Rail, under the title 'Inter-City 125', are basically a development of existing rail technology with a maximum service speed of 200km/h (125mph), although the prototype has already set a world speed record for diesel traction of 230km/h (143mph). They are formed into sets, with two streamlined 2,250hp power cars flanking the latest air-conditioned, fully carpeted double-glazed coaches. The redesigned bogies are air-cushioned, to ensure smooth, quiet riding, and are equipped with disc brakes so that a train travelling at the full 200km/h (125mph) can be brought to a stand within the same distance as conventional trains braking from 160km/h (100mph). As a result, no major resignalling has been necessary and HSTs share tracks with slower-moving local passenger and freight trains.

The Advanced Passenger Train, embodying many techniques borrowed from the aviation industry, is an altogether more novel concept. During the 1960s railway managements in several countries began to realize that further significant increases in speed could only be obtained by either the major realignment of existing railways or the construction of entirely new lines. All, that is, except the scientists at British Rail's Research Centre at Derby who, realizing the enormous asset of the existing railway, set about exploiting the potential of guided wheels on steel rails to the fullest extent. Much of their work centred on the behaviour of railway wheels and bogies when cornering, since curves, accounting for as much as 50 per cent of the mileage on almost all existing railways, are the major bar to really high-speed running.

The research led to the development of an entirely new bogie of unique geometric design. Unlike conventional bogies, the new design has a self-steering characteristic which automatically positions the axles to the radius of any curve, thus eliminating the disturbing 'hunting' that often takes place when a conventional train corners at high speed.

But with the new design of bogie came a new problem—how to overcome the greater side forces on the passenger resulting from the train's ability to corner at higher speed. This has been resolved by the adoption of a tilting body which, as on an aircraft, balances the centrifugal force so that the passenger rides in much greater comfort. To allow for tilting within the existing loading gauge, APT coaches are slightly narrower than orthodox

The prototype APT, seen tilting through a curve (right) and flashing across country (below), is gas-turbine powered, but the first trains to enter commercial service are electric, to work over the 25,000V ac London-Glasgow main line at speeds up to 250km/h (155mph).

vehicles. It should be emphasized that the tilting is entirely for the comfort of passengers; should the system fail in any way, the train could still corner at maximum speed in complete safety.

Because of the problem of developing a lightweight power plant capable of developing the enormous thrust necessary to get APT up to its designed speed of about 250km/h (155mph), the first prototype trains for commercial use will be electric, running on the 25,000V ac overhead West Coast main line from London to Glasgow.

The production APT units have streamlined front ends similar in design to those on the High Speed Train 'Inter City 125' (left) units now in regular fleet service on both the Western and Eastern Regions of BR.

135

As in Britain, so in Europe high-speed rail travel has become fashionable in the 1970s. Pressure for faster centre-to-centre transit times, whilst at the same time conserving energy, has given rail a new edge over its energy-consuming and environmentally less acceptable road and air competitors, and already the French and Germans, like the British, are operating sections of line at 200km/h (125mph).

But whereas the British Advanced Passenger Train has been developed specifically to run over existing tracks, the French, German and Italian railways have all opted for new or substantially rebuilt lines for their next generation of high-speed trains to operate above 200km/h.

Current French proposals centre around an entirely new 388km (241 miles) long 'Sudest' line from Paris to Lyon, planned for completion by 1982 and to be electrified at 25,000V ac. Already the prototype high-speed, articulated five-coach gas turbine-electric (turbotrain à très grande vitesse) TGV001 has repeatedly shown its ability to break the 300km/h (187.5mph) barrier under test, and an orthodox electric version is now planned, although initially the maximum speed on the new Paris-Sudest line will be 260km/h (162.5mph), allowing the 388km sprint be-

The main railway systems of both Europe and America are pressing ahead with plans to increase train speeds. The Japanese are extending their entirely new High Speed 'Shinkansen' lines. In Canada, Canadian National Railways have introduced high-speed Turbotrains between Montreal and Toronto (right), while French Railways have built a prototype high-speed gas turbine electric unit for tests on their new 260km/h (162.5mph) Paris-Lyon line, and an electric version is planned. Setting the snow flying on a high-speed dash between Annecy and Lyon (below) is ETG 001.

tween Paris and Lyon to be covered in two hours at an average speed of 212.5km/h (132mph).

In Germany, too, there are plans for entirely new high-speed lines; the Federal Government has already approved the construction of a new 100km (62 mile) line from the outskirts of Mannheim to Stuttgart. To be electrified on the German standard 15,000V ac system, construction is expected to take 10 years. The line is to be built with curves of not less than 7,000m radius to a ruling gradient of 1:125 so as to allow maximum speeds of 250km/h (156mph) for passenger trains and 120km/h (75mph) for freight trains. An enlarged loading gauge will allow 'piggyback' working of heavy road vehicles.

A similar high-speed line, not yet approved, is proposed from Hanover to Wurzburg, but the original intention to build a new line southwards from Cologne to avoid the sinuous Rhine valley now seems likely to be shelved in favour of substantial rebuilding of the existing curvaceous lines along each bank of the river.

In Italy, where maximum speeds are somewhat lower than in Britain, France and Germany, a new high-speed 'Direttissima' line is being built from Rome to Florence. Already,

Because railroad development was neglected for many years, maximum speeds in the United States do not match those of the major European lines. But Amtrak is rapidly introducing new trains like the electric Metroliner (right) and improving tracks on its trunk routes.

the first 122km (76 mile) section from Settebagni to Citta della Pieve is open, electrified at 3,000V dc; completion throughout is scheduled for 1982.

But perhaps the greatest revolution in rail speeds has taken place in Japan, where a complete new high-speed rail network is under construction. Most existing railways in Japan were built to 1.067m (3ft 6in) gauge and are therefore not suitable for development as high-speed lines, so Japanese National Railways decided to build entirely new standard gauge high-speed lines.

The first section, the Tokaido line from Tokyo to Osaka, was opened in October 1964 with specially built Shinkansen 'bullet' trains operating at speeds up to 210km/h (131mph). Such has been the popularity of the trains that the level of service has had to be progressively increased from the 30 trains each way of 1964 to no less than 113 each way 10 years later. Such unexpected growth brought both maintenance and capacity problems for JNR, but, undeterred, they have pressed ahead with the extension through Hiroshima to Hakata, on the island of Kyushu, and the 16-car trains now cover the entire 1,074km (667 mile) line in just under seven hours at an average speed of 155km/h (96.5mph). Construction standards on the new section of line have been raised so as to allow for a future increase in maximum speed to 260km/h (162.5mph), whilst nevertheless significantly reducing noise and vibration levels. Three further Shinkansen lines are under construction: the Tohoku from Tokyo to Morioka (496km/308 miles); the Joetsu from Tokyo to Niigata (300km/186 miles), and the Narita from Tokyo to Narita Airport (65km/40 miles). A further extension, from Morioka through the new Seikan Tunnel to Sapporo on the island of Hokkaido, is also planned, for completion in 1982.

All the Shinkansen lines are electrified at 25,000V ac, and are designed with the minimum of curves and gradients so as to allow high speeds to be sustained over long sections of line.

Because Japan's railway system was originally built to 1.067m (3ft 6in) gauge, it is unsuitable for upgrading for high-speed trains, and Japanese National Railways are instead building a new network of high-speed standard gauge lines with Shinkansen 'bullet' electric trains (above) operating at speeds up to 210km/h (131mph). First section to open was the busy Tokaido line from Tokyo to Osaka.

Trans Europe Express

In the early 1950s the railways of Europe were still recovering from the Second World War. Steam locomotives were used on many long-distance services, some coaches dated from the 1920s and 1930s, and timings, except in France and Germany, were not often very fast. Frontier stops on international services were often of 30 minutes or more and station stops were often lengthy as coaches for different destinations were added to or detached from the main train. Many cities only 500km (300 miles) from each other could not be reached in time for the return journey in a day. The developing airlines looked like taking a good part of the railways' international business.

The then President of the Netherlands Railways, Mr Den Hollander, saw that the railways could still play an important part in European transport, and masterminded a plan for a new network of fast, modern international express trains. Agreement was reached

TEE trains provide express services over almost all the major routes of mainland Western Europe, and many are inter-connecting. Present-day services are mainly provided by luxury rolling stock powered by separate high-speed diesel or electric locomotives, such as the German Railways 'Rheingold' express, (below), which provides a daily service from the Netherlands down the Rhine through Germany to Switzerland.

minute, and customs and passport control to be carried out on the train while on the move. There was no question of steam haulage, and since many of the planned routes were not then electrified the trains had to be diesel worked.

Mr Den Hollander's dream came true in 1957 with the introduction of 12 new trains, serving such cities as Paris, Brussels, Amsterdam, Dortmund, Cologne, Hamburg and Zurich. Two services were isolated from the others, running from Munich to Marseille, and Lyon to Milan.

Five of the railways served provided the trains. All were self-contained diesel trains. The French and Italian railways provided two-car diesel trains which were upgraded versions of existing units, the German Federal Railway built new seven-car trains with a diesel-hydraulic power car at each end and five passenger cars, including restaurant and bar, in between, while the Dutch and Swiss

between seven European railways—those of France, West Germany, Belgium, Holland, Luxembourg, Switzerland and Italy—for the new services, which were to have common standards. All trains were to be first class only, with a supplementary fare, coaches were to be modern, with three-a-side seating in side corridor compartments or two-plus-one in open saloons, there was to be air-conditioning, restaurant and buffet facilities in nearly all trains, station and frontier stops were to be short; often no more than one

Federal Railways jointly produced some four-car diesel-electric sets.

From the start, as far as distances would allow, the services were intended to attract businessmen, who would normally travel with little luggage, and who wanted high standards of meals and accommodation. It was possible on many services to leave around breakfast time, travel during the morning, work during the afternoon with clients and return in the evening. Businessmen were not the only users, for tourists soon found the fast new

services were far better than existing trains and more reliable than air services when weather often brought delays or diversions.

In the early 1960s, the Swiss Federal Railways introduced new five-car electric TEE trains, capable of working from any of the four standard European electrification systems: 1,500V dc in France and Holland, 3,000V dc in Belgium and Italy, 15,000V ac $16\frac{2}{3}$ cycles in Germany and Switzerland, and 25,000V ac 50 cycles in France. The train could run through the changeover section without stopping, and an automatic current sensing device changed the electrical connections in the power car. The driver, though, had to select a different pantograph to collect the current because of the different mechanical construction of the various overhead wire conductor systems.

By the mid-1960s new locomotive-hauled Trans Europe Expresses (TEE) had been introduced in France and Germany and through Switzerland. This was because some then existing comparable express trains were brought into the TEE system, and some services had outgrown the short diesel units. With the establishment of the major European political and economic headquarters in selected cities, for example Brussels and Strasbourg, business travel expanded rapidly,

particularly by European Economic Community (EEC) staff. More services were added until today nearly 40 TEE trains operate across Europe daily. No fewer than six each way run between Paris and Brussels alone. The original concept of a self-contained formation, with its own power cars, has almost gone, and except for the Swiss four-voltage units, now expanded to six cars, on Brussels–Zurich–Milan services, all other TEEs are locomotive-hauled. One, the 'Rheingold', for several years had a dome observation car between Holland, Basel and Geneva. The 'Catalan' TEE, between Barcelona (for TEE services have spread to Spain) and Geneva, is a Talgo-type train, with low-slung two-wheeled articulated cars and has provision for the wheels to be widened or narrowed on their axles at the Spanish frontier between standard 1.435m (4ft $8\frac{1}{2}$in) and Spanish 1.676m (5ft 6in) gauge. Passengers do not realize what is happening, for it is all over in six minutes as the train runs slowly through the automatic gauge-changing equipment.

TEE trains, in their mostly red and cream livery, are today's luxury replacements of the old Pullman services but on a wider scale. Moreover they have all the modern facilities of internationally-linked seat reservations by computer from all reservation offices.

The railways of Europe work around the clock, and many long-distance passengers, especially those in the European business community, prefer to travel overnight in the comfort of the many TEN (Trans Europe Night) sleeping car trains (above). Aptly described as rolling bedrooms, the accommodation and facilities on most TEN trains are quite the equal of those to be found in a high-class hotel (inset).

Freight Trains

Freight is the lifeblood of railways. It was to carry freight more swiftly and efficiently than the canals that the railway was invented, and even today, though it is less glamorous than passenger traffic, freight is vital to any successful railway. In the early days most freight took the form of coal and iron ore, or farm produce, and it was carried in short, unsprung wooden wagons without brakes, which were only slightly improved versions of the 19th-century horse-drawn road wagon but fitted with rail wheels.

Today the picture is very different. Just as passenger train development has pursued ever-increasing speeds, so freight train development has centred around increased weight, both in terms of individual wagonloads and total train weight. And now almost anything can be—and is—carried by rail.

In the days of steam, there were special engines for freight work, with smaller driving wheels to give greater adhesion and pulling

The earliest railways were built to carry freight rather than passengers and even today many railway systems throughout the world thrive exclusively on freight traffic, especially in the United States. This Oregon-bound freight on the Union Pacific railroad (right) has four diesels at its head.

power. But small wheels do not make for high speed, so freight trains were by definition slow. And because they were slow, their braking was often primitive, sometimes, indeed, hand-worked, and many locomotive crews had to work their trains without the benefit of automatic brakes throughout the train. There was little incentive to work trains in multiple, because each steam locomotive still had to be separately manned, while the couplings and buffing gear on the small, wooden wagons would not have withstood the greater drawgear and buffing loads of long trains.

Then along came electric and diesel locomotives, with their ability to work in multiple under the control of one man in the lead unit,

In Eastern Europe, more freight is carried by rail than road, and many of the satellite countries rely on Soviet-built motive power to modernize their fleets. Here, a Russian-built Czechoslovakian Railways, Class T679.1 diesel-electric Co-Co (above) wheels a heavy freight on the Ceska Trebova—Brno line.

and practices began to change.

The North American railroads were the first to realize the potential of diesel traction for freight operation and the USA in the 1940s saw impressive 1.600km (mile-long) freight trains headed by as many as six locomotives, all under the control of one man. And if the weight proved too much for the couplings, they simply split the train in the middle and put in an additional locomotive to equalize the buffing loads. The combination of smaller trains into one giant unit such as this has many operating advantages, especially on lines with long single-track sections, where line occupation is always at a premium.

With large-scale electrification and dieselization of the European railways, the big train concept has now crossed the Atlantic. The line carrying Europe's heaviest trains is quite probably also its coldest, because it runs from the ore mines at Kiruna in northern Sweden across to Narvik, on the Atlantic coast of Norway, which is ice-free but well within the Arctic Circle. Over this almost permanently frozen, snowclad line the Swedish and Norwegian railway systems work 5,200 tonne trains composed of four-axle 100-tonne ore wagons with automatic couplers. They are powered either by Swedish Class DM3 three-section electric locomotives, or two Norwegian Co-Co electric locomotives working in multiple. Close on the heels of the Scandinavians are the Germans, for the German Federal Railway (DB) now runs 5,000-tonne mineral trains between Hamburg and Salzgitter-Reine, near Hanover, using six-axle 100-tonne capacity hopper wagons and two specially-equipped Class 151 electric locomotives.

Throughout Europe the trend towards longer, heavier trains has been boosted by the development of the block train concept. Block trains are usually run under contract between specific points for a particular customer, often using his own special wagons and running at express passenger speeds. Loads can be anything from coal to oil, wood, steel or even finished products like motor cars. Purpose-designed wagons are always provided, and sometimes special vehicles have to be designed for the conveyance of dangerous materials such as chemicals, acids or even waste nuclear fuel.

Britain's heaviest freight trains are also among its fastest, for the 2,000-tonne triple-headed iron ore trains which run between the deep-sea terminal at Port Talbot and the blast furnaces of Llanwern Steel Works in South Wales share the same tracks as British Rail's 200km/h (125mph) High Speed Trains, and are therefore designed for 96km/h (60mph) running so that they can be fitted into the busy timetable. Each of the four-axle 100-tonne wagons used on this service is fitted with rotary automatic couplings so that the entire train can be unloaded one wagon at a time by a huge automatic tipper which can rotate an entire wagon through 160deg around the axis of its coupling.

Car conveyance by rail is an important traffic for the major railway systems of Europe and America. Car carriers are used to transport new cars from manufacturers to dealers, and to ferry cars with their passengers. In North America the loading gauge allows as many as three tiers of cars to be loaded. This Canadian National tri-decker train is carrying no less than 18 cars per vehicle.

The British Rail electrically hauled freightliner (left) carries as much as 30 average long-distance vehicles.

Industry did not feature largely in the works of early 19th-century fiction writers. Railways must have made an impact on the private lives of authors—Charlotte Brontë's brother, Branwell, left home to become a booking clerk on the Manchester and Leeds Railway—but for their stories they tended to choose themes that were considered more 'romantic'. There are, of course, many passing references to railway travel. Dickens, in his *Pickwick Papers*, makes Tony Weller, Sam's coachman father, relate his experiences on a train journey to Birmingham at a time when passengers used to be locked in the carriages while the train was moving. In more sombre mood, the London and Birmingham Railway appears again in *Dombey and Son* when the villain is knocked down and killed by a train while fleeing from justice.

The fatal accident to a Member of Parliament at the opening of the Liverpool and Manchester Railway in 1830 seems to have drawn authors' attention to the possibilities of the railway for scenes of drama and tragedy which previously had been supplied by storm or shipwreck. In Elizabeth Gaskell's tale of village life, *Cranford*, Captain Brown is a retired army man employed on the nearby 'obnoxious railroad', as one of the characters calls it. He is killed while saving the life of a child who has strayed on to the tracks in the path of a train. In Mrs Henry Wood's novel, *East Lynne*, the mother who returns to her child as his governess is unrecognized by the husband from whom she is estranged because of scars received in a railway accident and the dark glasses she wears to hide them.

We must turn to French literature for a whole novel about railways and railwaymen. Emile Zola made the main line from Paris to Le Havre the central thread of *La Bête Humaine*, around which he weaves a tale of drama, mystery and intrigue. There are several sensational accidents in the story, but its most noteworthy feature is its presentation of the everyday life of railwaymen in every grade of the service. Zola's descriptions of the work of an engine crew on the footplate could almost serve as an engine-driver's manual. Writers who venture upon portraying railways are often criticized for inaccuracies. Zola was actually rebuked by a leading literary critic of

his day for being too accurate and piling on textbook detail which was irrelevant to his stories!

Certain passages of *La Bête Humaine* are set in the lonely cottage of a level-crossing keeper, where the tinkle of telegraph bells and the roar of passing trains are the family's only contact with the world of affairs beyond their horizon. They see life in brief, flickering glimpses through carriage windows as the trains rush past. Zola here touches on a theme which was to be used years later by Georges Simenon in *The Man who Watched the Trains Go By*.

Alphonse Daudet in *Fromont Jeune et Risler Ainé* and Balzac in *Le Père Goriot* both give memorable pictures of excursionists returning to Paris from a Sunday outing in hot, stuffy and crowded trains with the melancholy prospect of long hours of work and low wages in the week ahead. There is a more cheerful railway trifle from Daudet in *Tartarin de Tarascon*. Tartarin has boasted of his prowess as a big-game hunter until he is shamed by the sceptics in his circle into making an expedition to Algeria to shoot lions. The only lion he finds is a harmless, half-blind beast but a camel attaches itself to him and refuses to be shaken off. As the train takes Tartarin home from Marseilles, dwellers by the line are astonished to see the faithful beast trotting along the tracks in its wake.

The Russian novelists were quick to make use of railway scenes, and Tolstoy's Anna Karenina meets her death on the railway. In our own time Boris Pasternak opens his novel *Doctor Zhivago* with a chapter called 'Five o'Clock Express' in which Zhivago's father falls from a train and is killed. The attitudes of the various travellers to this interruption of their three-day journey across Russia tells us much about their characters.

A famous European international train inspired both Graham Greene's *Stamboul Train* and Agatha Christie's *Murder on the Orient Express*. Railways seem often to have fascinated writers of mystery and detective stories. As a 19th-century Londoner, Conan Doyle's Sherlock Holmes had perforce to use the hansom cab and the train on his journeys in an England that did not yet know the motor car. In one of his investigations a body found beside the Underground tracks is shown to have been placed on the roof of a train from a house overlooking the line. Holmes is usually the pursuer rather than the pursued, yet once, with the master criminal Moriarty on his trail, the great detective found it prudent to leave the country in the disguise of an Italian priest. He and Watson catch the Dover train from Victoria Station in London. Knowing Moriarty is hard on their heels, they give him the slip by alighting at Canterbury. Moriarty has hired a special to pursue them. Hiding behind a pile of luggage on the platform, they watch as the special, consisting of a locomotive and one carriage, dashes through the station and disappears in the direction of the coast. Holmes and Watson then emerge from their hiding place and make their way to Newhaven by local trains.

In modern fiction airports and aircraft have taken the place of railway stations and trains, but the age of the railway has been preserved for all time in the works of writers who lived through it.

A scene from a novel by Conan Doyle. Sherlock Holmes, the famous detective, disguised as an Italian priest, and Watson, his companion, hide behind some luggage. They watch as the special train hired by Moriarty to pursue them rushes through the station.

European Railways

From its small beginning between Stockton and Darlington in England in 1825, public transport by railway was gradually developed on the European mainland. A French Government surveyor had inspected some of the English colliery lines in 1818, but by the end of the 1820s the only lines which had been constructed in France were still using horse traction. The first steam railway in Europe was the line from Brussels to Malines, opened on May 5, 1835. Its construction owed much to the initiative of the King of the Belgians. In the aftermath of the political changes of 1830, Belgium was cut off from the mouth of the River Scheldt, and the King urged on his Ministers the need for good communication between his country and the Rhineland to stimulate trade through the port of Antwerp. In 1834 an Act was passed by the Belgian Parliament authorizing the setting up of a State-owned railway system. This was the first measure of its kind in the history of rail transport.

Europe today has railways north of the Arctic Circle and on the shores of the Mediterranean. Its system all but touches Asia at Istanbul and crosses the frontier into its neighbouring continent in the Ural Mountains. The civil engineers who built the lines had to take them through terrain calling for feats of construction which have become world-famous. Other branches of engineering science were turned to railway use. In 1877 Werner von

The early electric locomotives in Germany and Switzerland had large locomotive-type driving wheels, coupling rods and jackshaft drives, and centrally-mounted cabs with pronounced bonnets. This vintage DB Class 194 Co-Co locomotive (above), although fitted with smaller wheels on motored bogies, is a direct descendant of those pioneers.

Siemens demonstrated an electric railway at an exhibition in Berlin and foreshadowed a form of traction that was to transform the European railway scene after the Second World War.

Europe has its transcontinental rail routes, but most of them pass through several countries. None the less, in normal times all have co-operated in the planning and operation of international services. Perhaps the most famous was the Orient Express, which began running through from Paris to Istanbul (then

Russia boasts both the most powerful electric locomotive and the longest section of electrified line in the world. This is a winter evening view of the Red Arrow at Moscow (right), electric locomotive at its head, as it awaits departure for Leningrad.

known as Constantinople) in 1888. It was organized by the International Sleeping Car Company, and at that time ran through the territories of nine different railway administrations. In later years there was a group of international expresses with the name 'Orient' in their titles—the Simplon-Orient, Arlberg-Orient, and Ostend-Vienna-Orient, as well as the original Orient Express. The best-known of these later versions was the Simplon-Orient with its through carriages between Calais and Istanbul. Air travel diminished the demand for through train services over such long distances. The Simplon-Orient became the Direct-Orient, with more numerous stops to cater for point-to-point traffic along its line of route, and from May 1977 ceased to run east of Venice.

In Russia the Trans-Siberian Railway crosses from Europe into Asia near the station of Urzhumka, 'in a place remote from all habitation' to quote the official guide to the line published in 1900. There were high hopes at first of this becoming an international route for travel from western Europe to the Far East, supplanting the steamship routes through the Suez Canal. It was a leisurely journey, however, with ten days in the train between Moscow and Vladivostok. In the early days of the route Lake Baikal was crossed by train ferry, although in 1904, when the lake was frozen over, rails were laid across the ice. Later in that year a rail link around the south of the lake was opened. Water transport along the Amur River was also necessary at first to connect the eastern end of the Trans-Baikal Railway with the Ussuri Railway at Khabarovsk. This section,

too, was later bypassed by rail. Construction of the Amur line began in 1908 and was completed in 1916. The distance from Moscow to Vladivostok by the present route of the Trans-Siberian Railway is 9,336km (5,801 miles), making it the longest railway in the world. It is electrified from Moscow to Irkutsk 5,213km (3,240 miles), which gives it another record in having the longest stretch of electrification. The Trans-Siberian Express runs daily over the whole route, passengers reaching their destination on the eighth day after departure from Moscow or Vladivostok.

Different systems of electrification meet at certain frontiers but there are now large numbers of electric locomotives in service capable of working on more than one system, a development made necessary by the fact that even within a country there may be two different electrification systems, one dating from before the Second World War and the other introduced later to take advantage of advances in electrical technology.

Water 'frontiers' complicate the railway geography of Denmark, with its numerous islands. Zealand and Falster have been connected since 1937 by the Storstrom Bridge, 3,200m (10,500ft) long and the second longest railway bridge in Europe, the longest being the Tay Bridge, Scotland, 3,552m (11,652ft). Plans for a Channel Tunnel between England and France are still in abeyance, but British Railways operate a ferry for freight vehicles across the North Sea from Harwich to Zeebrugge, and a cross-Channel passenger train ferry between Dover and Dunkerque, which conveys through sleeping cars between London, Paris and Brussels.

145

Railways in France

Railway development in France began with short lines in the Lyons and Paris regions. Saint Etienne was at the centre of two schemes, one to serve Andrézieux and the other to connect with Lyons. Part of the latter line was opened on June 25, 1830, but a year earlier it had been used for trial runs with the first steam locomotive in France. This had been built by Marc Séguin, who had designed a boiler with 43 fire tubes through which the hot gases from the furnace passed on their way to the chimney, heating the water throughout the boiler as they went. In the same year Stephenson's 'Rocket' won a competition at Rainhill, in England, largely as a result of being equipped with a boiler in which a similar method of increasing the heating surface was used.

Paris had its first railway in 1837 with the opening of the line to Saint Germain. Between 1841 and 1843 a line was built from Paris to Rouen, later extended to Le Havre. The engineer was the Englishman Joseph Locke, who thus had the honour of being responsible for the first French main line. While the work was in progress the French Government decided that future railway building in the country would follow a co-ordinated national plan, dividing France into six regions in each of which land was provided by the State and a concession was granted to a company to build and operate a railway. This was the genesis of the six major French railway systems which operated independently until all were merged in 1937 in the present French National Railways Company (SNCF).

In order of incorporation the original French railways were the Paris-Orleans (1838), the Nord and the Est (both 1845), the Midi (1852), the Ouest (1855, later becoming the Etat), and the Paris, Lyons et Méditer-

The ample proportions of the European loading gauge are well illustrated (right) in this massive SNCF ex-Paris-Lyon and Mediterranean Railway Class 231K Pacific waiting at Boulogne Maritime with a train for Paris. Notice the mass of external plumbing on the boiler as compared to British practice, the typically large electric headlights, and the highly-burnished buffers. French rolling stock cannot work over British lines, and special rolling stock of reduced dimensions has to be provided for train ferry traffic.

ranée (1857). The present organization of the SNCF still reflects the old company map. There are Nord, Est and Ouest Systems (Réseaux), the PLM has become the Réseau Sud-Est, and the combined PO and Midi network has become the Réseau Sud-Ouest.

The whole network is based on lines radiating from Paris. The Nord has main lines to the Belgian frontier and to the Channel ports of Boulogne and Calais. The Ouest serves Normandy and Brittany, including the ports of Dieppe, Cherbourg and Le Havre. The Sud-Ouest runs south to the Spanish frontier, with such important centres as Bordeaux, Toulouse, and La Rochelle on its routes. The Est is the main line to Strasbourg and Basle,

Although the Fades is the highest, France boasts several other lofty viaducts, including the elegant, spindly structure at Garabit (left).

'Etendard' express timed over the 581km (361 miles) between Paris and Bordeaux in 3hr 50min, an average speed of over 150km/h (94mph).

As early as 1953 French Railways showed their interest in high speed with electric traction by arranging a test run between Dijon and Beaune with an electric locomotive hauling three coaches, speed averaging 239.8km/h (149mph) for 4.8km (3 miles). A year later, on March 28, 1954, a locomotive of the same type achieved 330.8km/h (205.6mph) with a similar load on a test run between Facture and Morcenx on the Bordeaux-Hendaye line. A similar maximum was reached the next day with a smaller locomotive on the same section of line. The significant feature of these runs was that they were made with locomotives with all their axles motor-driven. Until then it had been normal practice to build electric locomotives for express service with non-powered guiding bogies, similar to those of a steam locomotive, in the interests of stable running at speed. The French tests showed that adequate stability was provided when all axles were powered and so the whole weight of the locomotive was used for adhesion. The 'total adhesion' locomotive, with four or six axles, soon became the general pattern throughout the world.

Another major French contribution to railway technology has been the development of electric traction using alternating current taken direct from the public supply network instead of through converting substations. After a pilot scheme in the Savoy in 1952, this system was extended to the important cross-country arterial route from Dunkerque to Basle, and then to the main lines from Paris to Lille and the Belgian frontier, to Strasbourg, and to Le Havre. To accelerate services on lines where electrification would be uneconomic, French Railways are making increasing use of gas-turbine traction.

with connections into Germany. The Sud-Est, still thought of by many as the PLM, is the great highway to Marseilles and the Riviera, with the major international routes to Switzerland, and to Italy via the Mont Cenis tunnel, diverging at Dijon and Mâcon respectively.

Since the Second World War France has held a pre-eminent position in railway speed, the most notable advance beginning with the electrification of the former PLM main line from Paris to Lyons in 1952 (later extended to Marseilles and along the Mediterranean coast). At that time the average speed of 124km/h (77mph) of the 'Mistral' express between Paris and Dijon was considered epoch-making. Later years were to see the

The French railways are acknowledged leaders in the development of lightweight gas turbine 'Turbotrains'; this handsome example (below) is one of the newer units pictured near Amplepuis while working between Lyons and Roanne.

German Railways

A scheme for a complete railway system for Germany was put forward in the early 1830s by Friedrich List, a one-time political exile who had returned to his homeland as American Consul at Leipzig in 1832. His plans were ridiculed at the time, but a more enlightened view was taken by King Ludwig of Bavaria, who approved a proposal for building a railway 6.4km (4 miles) long from Nürnberg to Fürth. It was opened on December 7, 1835, and known as the Ludwigsbahn in honour of the king.

A locomotive, the 'Adler' (Eagle), was supplied from England by the firm of Robert Stephenson, and arrived accompanied by an English driver, a Mr Wilson, who is reported to have earned double the money paid to the

The first railway in Germany, from Nürnberg to Fürth, was opened in 1835 and worked by this British Stephenson-built 2-2-2 (below) named 'Adler' (Eagle). The locomotive and rolling stock are now preserved, while the line itself now forms part of the Munich-Hamburg main line. The rail link with Scandinavia runs north from Hamburg via this impressive modernistic concrete bridge (bottom picture) across the Fehmarnsund to Puttgarden on the Baltic.

time. Some retained their independence, however, although Prussia was geographically in a dominant position and most of the lines in northern Germany were merged into the Prussian State Railways. Much of the through traffic for the other lines in Germany came via the Prussian network, which exercised considerable influence on the pattern of railway services in the country. In their classic work, *Express Trains, English and Foreign*, published in 1889, the British writers E. Foxwell and T. C. Farrer were scathing about Prussian influence, describing the London-Berlin rail service as 'an international disgrace'. In another passage they wrote: 'Now the Government have no interest in encouraging fresh lines of travel; they force all traffic into this route via Cologne and Hanover and have practically discontinued the international services via Aix, Bleyberg and Kreiensen, and of course have no interest in opening any new ways from Dresden to western Europe by more southern routes, since all such traffic must, as it is, pass over their existing lines in existing trains.'

The unification of German railways came eventually after the First World War with the creation of the German State Railway (Deutsche Reichsbahn) on April 1, 1920. Before many years had passed the Reichsbahn put itself in the lead of European speed with the introduction of the 'Flying Hamburger' express. This was a two-car articulated diesel-electric set placed on the Berlin-Hamburg run in 1932. At first it simply maintained the best steam timings, but in the summer service of 1933 began to make the journey of 286.6km (178 miles) at an average speed of 124.6km/h (77.5mph)—at that time an unprecedented speed for a regularly scheduled railway service. By 1937 a similar diesel-electric train, but with four cars, the 'Flying Cologner', was making the fastest start-to-stop journeys in

General Manager of the railway!

The Nürnberg to Fürth line was worked as a steam-operated railway until November 1, 1922, after which its track became part of the electrified main line from Munich to Hamburg.

Undeterred by opposition, List continued to press his support for rail transport and was behind the building of a line from Leipzig to Alten, 9.25km (5.75 miles). This was the nucleus of Germany's first inter-city main line. Opened to Alten in April 1837, it was extended eastwards and reached Dresden in April 1839.

At this period Germany was still a collection of separate kingdoms. When in 1870 Bismarck united them as Imperial Germany he had a plan to unify their railway systems at the same

Steam traction has now been replaced by diesel on all German non-electrified lines, but as in other European countries, the change was gradual and for several years both forms of motive power could be seen working in tandem, as in this 1970 view (right) of a Class 221 diesel hydraulic piloting a Class 003 Pacific into Ravensburg.

the world at that period with schedules of 132km/h (82mph) between Berlin and Hanover, and the same between Hanover and Hamm.

Germany began main-line electrification between the wars, choosing the 15kV system at a frequency of $16\frac{2}{3}$ Hz. In the late 1930s experiments were begun on a line in the Black Forest with a frequency of 50Hz (the industrial standard). These were interrupted by the war, but were revived and pursued after the war when the area came into the French zone of occupation. German engineers participated when the experiments were transferred to France, and there is some electrification on the 50Hz system in East Germany, but West Germany decided to retain and greatly extend its low-frequency $16\frac{2}{3}$ Hz system.

When Germany was divided into Western and Eastern Zones after the war the name Reichsbahn was kept for the part of the system east of the frontier, but the western part became the Deutsche Bundesbahn (German Federal Railway). At the end of 1975 the Bundesbahn was operating 28,771km (17,877 route-miles), of which 10,011km (6,220 miles) were electrified. Corresponding figures in East Germany were 14,252km (8,856 miles), with 1,406km (874 miles) electrified. Diesel traction is used on non-electrified routes in both halves of the country.

Germany has a long record of interest in high-speed rail traction, and as early as 1903 experimental electric vehicles on a test track attained speeds of 203km/h (126mph) and 210.2km/h (130.5mph). In 1931 a propeller-driven electric railcar attained 230km/h (143mph). Today new electrified main lines are planned to permit speeds up to 300km/h (186mph).

The Prussian Railways were a major constituent of the Nationalized German railway network. The versatile and robust Prussian Class P8 4-6-0s, soon became the work-horses of the entire system, some examples of the once-numerous class surviving well into the 1970s, including 038 65-8 (left), making a spirited departure from Freudenstadt.

149

Swiss Railways

With two-thirds of Switzerland consisting of mountain ranges early railway engineers were faced with enormous problems. Only on the Central Plateau, which occupies about one-third of the country, and stretches north-east from Lake Geneva in the west to Zurich and on to Lake Constance in the east, was the ground more gently undulating and favourable for railway construction.

The first railway on Swiss territory was in fact French, coming in from Strasbourg to Basel and completed in 1844; just three years later the first purely Swiss line was built between Zurich and Baden. The British railway engineer Robert Stephenson was asked to plan a railway network for Switzerland, as much for speedy transport for defence as for commercial use. His plan of 1850 provided for a south-west–north-east trunk line from Geneva through Lausanne, Neuchatel, Olton, Zurich and Rorschach to Lindau in Germany, with a north–south main line from Basel through Olten to Lucerne, and branches to Bern, in the centre of the country, and up the Rhine valley in the east to Chur. Apart from the Basel–Olten section, which climbed over the Jura mountains and included a 2.4km (1.5 miles) tunnel, none of these lines went through any major mountain ranges. Most were built as planned and they still form part of the system. More railways were built during the second half of the 19th century, but the most pressing need then was for a through route across the Alps to Italy, which would give direct communication from Germany. After much planning and ten long years of construction the 14.9km ($9\frac{1}{4}$ mile) long Gotthard tunnel between Göschenen and Airolo was opened in 1882, together with a new through route from Basel and Lucerne to Italy. Much of the line in the mountains was steeply graded at 1 in 37-40.

A second trans-Alpine route was built when the Simplon tunnel, a single line bore, was completed in 1906 linking west Switzerland with Italy. A second bore, at just over 19.7km ($12\frac{1}{4}$ miles) the longest main-line tunnel in Europe, added a second track and was opened in 1921. Meanwhile the 14.5km (9 mile) Lötschberg tunnel was built to give a through route from Bern to the Simplon line.

The Gotthard and Lötschberg/Simplon routes have remained the only two major through rail routes to cross the Alps, but another line, the Bernina, a metre gauge local railway in south-east Switzerland, goes up and over the Bernina pass at 2,255m (7,400ft) between St Moritz and Tirano in Italy. This line includes some spectacular climbs including grades of 1 in 14 (7 per cent) worked entirely by adhesion. Loads are light, normally no more than a motor coach and two trailer cars or freight trains of up to ten wagons hauled by two electric motor coaches.

Virtually all of Switzerland's railways are electrified; dwarfed by the mountain backdrop (left), two Swiss Federal Railways powerful Ae 6/6 6,000hp electric locomotives approach Goschenen with a Basle-Chiasso train.

The Bernina line is part of the Rhaetian Railway, one of the many private railways in Switzerland. The Rhaetian is the largest private line, and serves the whole of the southeast; together with the Furka-Oberalp and Brig-Visp-Zermatt lines it forms an important metre gauge link across southern Switzerland, so important that another new Alpine rail tunnel 15.3km (9.5 miles) long and due for completion in 1979 is being built under the Furka pass to avoid a 2,134m (7,000ft) summit which is snow blocked and closed to trains for six months of the year.

Of the 4,988km (3,100 route miles) of railway in Switzerland about 2,896km (1,800 miles) are operated by the nationalized Swiss Federal Railways. The rest are private lines owned variously by, for example, banks, commercial organizations such as large hotel groups, local authorities and particularly the cantons, the individual states forming the Swiss Confederation. Apart from one metre gauge line between Lucerne and Interlaken, all Swiss Federal lines are standard gauge, but the private railways consist of both standard and narrow gauge lines.

Nearly all railways in Switzerland are electrified. First experiments in electric working were carried out around the turn of the century and, since Switzerland has no coal but much hydro-electric power, electrification was carried out generally from the First World War. Some of the latest locomotives are the most powerful in Europe at over 10,000hp. Passenger motor coaches work trains on many local lines.

Some of the through routes and local lines in the mountains have gradients as steep as 1 in 8 (12.5 per cent) or more and have rack and pinion working. This system works by having cog wheels on the train engage a toothed rail on the centre of the track for power and braking. Rack and pinion operation is also used by the purely tourist lines to mountain summits on grades as steep as 1 in 2 (48 per cent) such as those to the Jungfraujoch 3,454m (11,333ft) above sea level, Pilatus 2,066m (6,778ft), Gornergrat, near Zermatt, just over 3,048m (10,000ft) up, or the Rigi railway from Vitznau 1,750m (5,741ft) high and the first rack and pinion railway in Europe.

Switzerland's railway system straddles the crossroads of Europe, and many International trains criss-cross the country, including several Trans Europe Express services. This is the Swiss Federal 'Cisalpin' (above) hurrying through the Rhone Valley on its daily dash from Milan through Lausanne to Paris.

Railways in the USA

Railways in many countries were built to serve societies which had been developing over periods of many centuries. In North America the railways grew up with a new society and kept pace with its expansion. Early railways in the United States linked the cities along the eastern seaboard and ran generally north and south. Penetration westward came later as immigration from Europe increased and the Federal Government made grants of lands to railway companies which they could sell to the new colonists. With this encouragement lines were extended westwards into the prairies and the great grain-growing areas were opened up, served by railways to take their products to the cities and to the ports for shipment.

By the time of the American Civil War in 1861 the railway network linked the eastern seaboard with the Middle West and the growing cities of Chicago and St Louis. Impetus for a transcontinental route was given during the war when, partly for strategic and political reasons, Congress passed an Act authorizing the Union Pacific Railway Company to build a line to connect Omaha, in Nebraska, with Sacramento, in California. It was a joint venture with the Central Pacific Railway of California, one line pushing westwards and the other eastwards and both anxious to lay as much track as possible to qualify for Government loans and grants of land. In fact, in the absence of a specified meeting place the two lines finally overlapped each other, but it was then agreed that they should link up at Promontory, north of the Great Salt Lake in Utah. The last spike was driven there in a ceremony on May 10, 1869.

Further transcontinental and inter-city routes followed in a period of railway and commercial expansion on a scale the world had not seen before. By 1900 there were 309,000km (192,000 miles) of railway in the United States compared with 32,200km (20,000 miles) in Britain, and the network of 418,000km (260,000 miles) existing in the USA in 1920 formed one-third of the world's total railway mileage.

There were numerous competitive routes, and some fast running to capture traffic. The New York Central and the Pennsylvania Railroad both ran between New York and Chicago, the former with a route 96km (60 miles) longer although much more easily graded. Up to 1893 the crack trains of both railways made the New York-Chicago journey in 24 hours, but in that year there was an international exhibition in Chicago and the New York Central put on a train that ran between the two cities in 20 hours, an average speed of 78.9km/h (49mph) for the journey of 1,547km (961 miles). After the exhibition the time reverted to 24 hours but in 1905 both railways put on a 20-hour service. The New York Central's train was the famous Twentieth Century Limited, accelerated to 18 hours in 1908, and eventually to 16 hours in 1938 with new streamlined steam locomotives and rolling stock. The Broadway Limited of the

Below is a replica of the De Witt Clinton 0-4-0 and its carriages reminiscent of stagecoach design. It depicts the first train to run on the New York Central Railroad, and shows the strong British influence on early American practice.

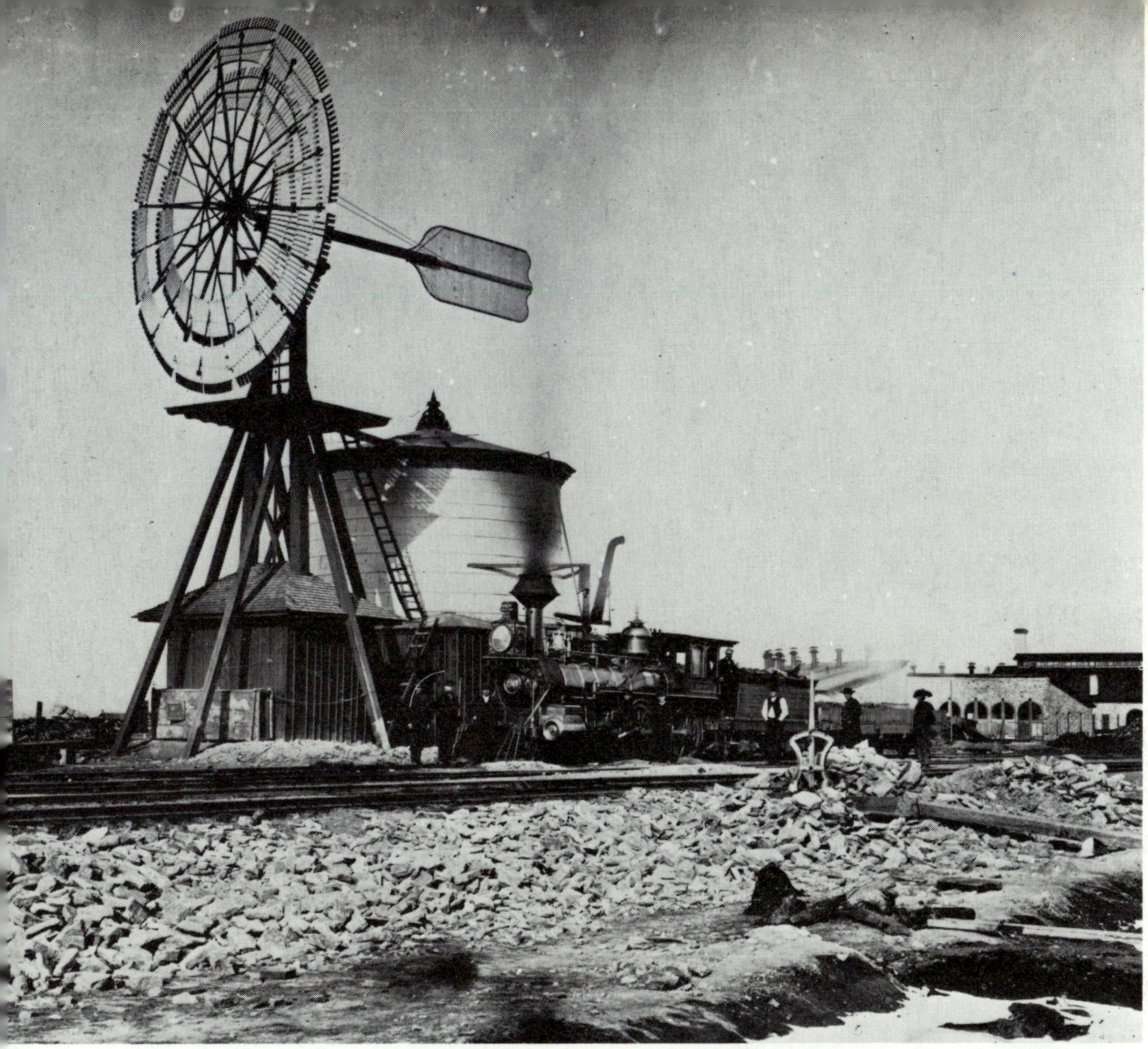

Whilst railways speeded the industrial revolution in Europe, in America, and particularly the mid-West, they quite literally opened up the country. Aided by Government grants, the Union Pacific and Central Pacific railroads joined forces to build a new transcontinental line from Omaha in Nebraska to Sacramento in California, opened in May 1869. This late 1860s view (left) of the Union Pacific complex at Laramie shows the typical wind pump and water tank, the surprisingly substantial stone-built roundhouse and an equally typical wood-burning 4-4-0.

Although most American railroads were dieselized long before their European counterparts, the last years of steam traction in the USA saw the development of some huge and powerful locomotives of impressive proportions. Even when some of the first diesels were taking to the rails in 1941, the Union Pacific Railroad introduced the first of its huge 'Big Boy' articulated 4-8-8-4s (below) for heavy freight.

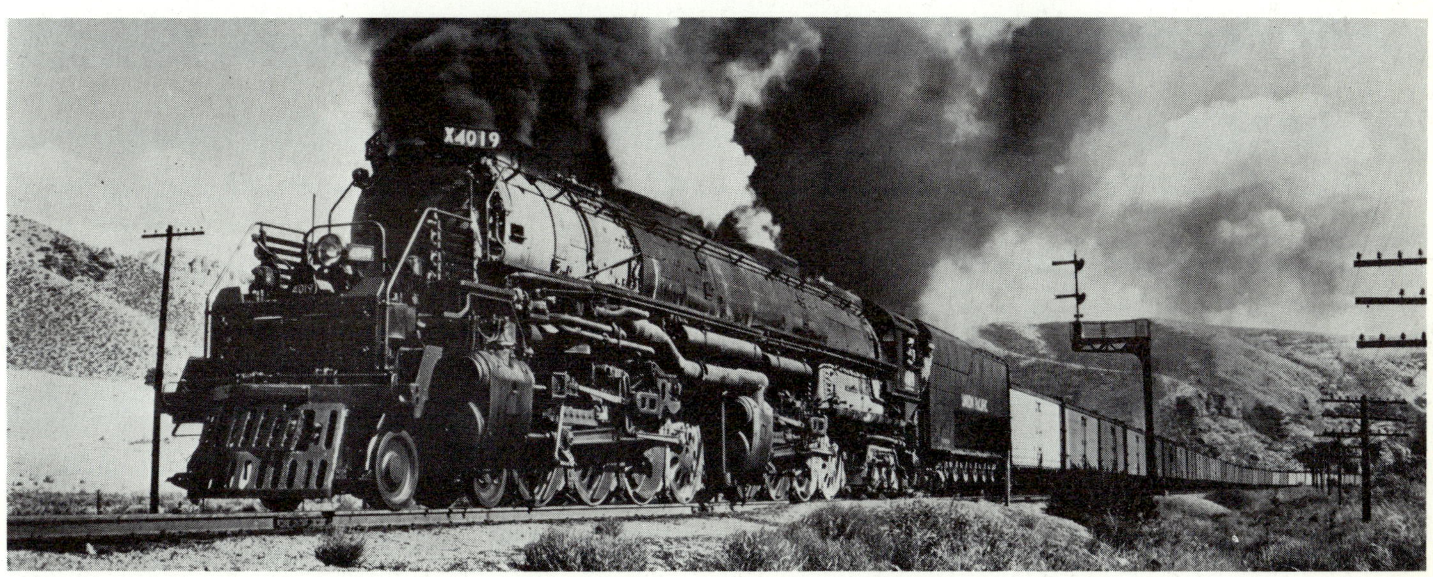

rival Pennsylvania Railroad ran to similar timings. Both trains were diesel-hauled in their later years.

The middle 1930s saw the introduction of main-line diesel locomotives on the US railways through the enterprise of the General Motors Corporation in developing standard units that could be bought 'off the shelf' and operated singly or in multiple according to the power required for a particular train. An 1800hp General Motors main-line passenger diesel was put in service by the Baltimore and Ohio in 1935, soon followed by the Atchison, Topeka and Santa Fe with two similar units operated as a coupled pair to form a 3,600hp locomotive. Economy and efficiency were the motives at first rather than spectacular speeds, but the picture was changing with the introduction of high-speed lightweight diesel trains. The Burlington Zephyr trains of the

Chicago, Burlington and Quincy were covering the 693.6km (431 miles) between Chicago and St Paul at an average speed of 106km/h (66mph) by the winter of 1934-35. This was a highly competitive route and 1935 saw the introduction of a high-speed streamlined steam train, 'The Hiawatha', by the Chicago, Milwaukee, St Paul and Pacific Railroad. Speeds of 160km/h (100mph) now became commonplace, and on one section of its run 'The Hiawatha' was scheduled to cover 126km (78.3 miles) in 62 min, an average speed of 121.8km/h (75.8mph). The Chicago and North Western also served the 'Twin Cities' of Minneapolis and St Paul and operated a train called 'The 400', which tied with the speed of 'The Hiawatha' over a section of its run. By 1939, however, diesel power was at the top of the US speed tables with ten runs

After two decades of decline in the face of immense competition from road and air transport, recent years have seen something of a revival in passenger traffic in US railroads. Spearheaded by Amtrak, the federal authority set up to operate the principal passenger services of the 22 major US railroads, new trains and services have brought traffic back to rail for intercity services. On the electrified Northeast corridor from Boston and New York to Washington, Amtrak's new locomotives and Amfleet cars (above) and Metroliner multiple-units (left) together provide a new level of fast, air-conditioned inter-city travel, competing for the first time in comfort, speed and reliability with airlines.

faster than those of the Chicago-St Paul steam fliers and a best performance of 131km/h (81.4mph) by the Union Pacific's 'City of Denver' express.

Railway electrification in the United States can be dated from August 4, 1895, when the Baltimore and Ohio introduced electric locomotives on a tunnel section of its line in Baltimore. In later years the tracks into the Grand Central Terminal, New York, were electrified after a collision in a smoke-filled tunnel, but the trains of the New York Central using the terminal changed to steam haulage at Harmon outside the city. This electrified section was shared for part of its length by the New York, New Haven and Hartford, which electrified its own tracks further out at 11,000V ac, with overhead collection of current. Since the Grand Central Terminal lines were electrified on the low-voltage dc system with third rail, the NYNH&H locomotives were designed to operate on both systems, and to pass from one to the other without stopping—a pioneer example of dual-system working. An important 11,000V ac main-line electrification was carried out by the Pennsylvania between New York, Philadelphia, Harrisburg and Washington, while the Chicago, Milwaukee, St Paul and Pacific was responsible for the first main-line electrification at 3,000V dc. Although the US ac lines have been supplied at the sub-standard frequency of 25Hz, the prospect of changing to the American industrial standard of 60Hz was studied soon after the Second World War and the Pennsylvania Railroad was early in the field with a rectifier motor coach and freight locomotives which would have been suitable

by a dwindling number of passengers. By early 1971 there were only about 500 passenger trains a day in the United States compared with around 15,000 at the outbreak of the Second World War. By this time, however, there was considerable public disquiet at the decline of passenger service. Concern at congested highways, pollution, and extravagant use of fuel caused the Federal Government to step in.

Despite bitter opposition from road haulage interests, the Rail Passenger Service Act passed in 1971 set up the Amtrak organization to take over and operate the passenger services of 22 principal railways (excluding commuter services). At first the number of trains a day

for working on the industrial frequency if it had been adopted. The country's first 60Hz line, however, was a fully-automated industrial railway linking the Black Mesa coal mines in Arizona with the Navajo power station. Electrified at 50,000 volts in 1974, it was the first in the world at so high a voltage. Power is fed in at one end of the 125.5km (78-mile) line, and no intermediate feeder stations are required. On lines electrified at the more common maximum of 25,000V it is usually necessary to feed power at intervals of 50 to 65km (30 to 40 miles).

Before many years had elapsed after the end of the Second World War, air travel and the motor car made such serious inroads into passenger services on the US lines that some companies preferred not to operate them and to concentrate on freight. Loads handled in a single train may be as high as 12,000 tonnes with one locomotive at the head controlling four 'slave' units marshalled at different positions in the train over a radio link. It is an economical method of working traffic, requiring only one engine crew per train, and there was progressively less inducement to provide the more expensive type of service required

was still further cut to 184 long-distance services but the routes were carefully selected and the basic Amtrak network was a sound foundation for future development. Sleeping cars now run through from New York to Los Angeles, and the San Francisco 'Zephyr' takes the historic transcontinental route from Chicago through Omaha to Sacramento and Oakland (for San Francisco). Much of the patronage of these trains comes from tourists, but Amtrak has also developed fast services for the business community along what is known as the North East Corridor from Washington to New York and Boston.

At first, Amtrak leased all its motive power and rolling stock from the railways which joined it but after a few years it began to buy its own equipment, both locomotives and rolling stock. There have been experiments with gas turbine trains on the New York-Boston section of the North East Corridor, and the switch of the New York-Boston trains from the Grand Central to the Pennsylvania terminal in New York improves the connection between the two sections of the Corridor route, enabling through coaches to be run between Boston and Washington.

Even on the non-electrified lines, Amtrak is determined to provide modern, fast, air-conditioned trains. This is one of the seven new turboliners (above) entering service on these routes; its blend of American and French design emphasises the current trend back towards the European standards of service and frequency which had until recently all but disappeared from the increasingly freight-orientated American railroads.

Canadian Railways

While the interior of Canada was still unexplored, seamen from Europe were probing the Atlantic coast in the hope of finding a passage to the Pacific. Exploration continued into the railway age, but by that time it was known that such a voyage could only be made through Arctic waters. Railways offered a new and at first unbelievably rapid means of transporting freight and passengers between the Atlantic and Pacific coasts. The dream of the transcontinental train dawned early, but the first lines were of more local interest, built to by-pass difficult or circuitous sections of the old trade routes by waterway in the eastern part of the country. Thus the earliest railway in Canada, opened on July 21, 1836, connected La Prairie, opposite Montreal on the St Lawrence, with St Johns on the Richelieu River, which flows into Lake Champlain, the southern end of which is close to the Hudson River

Dwarfed by the magnificent scenery as it soars over the Stoney Creek Bridge, the Canadian Pacific's transcontinental 'Canadian' express shows the sheer scale of the rough and inhospitable terrain which the CPR engineers had to tackle in the 1880s.

and the route by water to New York. Before the railway came, the traveller from Montreal had to first sail north for 64km (40 miles) down the St Lawrence to join the Richelieu at Sorel before heading south.

Later years saw the cities of eastern Canada being linked direct by rail, an important step being the opening of the Grand Trunk Railway between Montreal and Toronto in 1856.

When British Columbia united with the Dominion of Canada, the Canadian Government undertook to begin construction of a railway to link the province with the railways of eastern Canada within two years. A start was made in British Columbia in 1880, but progress was slow, and after a change of Government the remainder of the work was entrusted to a group of businessmen who had already made proposals for carrying the line forward when it was seen to be in difficulties. They formed the Canadian Pacific Railway Company (CPR), which was formally incorporated on February 17, 1881.

Surveys and building of the Canadian Pacific Railway proceeded with exemplary energy, daring and highly competent organization. The eastern and western sections of the railway linking Montreal and Vancouver met in Eagle Pass, British Columbia, on November 7, 1885, and the first transcontinental train left Montreal on June 28, 1886. On this route the Rockies are crossed in the Kicking Horse Pass, but the highest summit on the line (and on any railway in Canada) is at the Great Divide on the boundary between British Columbia and Alberta, at an altitude of 1,435m (5,332ft).

A second transcontinental undertaking, in which the Grand Trunk Railway was active, got under way in 1905 with the work shared between contractors for the Government and a Grand Trunk subsidiary, the Grand Trunk Pacific. The route through to the Pacific coast at Prince Rupert was completed in 1914. It crosses the Rockies in the Yellowhead Pass and is less severely graded than the Canadian Pacific, which chose the more southerly route to be closer to the United States border and forestall competition by any US transcontinental route that might be contemplated.

A third transcontinental line was built by the Canadian Northern Railway, opened throughout between Quebec and Vancouver in 1915, but it soon had financial problems and was taken over by the Canadian Government as the nucleus of the Canadian National Railways, while later, in 1920, the government took formal possession of the Grand Trunk, which was already in receivership, and absorbed it into the new Canadian National system.

The Canadian Pacific and Canadian National lines stretch from coast to coast, but

their importance is for heavy freight across the continent. Air travel has reduced transcontinental rail passengers to a trickle, and at one time the Canadian Pacific sought leave to discontinue its transcontinental passenger train, 'The Canadian'. This was refused and trains run between Montreal and Vancouver, but the thrice-weekly trips now combine with Canadian National's transcontinental service between Sudbury and Winnipeg in winter.

The principal railway passenger activities in Canada are now on the inter-city lines in the east, particularly between Quebec, Montreal and Toronto. High-speed gas turbine trains —the Turbos—run on the Montreal-Toronto route and high speed LRC (Light, Rapid, Comfortable) diesel sets with tilting coaches are coming into service on both the Quebec-Montreal corridor and the new combined CP/CN transcontinental services.

Australian Railways

Rail transport in Australia did not begin on the mainland but on the island of Tasmania, where in 1836, a line with wooden rails was laid across the Tasman Peninsula, a distance of about 7.2km ($4\frac{1}{2}$ miles), to save passengers by sea the notoriously rough passage round Cape Raoul. The 'trains' were individual four-wheeled trolleys and they were propelled by manpower drawn from the nearby convict settlement. It appears from early accounts and drawings that the men pushed the trolleys by means of poles extending outwards on each side, and that on down grades they jumped on board to ride until more pushing was needed.

In later years a number of short railways were opened on the mainland and worked with horses, both for freight and passenger traffic, but the first steam-operated line was the Melbourne and Hobson's Bay Railway, opened in 1854. It had a gauge of 1.6m (5ft 3in).

Australia in its early days was a collection of separate colonies, each looking to Great Britain for most of its trade. Railways radiated from the main ports and transport across the borders was relatively unimportant. Different gauges were chosen in different parts of the country, and this led to obvious problems when Australia had become a federal commonwealth with trade flowing from State to State. Australia has three principal railway gauges. Nearly half the total mileage is 1.067m (3ft 6in) and the remainder roughly evenly divided between the standard gauge of 1.435m ($4ft 8\frac{1}{2}in$) and 1.6m (5ft 3in).

Each of the present Australian States operates its own railway system and these are now interconnected, although sometimes with a break of gauge. There is also the Australian National Railways system, owned and operated by the Commonwealth Government. Of the five sections of this system the longest is the Trans-Australian Railway, built across the

Each State in Australia has its own railway system, and although all but the lines in Northern Territory interconnect, the various gauges in use often make through running difficult. Nearly half Australia's rail mileage is laid to 1.067m (3ft 6in) gauge, including the Queensland system, traversed here (right) near Cairns on the Pacific Coast by the diesel-hauled 'Sunlander' express.

virtually unpopulated desert country in the south to connect Western Australia with the eastern States. It is a standard gauge line 1,783km (1,108 miles) long, from Kalgoorlie in Western Australia to Port Pirie, South Australia. The Western Australian system is basically 1.067m (3ft 6in) gauge, but in 1968 a standard gauge line was completed from Kalgoorlie to Perth and Fremantle to connect with the Trans-Australian. Two years later South Australia adapted its line from Port Pirie to Broken Hill in New South Wales to take standard gauge trains, and since the New South Wales system is standard gauge through running between Perth and Sydney at last became possible. Three track gauges are found in South Australia and at one point on the Point Pirie-Broken Hill line the track is laid with additional rails to make it triple gauge.

For many years the break of gauge at Albury, the border meeting point of the Victorian Railways 1.600m (5ft 3in) system and the New South Wales Standard gauge lines, precluded through running between the major cities of Melbourne and Sydney. Even passengers on the crack, streamlined, air-conditioned 'Spirit of Progress' express had to change trains at Albury until 1962, when the Victorian Railways Melbourne-Albury section was equipped with standard gauge track and for the first time through trains could be run over the entire 961 km (596 mile) route. The standard gauge 'Spirit of Progress' (left) heads south from Albury, flanked on the right by a VR broad gauge train.

The first through service between Perth and Sydney was introduced in 1970 and named the Indian-Pacific after the two oceans it links. In the course of its journey across the desert the train traverses the celebrated section of 478km (297 miles) of dead straight track over the Nullarbor Plain. The total distance from Perth to Sydney is 3,960km (2,461 miles). There are four departures a week by the Indian-Pacific service in each direction, and the traveller reaches his destination on the fourth day after departure.

Another important development in the improvement of Australian train services was the opening in 1962 of a standard gauge line from Melbourne to Albury, connecting with the standard gauge New South Wales Railways. Through running thus became possible between Melbourne and Sydney. The Melbourne-Sydney service saw the first streamlined train in Australia, the Spirit of Progress, introduced by the Victorian Government Railways in 1937. In those days the train ran between Melbourne and the New South Wales border at Albury, being built for the 1.6m (5ft 3in) gauge, and passengers changed at Albury into the standard gauge Sydney Limited of the New South Wales Government Railways. With the opening of the standard gauge line between Melbourne and Albury a number of through trains between Melbourne and Sydney were introduced and one of them was named 'Spirit of Progress' to keep the title of the pre-war pioneer Australian streamliner in being.

Diesel traction predominates on the Austra-

lian railways, but the States of Victoria and New South Wales have electrified suburban networks serving Melbourne and Sydney respectively. In both States, also, electrification has been extended from the city suburbs over certain sections of main line. In Victoria the Gippsland line has been electrified to Traralgon. In New South Wales the line through the Blue Mountains from Sydney to Lithgow is electrified for 156km (97 miles), and the line running northwards from Sydney to the Queensland border is electrified as far as Gosford, 80km (49.7 miles). The electrifications in both States are at 1,500V dc with overhead contact wire.

New South Wales has 446km (277 miles) of electrified line, and Victoria 421km (261 miles). The most powerful electric locomotives in Australia are Class 46 on the New South Wales Railways, rated at 3,780hp (2,819kW).

The standard gauge Trans-Australian Railway, operated by the Commonwealth Government, connects the Western Australian system at Kalgoorlie with the South Australian lines at Port Pirie, and crosses the Nullarbor Plain (above), a vast waterless, treeless desert. The line travels for nearly 482km (300 miles) without a single curve. In recent years, both the Western Australian and South Australian systems have added standard gauge rails to their existing lines, and since 1970 the Indian-Pacific express has been running four times a week over the entire 3,960km (2,460 mile) route from Perth on the west coast to Sydney in the east.

Fairlies, Mallets and Garretts

The tractive effort (pulling power) of a steam locomotive can be calculated from a formula based on piston size and stroke, steam pressure and wheel diameter. If the wheels do not grip the rails, however, the figure is only of theoretical interest, for the locomotive will be unable to move its train. Tractive effort is measured in pounds or kilogrammes, and the effort that can be used is equal to about one-quarter of the locomotive weight carried on the driving wheels. In conventional locomotives the number of driving wheels rarely exceeds ten because the practicable length of driving wheelbase is limited by the curvature the locomotive has to negotiate. For very high tractive efforts the designer may have to

best known of these early articulated locomotives are the Fairlie, the Mallet, and the Kitson-Meyer. Fairlies have two boilers back to back with an engine (ie cylinders, motion and driving wheels) under each. The cab is between the boilers. The others have one large boiler and two engines. In all cases the engines are pivoted below the main frame which carries the boiler.

In 1908 a British engineer, H. W. Garratt, was awarded a patent for the type of articulated locomotive which now bears his name. Manufacture was undertaken by Beyer, Peacock and Company so that the type is often called the Beyer-Garratt. Its articulation is quite different from those mentioned above,

choose between increasing the weight on the driving wheels and having more of them. The first choice may be ruled out by the civil engineer, who sets a limit on the load per axle that can be allowed on the rails and bridges. The second presents the problem of rigidity.

In the second half of the 19th century various designs of locomotive appeared in which the driving wheels were in two groups, each group able to pivot independently. The

for the Beyer-Garratt consists of two steam engines with the boiler and cab carried between them on an independent supporting frame. At each end of the frame there is an articulated joint with the separate frame of one of the steam engines. All wheels, driving and carrying, are in the steam engine frames. Those at the inner ends are often under the smokebox and cab, but under most of the boiler length there are no wheels, and this

The most prolific users of Garratts were the 1.07m (3ft 6in) gauge South African Railways and the metre gauge East African Railway system. This is a South African Railways Class GMAM 4-8-2+2-8-4 (above).

enables a boiler of large size to be used.

Coal is carried in a bunker mounted above the engine at the cab end of the locomotive, and water supplies are in a tank over the other engine. Cylinders are normally at the outer ends of the engine units, but in the first two Garratts built were at the inner ends. These were supplied in 1909 to a light railway in Tasmania. The wheel arrangement of each engine unit was 0-4-0 and the gauge 610mm (2ft). One of the pair has been preserved in Great Britain in the National Railway Museum at York. In describing a Garratt locomotive the usual wheel notation is used with a plus sign between the two sections, for example, in the case of the Tasmanian Garratts 0-4-0+0-4-0.

The modest size of the first Garratts underlines the fact that the importance of the principle is that axle-loads can be kept low in building for railways where economic factors have imposed the use of light rails and avoidance of heavy engineering works. These conditions often lead to steep gradients and severe curvature and so the need for high tractive efforts. Operators of such railways are more interested in hauling heavy loads at low speed than in running a frequent express service. This is the background against which the Garratt locomotive has been developed from its first small beginnings to giants developing over 31,750kg (70,000lb) tractive effort. Some of them are still at work, mainly on the continent of Africa. The most powerful locomotives in South Africa are the 4-8-2+2-8-4 Garratts of the GL Class, a 1.07m (3ft 6in) gauge design capable of a tractive effort of 35,675kg (78,650lb) spread over 16 driving wheels, while on the metre gauge lines of the East African Railways the 59 Class Garratts of the same wheel arrangement will develop 33,339kg (73,500lb) tractive effort, making

them the most powerful metre-gauge steam locomotives in the world. Rhodesia has also been an enthusiastic user of Garratts and finally standardized a 4-6-4+4-6-4 for mixed passenger and freight duties on all lines still worked by steam. Its most powerful freight Garratt is the 20th Class 4-8-2+2-8-4.

The number of Garratts in service is declining fast with the spread of diesel traction and electrification, and those which have survived are mainly in situations where electrification is not yet economic and the import of oil fuel exceptionally expensive. The type will be remembered for its exploits in heavy haulage, but Garratts have also been built for fast passenger work. A 2-4-0+0-4-2 was supplied for this purpose to the Sao Paulo Railway in Brazil in 1915 and proved so successful that its successors were later converted to the 4-6-2+2-6-4 wheel arrangement to increase their capabilities.

This works view (above) of a small-wheeled 2-8-2+2-8-2 built in 1926 shows the Garratt principle. One single boiler and cab is carried on a mainframe supported at each end by two entirely separate steam engine chassis. Water is carried in a large tank above one set of wheels, while the oil—or coal—is carried above the other adjacent to the cab.

In Britain Garratts were often used on coal trains with the engines having rotary coal-bunkers (below).

The Underground

The first underground railway in the world was opened in London at the beginning of 1863. Although a few main-line railways had managed to penetrate into the heart of the City of London, to Liverpool Street, Fenchurch Street and Cannon Street for example, many of the main line companies had been required to build their London termini on the outskirts of the capital. Although it may now be hard to believe, the termini of the London and Birmingham Railway (later the LNWR) at Euston, of the Great Western Railway at Paddington and of the London and Southampton Railway (later the LSWR) at Nine Elms were constructed on the edge of open country inconveniently placed for the city.

Even in the mid-19th century traffic congestion was a problem in London and as early as the 1830s an urban railway was proposed between King's Cross and Snow Hill (near the Old Bailey). Later a line had been planned between Paddington and Shoreditch under the New Road (later known as the Marylebone Road and Euston Road) and in 1851 Charles Pearson, a city solicitor, had conceived a 30.5m (100ft) wide road from Holborn to King's Cross to be supported on arches wide enough to cover no less than six standard-gauge and two broad-gauge lines.

It was as the result of Pearson's perseverance and tenacity that parliamentary powers were obtained in 1854 for the construction of an underground railway from Paddington to the Post Office, near St Paul's. Financial support from the GWR—anxious to obtain access to the city—enabled work to commence and the line opened on January 10, 1863 using broad-gauge trains hauled by GWR 2-4-0T locomotives especially designed with condensing apparatus by Sir Daniel Gooch. An earlier experimental fireless locomotive, now known as Fowler's Ghost, designed 'to consume its own smoke' had proved a failure, although it had probably been used to haul an inspection train in 1862 when the line was visited by such notable figures as the Prime Minister, Mr Gladstone, and Lord Grosvenor. When the GWR fell out with the Metropolitan Railway in the summer of 1863, temporary assistance was obtained from the Great Northern Railway which enabled it to operate a standard gauge emergency service until new 4-4-0T locomotives were designed and delivered by Beyer Peacock and Co. of Manchester. Similar locomotives were ordered by the District Railway and ultimately 66 similar locomotives were constructed, one of which (No.23) is now preserved by London Transport.

The first section of the Metropolitan Railway was opened between Paddington and Farringdon Street, and was soon extended eastwards to Moorgate. In the west the line was extended to South Kensington in 1868, where it met end-on with the Metropolitan District Railway, which operated thence to Westminster Bridge and Blackfriars. After initial rivalry, the two companies later worked in harmony and jointly operated the Inner Circle service which still operates today under the auspices of London Transport.

The Metropolitan and District Railways were built by the cut-and-cover system: the cuttings were dug out, usually under existing roadways to avoid legal complications, and later covered over again, and this system has subsequently been used throughout the world in the construction of underground systems where deep-level tubes are not required. To facilitate the dispersal of locomotive smoke, gaps were left in the covering at intervals, as can still be seen today on the Circle Line along the Embankment between Westminster and Blackfriars.

Although not 'underground' in the literal sense, it is appropriate to mention here the later extensions of both the Metropolitan and the District Railways at ground level that took 'underground' trains out into the country, westwards to Hammersmith and Wimbledon and northwards into 'Metroland' in Buckinghamshire. Inspired by the hope of becoming a main-line railway, the Metropolitan eventually extended over 50 miles from its headquarters at Baker Street, to Brill and Verney Junction.

The Metropolitan had endeavoured to be excluded from the London Transport reorganization plans that ultimately resulted in the formation of the LPTB in 1933 and, although

The extensive Underground railway system in Paris—the 'Metro'—now enjoys a high level of public subsidy and much of the older stock has been replaced in recent years. The famous rubber-tyred trains introduced on Line 11 in 1956 have not found favour elsewhere, and the most recent rolling stock, such as this unit entering (above, left) Pyramines station on Line 7, is of more orthodox construction.

In complete contrast to the clean, functional lines of most of the Underground systems of the Western world, Moscow's Underground system (left) boasts lavish, spacious stations of grand proportions, often finished in marble, with ornate columns and arches. There is also a complete absence of the all-pervading advertising material of Western systems.

Unlike the Parisian Metro, which was planned from the outset as a complete system, London's Underground railways grew in a rather piecemeal way. Indeed, London's first Underground line, the first in the world, opened in 1863 from Paddington to Farringdon Street as virtually an eastward extension into the heart of the City of the Great Western Railway. As can be seen in this contemporary view (above) of King's Cross Metropolitan line station shortly after opening, broad as well as standard gauge rails were provided, allowing the use of GWR broad gauge locomotives and rolling stock.

unsuccessful, maintained its main-line image by continuing to run two Pullman cars (introduced in 1910) until the outbreak of the Second World War and by operating electrically-hauled compartment coaches until the completion of the electrification of the line to Amersham in 1961.

Many 'underground' railways elsewhere in the world are also built partly above ground. The first overseas underground railway was the Paris Metro, and the earliest lines in Paris were also constructed by the cut-and-cover system. Unlike in London, where the underground system was developed piecemeal by private enterprise to no overall plan, the French network was planned as a co-ordinated whole unconnected with the main lines. The first section of line in Paris, which linked the Place de Nation, the Place de la Bastille and the Arc de Triomphe, opened in July 1900, and as early as 1904 the Place de l'Etoile—in the middle of which stands the Arc de Triomphe—had become the meeting place of no less than five underground lines. In parts of Paris, and particularly wherever a crossing of the River Seine is required, the underground lines are carried on overhead sections which give passengers good views of the city—as at Montmartre—but which are not an asset to the city scene.

In the 1950s much of the stock on the Paris Metro appeared old-fashioned, but that could not be said of the pneumatic-tyred trains that were introduced to give a quiet and comfortable ride on Line 11 in 1956. Similar stock has since been introduced on other lines in Paris and on the underground system opened in the 'Paris of Canada'—Montreal—in 1966 in preparation for the Expo '67 exhibition and the 1976 Olympics. Much of the Montreal system is in deep tunnel, however, and should more properly be described as a tube rather than an underground railway system.

Not long behind Paris in the introduction of underground railways was New York. Elevated railways had expanded rapidly after the first section had opened in 1872, but by the beginning of the 20th century public demand for further passenger lines to be built underground was growing. Work commenced on the first 'subway' in March 1901, and the new lines were built on a grand scale, wide enough (no doubt assisted by the wide and straight character of North American streets) to permit four tracks and therefore both all-station and express services. Even the Harlem River was crossed by cut-and-cover methods, sections of tunnel being protected by coffer dams during construction.

If the New York subway was constructed on grand lines, its stations cannot be compared with the grandeur of the buildings of the Moscow system. Unlike in London or New York, where financial pressures determine the simple design of the stations and attract advertising revenue on the platforms, the Moscow underground system is graced with lavish and spacious stations designed in grand style and finished in white and black marble. Part of the system was built by cut-and-cover, but in parts deep tunnelling was also necessary.

Underground systems, often developments of tramway systems, are multiplying throughout the main cities of the world as the traffic congestion justifies the high capital cost of such construction. Although the first line had opened in Madrid as early as 1919, new lines have been regularly opened since that date and two are still being constructed; in Rome a line was planned in 1938 but not brought into service until 1955; a Metro was introduced in Milan in 1964 and Munich opened its first lines in preparation for the Olympic Games there in 1972. Elsewhere in Germany, the divided city of Berlin had enjoyed underground and elevated services since 1902, and today enjoys the unenviable distinction of running underground services beneath the Iron Curtain.

In Hong Kong, an entirely new system, using British rolling stock, is under construction.

Even in the USA, a new high-speed semi-underground commuter railway—the Bay Area Rapid Transit (Bart) System—has opened in San Francisco. If underground railways can be built in the home of the motor car, it is not surprising that throughout the world the cities which are building or contemplating underground systems are too numerous to mention individually: it is all a far cry from the early days of steam on the Metropolitan Line in 1863.

Tube Railways

The oldest tube tunnel on London's Underground system carries a section of the Metropolitan East London line beneath the River Thames between Wapping and Rotherhithe. Although the East London Railway did not open until 1869, the tunnel was of much older construction and had been purchased by the railway in 1865 after it had failed to make a profit in its original role as a pedestrian tunnel.

Plans for tunnels under the River Thames had been proposed as early as 1798 and 1805, and work commenced on the latter scheme under the direction of Richard Trevithick, the Cornishman generally acknowledged to be the inventor of the railway locomotive. In 1808 the works were abandoned after the river broke in, and no further attempts were made to build under the river until a tunnel shield was invented by Sir Marc Brunel—father of the great engineer Isambard Kingdom Brunel —and a New Thames Company formed. Isambard was appointed resident engineer on site in 1826 and, after disheartening delays, flooding and temporary abandonment, the tunnel was opened for pedestrian traffic in 1843. It speaks volumes for the skill of the designer and the quality of the work that the pedestrian tunnel has been used for over a century for railway use without problems.

Its construction was made possible by the development of the 'shield' designed by Marc Brunel, whereby massive cast-iron frames were inserted as the tunnel was built to support the land above until each section of brickwork had been completed. The shield could then be moved forward and the tunnel progressed. The shield invention was later further developed by Peter Barlow and James Greathead, and they built a tunnel under the Thames in 1870 by this method. The first passenger railway tube service commenced in that year on a 0.762m (2ft 6in) gauge cable-hauled railway through Greathead's tunnel, but the project was not a financial success and the service ceased after but a few months.

The feasibility of building tunnels through London clay had, however, been clearly demonstrated. Greathead was appointed Engineer of the City and South London Railway which opened in 1890 the first section of purpose-built 'tube' in London. The line, opened by the Prince of Wales, ran between King William Street and Elephant, using electric traction, and now forms part of the present Northern Line of London Transport.

Within 20 years the greater part of the Inner London Tube system had been constructed, the majority of lines being built by separate

One of the newest systems to include tube tunnels is BART, the Bay Area Rapid Transit system in San Francisco. BART is highly automated, the trains, like those on London's Victoria and Jubilee lines, controlling themselves. Here (right) a BART train speeds through the spacious tube tunnel 135ft below the surface of San Francisco Bay.

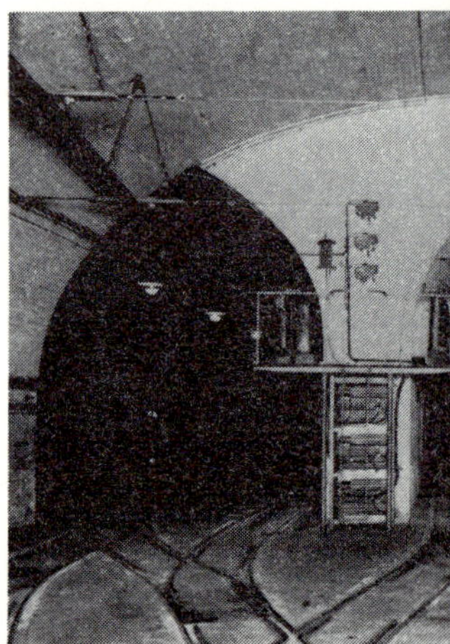

The world's first electric tube railway, the City and South London (below right), opened in 1890. Today, the original City and South London line forms part of London Transport's Northern Line. London's newest tubes are the Victoria and Jubilee lines (below left). London's extensive Underground system is familiar to residents and visitors alike, but one line the public never see is the Post Office Tube (below, centre) built in the 1920s to link the major London railway termini with the central post and sorting offices.

companies but all under the influence of an American, C. T. Yerkes. Over fifty years were to pass before new inner London railways were authorized, the Victoria Line (opened in 1968-69) and, more recently, the Jubilee Line. Outside the Yerkes' empire were the Waterloo and City Railway, purchased in 1907 by the London and South Western Railway and still owned and operated by British Railways; the Central London Railway that later formed the Central Line of London Transport; the Post Office Railway and the Great Northern and City Railway.

There could be no greater contrast than between the last two named. The Post Office Railway was opened in the 1920s to provide a non-passenger service between the main post offices between Paddington and Liverpool Street and was built to 0.610m (2ft) gauge in 2.74m (9ft) wide tunnels. In contrast, the GN & City was built between Finsbury Park and Moorgate in tunnels capable of accepting main-line rolling stock at a time when it was hoped that through trains would be run from the Great Northern Railway. Opened in 1904, over 70 years were to pass before the directors' plans were to come to fruition; since November 1976 the line has been operated as part of the Eastern region of British Rail to provide through electric services to Hertford and Welwyn Garden City.

Few underground systems elsewhere in the world incorporate as many 'tube' (as opposed to cut-and-cover) railways as in London, although parts of the systems in Glasgow and Moscow, and the Montreal Metro, were constructed by tube methods as have been the extensions to Merseyside's underground lines, and the new section of Tyneside's Metro. Special mention must be made, however, of the new express deep-level tubes that have been built and are being projected under Paris. The first underground section of the express metro opened between L'Etoile and La Défense in 1970, when the spacious high quality of the new stock and stations became immediately apparent. Unusually for tube railways, but indicative of the large scale of the project, the trains are supplied with 1,500V dc current collected by pantographs from overhead wires, whilst the stations have been built to main-line standards.

London's tube travellers are now able to reach the main terminals at Heathrow Airport direct from central London on the new Piccadilly Line extension into the heart of the complex, and construction of the new Jubilee Line tube is well advanced. As on the Victoria Line, Jubilee Line trains will be automatically controlled, while passenger movements will be controlled by automatic ticket machines and supervized by closed circuit television.

165

Great Engineers

The railway systems of the world could never have been constructed without the help of a great number of railway and civil engineers, by whose efforts mountain ranges were crossed, rivers bridged and deserts defeated, and by whom ever more powerful locomotives and improved coaching stock have been designed to improve the lot of the travelling public.

George and Robert Stephenson, with Isambard Kingdom Brunel, are regarded by many as the greatest railway engineers of all time. Other engineers may subsequently have had to conquer barriers of greater physical size—such as the Alps in Europe or the Rocky Mountains in Canada—but the Stephensons and Brunel stand alone by reason of their vision and diversity of skills. Robert Stephenson and Brunel were, in fact, almost exact contemporaries, and they strove to develop the British Railway system sometimes in competition and sometimes in harmony during the heyday of British railway expansion.

George Stephenson was born in 1781, the second son of a fireman at Wylam Colliery near Newcastle-upon-Tyne. Born of poor parents, he did not enjoy the benefit of formal

Along with George and Robert Stephenson, Isambard Kingdom Brunel (right, in typical Victorian attire and stovepipe top hat) was perhaps one of the greatest railway engineers of all time. Not only did he plan and begin work on the Great Western Railway while still in his twenties, he also designed and built all the major bridges and viaducts on the line, including the Royal Albert Bridge at Saltash, and managed to find time to design ships, including the 'Great Britain' (below), one of the first with an iron hull and screw propulsion.

education and developed his engineering skills working at a number of collieries. At Warbottle Colliery he worked closely with the engineer Robert Hawthorn, whose sons were later to found the famous Newcastle engineering firm that was closely connected with railway development. George Stephenson was associated with railways from birth, for his birthplace at Wylam was immediately adjacent to a long-established horse-powered wagonway, and after his move to Killingworth Colliery in 1804 he was in contact with the great railway engineers of the day, including Richard Trevithick. In 1813 he was invited to supervise the construction of a locomotive for the Killingworth tramway and his 'Blucher' was successfully steamed in July of the following year. This success and his established reputation locally led to his being invited to survey the line of the proposed Stockton and

Not unnaturally, British engineers were much sought after abroad in the early days of railways, and while Stephenson and Brunel were busy extending railways across the length and breadth of Britain, others were tackling the problems of construction overseas. Joseph Locke (centre left) engineered the line from Paris to Rouen, after successfully building lines in Britain from London to Southampton, Birmingham to Warrington and Manchester to Sheffield, while Thomas Brassey (near left) was responsible for lines as far afield as Canada, Australia, South America and India.

Just as British engineers were much in demand for the construction of new lines, so too were the products of British locomotive works. This early Hackworth 0-6-0 (right), with the original 'footplate' running the length of the boiler, and bar-type coupling rods, was built in about 1830 for use in Nova Scotia and was still at work many years later.

Darlington Railway after it had been authorized by Act of Parliament in 1821 and, assisted by his then 18 year-old son Robert, he completed his plans, reports and estimates by January of the following year.

In 1823 a locomotive manufacturing company was formed—Robert Stephenson and company—which gained the orders for the first four locomotives for the Stockton and Darlington Railway. Number 1 'Locomotion' survives to this day. George Stephenson was later engaged as engineer for the Liverpool and Manchester Railway, which opened in 1830 using Stephenson locomotives after the company's 'Rocket' had defeated all opponents at the Rainhill trials in 1829, a competition open to all and designed to determine the best locomotives of the day. The construction of the Liverpool and Manchester Railway involved the building of the great Sankey viaduct and the embankment across the great bog of Chat Moss, a feat that had been considered impossible by many engineers of repute.

After 1830, Robert Stephenson increasingly took over the day-to-day control of the Stephenson businesses and it was he who surveyed the main line of the 180km (112 mile) London and Birmingham Railway to which he was appointed engineer-in-chief before his thirtieth birthday. His father (who died in 1848) lived long enough to see many of Robert's great schemes come to fruition and to see, at least, the commencement of works on the great bridges for which Robert is famous, the High Level Bridge at Newcastle, (opened in 1846) and the Conway Bridge (opened in the same year), although he died before the completion of Robert's greatest works, the great tubular bridges at Montreal and over the Menai Strait.

In the erection of the Britannia tubular bridge over the Menai Strait, Robert Stephenson was assisted by the presence of I. K. Brunel, with whom he formed a close friendship in his later years. Brunel was born in 1806, the son of an émigré French engineer who was later to achieve fame and a knighthood on the completion of the first tunnel under the River Thames and, like Robert Stephenson, so assisted his father as to be given enormous responsibility at an early age. At the age of 27, in 1833, he was appointed engineer of the Great Western Railway (GWR) and planned the beautifully engineered main line between Paddington and Bristol that is used to such advantage today by British Railways High Speed Trains, whilst (like Robert Stephenson) his skills were such as to enable him to excell in other fields, designing the impressive Royal Albert Bridge at Saltash and great steamships far in advance of their time. The steamship *Great Britain* (built 1845) had an iron hull and was screw driven and has recently been returned to Britain for restoration from the Falkland Isles. Less successful was his largest ship, the *Great Eastern*, the construction, launch and operation of which caused him so many anxieties that it almost certainly contributed to his early death in 1859. He did not live to see the complete destruction of the broad gauge for which he had fought so hard on the GWR and the conversion of all lines to the standard gauge favoured by the Stephenson family.

Although the first main lines of the GWR and the London and Birmingham Railway could be personally planned and engineered by Brunel and Stephenson, they could not be

Despite their lack of information on the strength and durability of materials, and the need to build everything piecemeal because cranes were then virtually unknown, the 19th Century railway engineers were at the same time both bold and ingenious. Faced with the prospect of carrying the railway from Chester to Holyhead across the Menai Strait in Britain, Robert Stephenson devised his ingenious box girder Britannia Tubular Bridge (right). Two sets of tracks were carried high above the water in twin cast iron 'tubes' of box section, supported on elegant brick piers. As this contemporary print reveals, each tube was erected on the shore, floated into position and slowly jacked up onto the supporting piers. The bridge was opened in March 1850, and despite its novel form of construction, remained in use carrying ever-increasing loads until damaged beyond repair by fire in 1970, completely cutting off the important Container terminal at Holyhead from the remainder of the British railway system. Within two years, British Rail replaced the scorched, twisted girders with an entirely new bridge, but using the same brick piers, which had survived virtuaiiy intact.

expected to carry out similar surveys of all the numerous lines that proliferated during following decades. Other great engineers too numerous to mention individually, such as Joseph Locke (1805-60) and Thomas Brassey (1805-70) began to make railway history. Locke planned such lines as the Grand Junction Railway between Birmingham and Warrington, the London and Southampton Railway and lines between Sheffield and Manchester and Paris and Rouen, whilst Brassey was responsible for the Grand Trunk Railway in Canada and many lines in Australia, South America and India.

Without such engineers, many of whom died from exhaustion from their efforts, the great railway systems of the world could not have been built.

The first steam locomotives carried their coal and water supplies in a special wagon, or 'tender', immediately behind the engine. But after George England exhibited his lightweight 2-2-2 'little England' (left) at the 1851 Exhibition, his design became very popular, and the modern 'tank' engine, in which both water and coal are carried on the locomotive itself, was born.

Stations of the World

When the Stockton and Darlington Railway opened in 1825, its primary traffic was coal, and any passenger traffic was incidental to the haulage of freight, so the facilities for passengers were fairly spartan. In contrast, the Liverpool and Manchester Railway, opened just five years later, was intended to encourage the substantial passenger traffic between the two industrial towns, and from 1830 onwards the needs and comforts of passengers became of much greater importance to railway companies.

The London and Birmingham Railway,

wick, the passenger waiting hall and shareholders' and Directors' Room were also built in grand style. Sadly, all these features were swept aside when Euston Station was entirely rebuilt in the early 1960s.

At the other end of the line, in Birmingham, the original Curzon Street Station remains in existence, although its massive Ionic columns and stonework are in need of considerable restoration work, because its life as a terminus was short and it has not been used as a passenger station ever since Birmingham New Street was opened in 1852. After over a century of use as a freight depot, there is hope that it will be restored to its former glory to commemorate the original style and grace of

opened in 1838, spared no cost to impress its passengers. At Euston, the London terminus, passengers entered the station through a massive Doric arch, probably the most outstanding example of early railway architecture in the world, provided by the directors of the company as 'an embellishment' at the then enormous cost of £35,000. Inside the station, designed, like the Doric arch, by Philip Hard-

The ornate and extravagant Milan Central Station (above) was built on an entirely new site in the 1920s under the direction of the dictator Mussolini.

the London and Birmingham Railway. Elsewhere in Birmingham, the original and even older terminus of the Grand Junction Railway—which joined with the London and Birmingham to form the nucleus of the London and North Western Railway in 1846—was demolished in 1871, while the Great Western Railway's cavernous Snow Hill Station has now been closed. Western Region services

The entrance to the original Euston station, opened in 1838 as the London terminus of the London and Birmingham Railway, was graced by this massive Doric Arch, designed by Philip Hardwick (right). Despite protestations from the preservationist lobbies, the Doric Arch, together with Hardwick's adjacent Great Hall, was demolished in the mid 1960s to make way for the new Euston station (below right) which is undoubtedly more suited to the demands of present day rail travel.

now use New Street Station, which was completely rebuilt beneath a new shopping centre, as part of the West Coast main line 25,000V ac overhead electrification scheme. Some critics, used to Victorian grandeur, have decried the rebuilt stations as lacking in character, but there is no doubt that they are much more efficient from an operating point of view, and present a welcoming modern image to the intending passenger. Sadly, operating needs and the cost of maintenance demand simple, easy-to-run station structures in maintenance-free materials, and this is resulting in the demolition of fine stations erected in the early years of the railway age but now quite hopelessly out of date.

At about the time when the Curzon Street terminus was being abandoned, I. K. Brunel was putting the finishing touches to the London terminus of the Great Western Railway at Paddington. This magnificent station remains in use today, extended but otherwise unchanged from Brunel's light and airy design. Its triple roof spans, interupted by cross-transepts, have recently been enhanced by repainting in the original colour scheme of grey and red. Paddington Station has been scheduled as a building of great architectural and historic interest, as indeed have lesser examples of Brunel's work, such as Lostwithiel Station in Cornwall.

The St Pancras terminus of the former Midland Railway has also been scheduled as a building of great historical and structural interest. Although the station is smaller than Paddington, the great train shed at St Pancras has a single span of 73m (240ft), designed by W. H. Barlow, and over a hundred years later it still impresses passengers with its lightness and simplicity—particularly when compared with the over-ornate Gothic style of the adjoining station buildings and now empty hotel designed by Sir Gilbert Scott.

Elsewhere in Britain, other Victorian stations still in use include the great curved train sheds at York and Newcastle, the hammerbeam roof at Bristol Temple Meads, and the classical porticos at Huddersfield and Monkwearmouth—the last now closed and used as a local museum. Each of the pre-grouping railway companies developed quite recognizable architectural styles for their small stations as well as their main termini—Jacobean styling was the rule on the East Grinstead-Lewes line in Sussex, for example, while mock Gothic ruled in Wales.

Railway passengers in Britain are provided

Despite the delusions of grandeur of some of the early railway barons, small stations often proved to be most effective. The simple station in Sumatra (above) with its single, low island platform and basic awning is typical of wayside stations throughout the world.

with a raised platform giving easy access to trains, but in contrast, elsewhere in the world, low or non-existent platforms are the rule in all but the largest of stations, and most Continental and American railway carriages are fitted with steps to enable passengers to 'climb aboard' from track level.

The main termini in the capitals of France and Germany are graced with massive train sheds, as epitomized by the imposing Gare du Nord in Paris, rebuilt in the 1880s, and the original Berlin Anhalterbahnhof. As in London, Paris and Berlin are ringed with numerous railway termini, each serving lines reaching to the far corners of their countries. But whereas those in Paris are still very much in use, the partition of Germany and the isolation of Berlin has resulted in the closure of the main stations in the former German capital.

In Italy, Milan Central was rebuilt on a new site on a scale worthy of the worst Victorian extravagances as late as the 1920s under Mussolini. In North America, Grand Central Station in New York was rebuilt at the beginning of the century on two levels, both below street level. There were 29 express platforms and 13 storage lines on one level, and a further 15 suburban platforms at the lower level. Some of the low-level lines were extended right round the station to form a loop and thus obviate reversal. The palatial terminal building is 183m (600ft) long and 91.5m (300ft) wide, and is more reminiscent of a cathedral

The closing decades of the 19th Century were expansionist times for the railways of Europe; encouraged by soaring traffic, the Directors of many companies embarked on plans for sumptuous and ornate termini. In England, the Directors of the Midland Railway spoilt Barlow's magnificent train shed at St Pancras by sanctioning the construction of Sir Gilbert Scott's huge over-ornate mock-gothic facade (left) for the station and hotel. Even then an extravagance, the building has been an embarrassment to successive railway administrations, and today stands as preserved but rotting railway offices. No less extravagant, but somewhat more practical, was the wide frontage of the Gare du Nord in Paris (right), completely rebuilt in the 1880s.

than a railway station, although it has long since been dwarfed by neighbouring skyscrapers.

Many of the major cities in North America had 'Union' stations, built as joint projects by several railroads to include shops, arcades, restaurants and hotels. One of the most luxurious, in Chicago, is said to have cost £4.75 million at the turn of the century.

In Canada, too, the Canadian National Railway station at Montreal has been rebuilt below ground, beneath the palatial Queen Elizabeth Hotel from which direct access to the station can be obtained, but elsewhere in Montreal the faded grandeur of the Canadian Pacific Railway's Windsor Station is being replaced by more basic facilities. Throughout the world stations are being re-developed more along air terminal lines, while in some places the city termini are being moved away from city centres—as in Quebec; such moves, although no doubt welcome to city planners, seem unlikely to assist in the retention or increase of passenger traffic!

Many cities in Europe have clean, modern stations built to replace earlier structures destroyed during the Second World War. The main station (Hauptbahnhof) at Munich, dating from the 1840s, was destroyed by Allied bombing and has been replaced by a modern and functional building, while Rotterdam has a new city-centre terminal.

Although unaffected by wartime action, the

As railways spread across the world, British engineers and engineering were much in demand, especially in the Commonwealth countries. And the stations, like the railways they served, were very British in concept and design as evidenced by the ornate frontage of the Victorian State Railways Flinders Street station (left).

main station at Basle, appropriately situated astride the frontier, has been reconstructed in recent years to deal with the rapidly increasing international traffic, while in Italy the main station in Rome has been rebuilt. Here, the architect has managed to successfully incorporate a piece of the original Roman city wall in the design without detracting from the modern image of the new station, but it seems likely that more and more stations will be rebuilt along functional lines in the next few years, and although this may dismay students of architecture, there is little doubt that in many cases, in both Europe and America, modernization is long overdue.

Preserved and Miniature Railways

Barely a year now passes during which a line closed by British Railways does not reopen as a privately owned steam-operated railway. So far, none have suffered the ignominy and distress of re-closure, but there are now so many that it seems inevitable that financial stresses and the increasing age of the steam locomotives in operation will eventually take their toll.

Britain is in the forefront of the preserved railway league—perhaps appropriately for a nation renowned for its amateur attitude to life. First in the field was the Talyllyn Railway in Wales. Plans for the construction of a narrow-gauge railway from the Welsh coast at Towyn, north of Aberystwyth, to the slate quarries at Abergynolwyn were inspired by the construction of the nearby Festiniog Railway and its successful introduction of steam

One of the longest-ever enthusiast trips was the 5,000 mile round trip (below) of the "Western Endeavour" from Sydney to Perth and back in August 1970. Ever since the line was opened throughout, diesels have worked the trains, so this all-steam trip behind preserved 38 Class Pacifics was both a first train and a last!

power in 1863. Parliamentary powers were obtained in 1865 for the construction of a 686mm (2ft 3in) gauge line, and the Talyllyn Railway duly opened the following year.

At the opening, the railway was the proud owner of two locomotives, 0-4-0T No. 1 'Talyllyn' and 0-4-0T No. 2 'Dolgoch'. The first was soon rebuilt as an 0-4-2T, but few other changes affected the railway as the years passed, and because of its relatively remote position, the line survived competition from motor vehicles and two world wars. Despite cessation of quarry traffic in 1946, Sir Haydn Jones, who had acquired control of the line in 1911, gave an undertaking that the line would not close during his lifetime, and services

continued until his death in 1950. It seemed certain that the railway would not re-open in 1951 and that the line would be sold for scrap. But then a group of railway enthusiasts, led by L. T. C. Rolt, conceived the idea of forming a non-profit-making voluntary society to save the line. Public meetings and letters to national newspapers produced enthusiastic and monetary support, and in late spring 1951 the new summer season commenced, albeit on only part of the line, under new management.

Another leading member of the group of Welsh narrow-gauge lines is the Festiniog Railway, between Blaenau Ffestiniog and Porthmadog. Older than the Talyllyn, the first section of the Festiniog opened as a 'force and gravity' line in 1836, and steam locomotives were not introduced on the 600mm (1ft 11½in) gauge line until 1863. It is most widely known for its use of double-boilered Fairlie articulated locomotives, two of which survive today, but it was also an innovator in the coaching stock field, introducing bogie coaches in 1872 many years before they became common on main-line railways. In more recent years, the railway has kept in the van of coaching stock innovation by introducing the first buffet car to serve draught beer.

Unlike the Talyllyn, the Festiniog cannot claim a history of uninterrupted service, for the line closed in 1946 and the first section was not reopened until 1955. The company has progressively opened further sections of line, and is now carrying out new works to restore services through to Blaenau, despite the fact that flooding of part of the line by a new reservoir has necessitated the construction of a deviation line and a new tunnel.

The success of the Talyllyn encouraged the reincarnation of the Festiniog, and other narrow-gauge lines, in Wales, and later inspired enthusiasts to endeavour to reopen a standard gauge railway.

In the south of England in Sussex, the LBSCR had opened a line between East Grinstead and Lewes in 1882, partly in the hope of establishing it as an alternative route to the main Brighton line, but it had never realized such hopes and BR withdrew all services in June 1955. But a local resident unearthed a clause in the original Act of Parliament authorizing construction of the line which required no less than four trains a day to be provided, and in 1956, with noticeable ill grace, British Railways was required by legal action to restore the service until parliamentary approval could be obtained for its re-closure.

The reopening, and the associated publicity,

Preserved railways tend to collect a large number of locomotives in varying stages of repair, and because of the time and cost, it is unusual to find many locomotives in steam on a line at any one time, and doubly unusual to find them all assembled in one train, as in this centenary cavalade on the Kent & East Sussex Railway, (above).

inspired local enthusiasts to attempt to emulate the successful preservation schemes in Wales and, in 1960, passenger services were restored between Sheffield Park and Horsted Keynes, at that time still a junction with the electrified line to Haywards Heath. At the outset, the line was worked by two diminutive veteran locomotives, an ex LBSCR 'Terrier' 0-6-0T No. 55 'Stepney' and an ex-SECR Class P No. 323, hauling the line's only two coaches. Since then both the rolling stock and locomotive stud have greatly increased, and latest developments include proposals to extend the line northwards over the old track-bed towards East Grinstead.

The success of the Bluebell Railway

The only steam engines still at work on British Rail are the three 600mm (1ft 11½in) gauge locomotives on the Vale of Rheidol line from Aberystwyth to Devil's Bridge in Wales (above, left); all the other Welsh narrow-gauge lines are worked by Preservation Societies or Private Companies. Several preserved lines have acquired redundant steam locomotives from overseas; one such example is this ex-Norwegian Railways 2-6-0 (above right).

inspired a considerable number of similar preservation schemes, and the needs of steam enthusiasts are now catered for in most parts of Britain. Close to the Bluebell is the Kent and East Sussex Railway at Tenterden in Kent, whilst in the West Country beautifully restored ex-GWR locomotives and carriages are in use on the Dart Valley and Torbay railways in Devon. In Somerset the West Somerset Railway is endeavouring to open the whole of the Taunton-Minehead line, while in the West Midlands, the Severn Valley Railway has already expanded from its original base to run trains between Bridgnorth and Bewdley, and a further extension to Kidderminster is planned. In the East Midlands there is the Main Line Steam Trust, based at Loughborough, while further north in Yorkshire are the Keighley and Worth Valley and North Yorkshire Moors Railways. In East Anglia there are the North Norfolk and Stour Valley Railways, while in Scotland there is the Strathspey Railway. But perhaps the greatest single centre for railway enthusiasts, attracting visitors from all over the world, is the recently-opened National Railway Museum at York. Housed in a refurbished part of the disused locomotive shed, the many exhibits include the record-holding Gresley Pacific 'Mallard', the last steam locomotive to be built by British Rail, 'Evening Star', and the prototype vehicle of the Advanced Passenger

There are probably more miniature railways—scaled down replicas of the standard gauge prototypes—in Britain than anywhere else in the world, and the British influence is strong. Even this 260mm (10¼in) gauge locomotive (above) at work in Bulawayo, Rhodesia, is based on the British 'Royal Scot' prototype.

Train, as well as many other locomotive and carriage exhibits.

Railway preservation is not confined to Britain and similar developments have taken place both on mainland Europe and in America. In Switzerland the metre-gauge line from Chamby to Blonay, above Montreux, was reopened in 1968 by railway enthusiasts and now operates steam locomotives built in no less than three different countries—Germany, France and Switzerland itself.

In France a number of old steam locomotives have been preserved under the aegis of the Fédération des Amis des Chemin de Fer Secondaires (FACS), and lines have been reopened by the Chemin de Fer Touristique de Meyzieu (CFTM) and the Chemin de Fer Touristique St Trojan on the Ile d'Oleron (off the west coast of France near Rochefort). More recently, an extensive (33km/20 miles) narrow-gauge system has been leased by the CFTM in the Rhone Valley; since 1967 goods and passenger trains have again been running on the line which runs eastwards into the Massif Centrale from Tournon, south of Lyon, and yet further preservation schemes are proposed. In Norway two 'preserved' steam railways are run by enthusiasts in

Many preserved railways now carry passenger traffic far in excess of that envisaged by the original builders, especially the narrow-gauge lines of Wales, which were essentially freight lines. To cope with the extra traffic, most lines have acquired additional 'foreign' engines; this powerful 2-6-2T (above, left) 'Mountaineer' at work on the Festiniog Railway in Wales was built by Alco in the USA.

Kristiansand and Oslo respectively, whilst elsewhere in western Europe preserved steam engines can still be seen at work on certain State-owned lines where the public enthusiasm for steam specials has been recognized by the State railway systems.

In North America, although the enthusiast owned-and-run concept epitomized by the Talyllyn Railway has not taken root, numerous railway companies in the USA have recognized the tourist potential of such lines, the most famous of which are probably the Washington Cog Railway, the Silverton Line in the Rocky Mountains, the Arcade and Attica Railroad in New York, and the Cass Scenic Railroad in West Virginia. The 1m (3ft 3in) gauge Silverton Line, for example, is operated by the Denver and Rio Grande Western Railroad, using steam locomotives

passengers to sit inside the stock, whereas on 0.185m (7¼in) gauge railways the engine driver sits astride the locomotive tender while the passengers ride on open trucks. In Britain the most famous miniature railways are the 0.381m (15in) gauge Romney, Hythe and Dymchurch Railway in Kent and the Ravenglass and Eskdale line in Cumberland. The former was constructed across Romney Marsh in 1926 to provide a passenger service for the area and was backed by the Southern Railway; during the Second World War it provided a strategic link along the coast, and a special armoured train was built. The Ravenglass and Eskdale line opened as a miniature railway shortly after the First World War, when a trackbed of an earlier narrow-gauge mineral railway was taken over and converted to 0.381m (15in) gauge.

The first preserved railway in Britain was the Talyllyn Railway, a 686mm (2ft 3in) gauge line in North Wales bought by enthusiasts in 1951. Rebuilt and refurbished, the line (left) carries holidaymakers from Towyn up into the Welsh hills at Dolgoch and Abergynolwyn, and has inspired scores of other schemes, both in Britain and around the world.

hauling rolling stock dating from the 19th century.

Restoration of passenger services on closed standard-gauge and narrow-gauge railways using preserved locomotives and rolling stock is to be distinguished from the running of trains on specially-built miniature railways with gauges as small as 0.185m (7¼in). On miniature railways the locomotives and rolling stock are scaled-down versions of standard gauge prototypes, and are almost always built and operated as tourist attractions. On 0.381m (15in) gauge lines, locomotives and rolling stock can be built to permit drivers and

These lines provide a regular public service during the summer months, but throughout Britain, Europe and North America there are numerous miniature lines that have been constructed for private use by locomotive owners and their friends. Generally built to 0.260m (10¼in) or 0.185m (7¼in) gauge, such railways are to be found in the grounds of stately homes and at seaside resorts, as well as in private gardens or fields. But whatever the gauge, or means of propulsion, such railways enable thousands of enthusiasts to actively pursue their interests while at the same time bringing pleasure to many more.

Unusual Railways

The majority of the railways of the world have been constructed to the standard gauge of 1.435m (4ft 8½in) or something similar, and almost all now employ steam, diesel or electric traction, with the conventional steel wheel running on steel rails. Variations on the theme, such as narrow-gauge lines, mountain railways and Brunel's broad gauge are described elsewhere in this book, but it should be recorded that, over the years, some very unconventional ideas have also been applied —usually unsuccessfully—to rail transport.

One of the earliest experiments that initially seemed likely to revolutionize the railway scene was the Atmospheric Railway. Within 20 years of the opening of the Stockton and Darlington Railway an idea was being tested as a result of which it was hoped that noisy

Over the years, almost every method of propulsion known to man has been hopefully put to test on rails, but so far none has supplanted the modern diesel and electric units. This (right) experimental New York Central jet-powered unit achieved a US rail speed record of 299km/h (185.85mph) on test between Butler, Indiana, and Stryker, Ohio, but would hardly find favour with today's environmentalists!

and dirty steam engines would be replaced by quiet air-operated machines. Particularly as it was hoped that the new machines would more easily cope with severe gradients, such a novel concept naturally found favour with early Victorian engineers, and by 1840 the ideas of Clegg and the Samundas brothers were sufficiently advanced for a demonstration section of line to be laid near Wormwood Scrubs in West London.

The late 19th century saw the first stirrings of discontent at the dirty, smoky nature of the steam engine. Hence the quaint coach-like appearance of this 1882 vintage Kitson-built unit for the Portstewart steam tramway (above).

The Atmospheric System depended upon air pressure. Tubes, generally 38cm (15in) in diameter, were laid between the railway tracks and the atmospheric vehicles were fitted with a piston that slotted into the tubes. At intervals along the line stationary engines were positioned to exhaust the air from the vacuum tubes in front of each train, so that each train was propelled by the pressure of air in the tube behind the train's piston. Under

this system, therefore, coal dust and smoke were confined to the stationary engine houses, and the trains themselves travelled cleanly and silently along the lines.

This system was adopted for a 2.8km (1.75 mile) planned extension to Dalkey by the Dublin and Kingstown Railway, and the line worked well from its opening in 1844. In that year parliamentary powers were obtained for the construction of another Atmospheric Rail-way, between London and Croydon, and the first section of that line opened between Forest Hill and Croydon early in 1846. But the system was less successful than in Ireland and opposition to the experiment steadily grew, fired by the inconvenience of the change of train at Forest Hill, increasing working expenses and the regularity of breakdowns. Eventually, the directors lost patience with the system and ordered that ordinary steam locomotives take over all traffic; one day's notice only was given and atmospheric working ended peremptorally on May 3, 1847.

This decision must have greatly shocked the directors of the South Devon Railway, the only other company to introduce the system in Britain, because their atmospheric services were not introduced between Exeter and Teignmouth until September 13, 1847, five months after the Croydon experiment had been abandoned. The South Devon experiment proved to be no more successful, and the

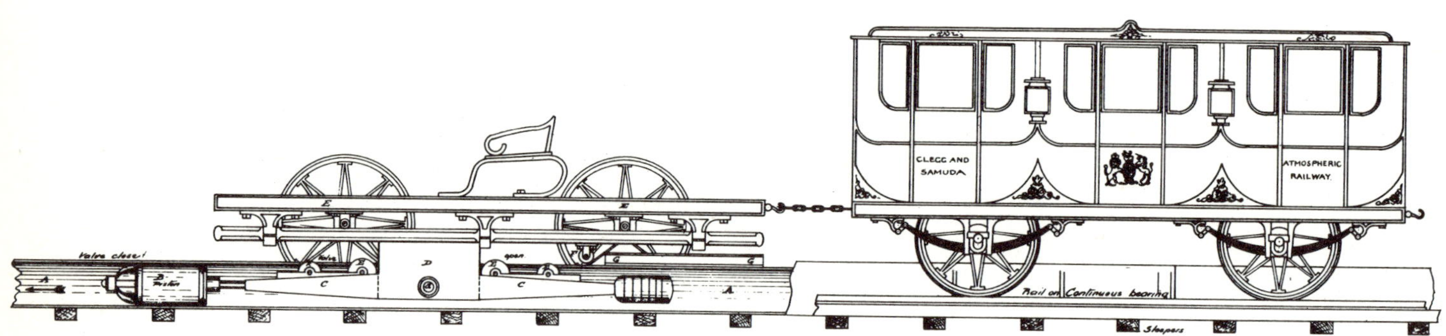

Perhaps one of the strangest railways of all time was the Lartigue Monorail line, built between the equally-unlikely named villages of Listowel and Ballybunion in Ireland in 1888. Using a lightweight, elevated track with a single running rail but two 'steadying' rails, both the twin-boilered locomotives (right) and the rolling stock sat astride the raised centre rail.

system was abandoned almost exactly one year later. As on the Croydon line, the system failed because of technical difficulties, mainly valve leakage, the rusting of the iron parts of the valve and the inadequacy of the pumps. In contrast, the Dublin line continued to operate successfully until 1854, whilst in France the Compagnie du Chemin de Fer de Paris St Germain used atmospheric working on the steep final stretch of its line until 1860.

No signs remain today to remind travellers on either the Croydon or the Paris suburban network of the atmospheric experiment.

Just as Ireland experimented with the Atmospheric System, so it was in Ireland that experiments also took place with the unique Lartigue Monorail System. Charles Lartigue designed an elevated track system using pre-fabricated metal sections shaped like a

One of the few successful monorails, still in intensive use today, is that at Wuppertal in West Germany. In contrast to the Lartigue System, the Wuppertal monorail is suspended from overhead girders, many of which span the River Wupper, and the electrically-powered system has now served the local inhabitants, despite war damage, for over 70 years.

The strangest 'railway' ever to have been constructed in Britain was the 'Railway in the Sea' at Brighton designed by Magnus Volk. In 1883 Volk had already achieved the distinction of introducing the first electric railway in Britain—the line still runs along the seafront at Brighton—and in 1896 he designed a 3.60km (2.75 mile) line to Rottingdean which ran through the sea. An electrically operated double-deck car was constructed on four legs

With the rise of electric street tramways and the electric suburban train, many railways throughout Europe sought to make their steam suburban and branch line trains look more progressive. One popular solution in the early years of the present century was the steam rail motor. Like the Brush-built 'steam autocar' for the Taff Vale Railway (above left) most were essentially a tiny (and often cramped!) 0-2-2 tank engine grafted onto one end of an orthodox bogie coach. Another innovation was the atmospheric railway system. In this system, trains were hauled not by locomotives but by vehicles fitted with large pistons which ran in pipes laid between the running rails (left). The theory was to use a series of stationary engines to exhaust air from the pipe so that trains would be hauled along by the resulting vacuum. But none of the lines survived for very long.

Probably one of the most successful of the unusual railways of the world, and certainly one of the longest lines, is the suspended monorail system at Wuppertal in West Germany. Built in 1901, several stretches straddle the course of the River Wupper through the town, as can be seen in this 1929 view of the line (below). Despite heavy war damage, the line continues to thrive and is now equipped with modern rolling stock.

triangle, straddling the top of which sat the train, for cheap erection in difficult country. The Lartigue train had to be balanced on a single rail on top of the triangle, and locomotives and loads—both passenger and freight—had to take account of this need for balance! The nine-mile line was opened between Listowel and Ballybunion in 1888 and continued in operation until 1924. A modern version of the Lartigue system opened in 1964 between Tokyo and the airport at Heneda.

that ran on parallel tracks 4.57m (15ft) below water at high tide: damage by storms in 1897 was subsequently repaired but the line ceased operating in 1901 and no signs remain today.

Many engineers continue to strive to invent systems of mass transport not dependent upon the iron rail, the hover and electrical levitation concepts being among the latest, but over the last 150 years no system has appeared which seems likely to replace the standard two-rail 'railway' with which we are so familiar.

Mountain Railways

Mountain railways are generally associated with the Alps, and particularly with Switzerland, in which mountainous country so many peaks have been conquered by the 'iron road'. It is surprising, therefore, to discover that the first mountain railway was built not in Europe but in America, where a cog railway was constructed on Mount Washington in New Hampshire in 1869 by an inventor named Sylvester Marsh.

The line ascends over 1,128m (3,700ft) in 6km (4 miles) on an average gradient of 1 in 4 and the line is still operated by steam locomotives, the earliest of which dates from 1870. The Washington Cog Railway is built to the 'almost' standard gauge of 1.422m (4ft 8in) while the only other major cog railway in the USA—up Pike's Peak in Colorado—is of standard 1.435m (4ft 8½in) gauge. The Pike's Peak Terminus at over 4,267m (14,000ft) holds the height record for rack and pinion railways, and the line is unusual in being operated by diesel traction.

The second mountain railway in the world—the Vitznau Rigi Railway in Switzerland—was also built to the standard gauge and opened one year after the Washington line, using a similar but modified rack system. In Europe the use of standard gauge for mountain railways is unusual, and the majority of lines subsequently constructed adopted a narrower gauge.

The Rigi line was engineered by Niklaus Riggenbach, who patented the idea of anchoring a steel rack between the running lines, with which pinions on the locomotives, driven by steam cylinders, engaged. The Rigi line climbed over 1,131m (4,300ft) above Lake Lucerne: the original vertical-boiler steam locomotives took 80 minutes for the journey

Switzerland is the traditional home of mountain railways. This dramatic view of the 4,165 metre high Breithorn is the reward of passengers on the rack-and-pinion Gornergrat Railway.

Britain's only true mountain railway is the Abt rack-and-pinion line up the slopes of Snowdon in North Wales. After a horrific runaway on the opening day in 1896, as a result of which a locomotive crashed down the mountainside, safety has been of the utmost importance on this and other mountain lines, and mountain railways in general enjoy a superb record for safety. The angled boiler and pinion wheels are clearly visible in this view (right) of Swiss-built Snowdon Mountain Railway No 3 'Wyddfa'.

up the 1 in 5 gradient but now modern electric motor coaches reach the summit in 35 minutes. Although Riggenbach's rack and pinion system was later improved upon by Dr Roman Abt, the system was inappropriate for gradients steeper than approximately 1 in 3. Success of the Rigi Railway soon inspired plans for the construction of railways up even steeper and higher mountains, and a unique rack suitable for use on gradients as steep as 1 in 2 was developed by Locher for the construction of a line to the summit of Pilatus. This system differed from Riggenbach's in that the centre rack had its teeth machined on the outside edges rather than the top and the locomotive pinions gripped the rack from both sides.

Like the Rigi and most other mountain railways in Switzerland, the Pilatus Railway is now electrically operated, but one rack and pinion line remains steam operated, the Brienzer-Rothorn Railway. This line climbs a total of over 1,670m (5,500ft) on an average gradient of 1 in 4, an onerous task for its small but powerful locomotives. Steam power would, however, be inappropriate for the rack and pinion system that reaches the highest station in Europe at 3,454m (11,333ft), as the last 7.24km (4.5 miles) of the Jungfrau Railway are built in a tunnel, including the terminus station at Jungfraujoch from which galleries run through the rock of the mountain to the icecap on the summit and the nearby meteorological station, from which impressive views can be obtained. The Jungfrau Railway uses a yet further development of the rack and pinion system, the Strub.

It is opportune to mention at this point a further system designed to assist railway engines to climb mountains under 'their own steam'. From a superficial glance, a railway fitted with the invention of John Barraclough Fell would look like a rack and pinion line; this system, however, does not require cogs and merely involves the laying of a further length of standard bullhead track on its side in the middle of the line to give two additional running surfaces against which are engaged four horizontal driving wheels to give greater adhesion. The Fell System was used by the railway which ran over the Cenis Pass pending the opening of Mount Cenis Tunnel and remains in use today on the Snaefell Mountain Railway in the Isle of Man. The most famous use of the Fell System was on the Wairarapa Railway through the Rimutaka Mountains in the North Island of New Zealand. Between 1878 and 1955, when the incline was replaced by a new tunnel, Fell locomotives successfully tackled the 1 in 16 gradients with passenger and goods trains, the incline's final years being graced by a Royal Train carrying

Although now the mountain railway centre of the world, Switzerland was not the first to boast a mountain railway. That honour goes to America, where in 1869 Sylvester Marsh opened his 'cog railway'—an early type of rack-and-pinion line—on Mount Washington in New Hampshire. Although refined in later applications, the system, with its toothed rack rail laid between the running rails, is much the same the world over, and pointwork is every bit as complicated as this turnout (left); all rack-and-pinion lines are worked with locomotive at the lower end of the train, in case of coupling or brake failure (below) and boilers are sloped so as to maintain water level on the ruling gradients (bottom).

Mountain Railways
(continued)

the Queen on her Royal Tour of New Zealand in 1954.

In Switzerland, pressing demands from tourists encouraged the Swiss to build railways up even steeper slopes than can be catered for by the rack and pinion systems. Cable cars and chair lifts suspended in the air from pylons may not be considered railways by purists, although their German names of Schwebebahn and Sesselbahn might suggest so, but funiculars are cable-operated vehicles that run on rails up gradients as steep as 1 in 1.5. Funiculars work on the principle of two cabins connected by a single cable passing round a winding wheel at the top end of the line, the power for working the system being reduced by the fact that the weight of the ascending cabin is balanced by the weight of the descending cabin. About 50 funicular railways were constructed in Switzerland, and

in Italy one was even built up the side of Mount Vesuvius. So steep are the funicular gradients that the passenger cars are often built with their seats on steps, as if the passengers were sitting on the stairs of an ordinary house. Some of the views obtained from the funiculars and the location of some of the railways themselves have to be seen to be believed.

Increased building costs and the development of modern technology means that there can be little chance of any further rack and pinion or funicular railways being built anywhere in the world. Cable cars, swinging on cables between pylons, can cross terrain over which no railway could be built, whilst over easier ground chair-lifts can be constructed at a fraction of the cost of a railway.

Mountain railways are not only to be found in Switzerland and in conclusion one must mention Britain's only mountain railway, up Snowdon, in North Wales. Using Swiss-built equipment and the rack and pinion system

For the almost unbelievable 1 in 2 gradient of the Pilatus line, Locher developed a horizontal version of the Abt rack-and-pinion system in which teeth were cut into the sides, rather than the head, of the rack rail, and horizontal pinion wheels gripped each side of the rail. The line is worked electrically, but this turn of the century view (right) shows one of the original steam rail motors, with its small transverse boiler and stepped passenger accommodation.

Swiss engineers may have beaten nature in their battle to build railways across the Alps, but each year brings a new battle to keep them open; snow is the ever-present enemy of punctual operation on most Swiss mountain lines, and ploughs are in action through most of the winter. Modern snowploughs, such as this small unit (left) at work on the Simplon line, not only clear the snow but throw it well clear of the line.

(Abt), this railway survives today using steam power, 80 uneventful years after the only too eventful happenings on its opening day in 1896 when one of the original locomotives ran away and crashed down the mountain. Mountain railways round the world learnt from that incident, and they now enjoy a deservedly high reputation for safety.

The last steam-worked rack-and-pinion line in Switzerland is the Brienzer-Rothorn Railway (left), which climbs over 1,600 metres from Brienz, on the lake near Interlaken, almost to the summit of the 2,350 metre high Brienzer-Rothorn.

Railways of the Future

Sadly for the romanticists, the railways of tomorrow are likely to be rather like the railways of today. Faster, quieter, cleaner and more comfortable they will certainly be, but it now seems that developments in the near future will continue to centre around the steel wheel running on steel rails—in other words, an extension of the present high-speed train technology.

The explosion of interest in advanced ground transport (agt) in the late 1960s spawned a decade of breakneck development of new railway technology in Britain, Germany and Japan, and has produced workable tracked air cushion (tac) and electro-magnetic levitation (maglev) vehicles. But it has also encouraged and produced startling developments in traditional railway technology; the early linear induction motors have been developed to a state whereby the technology can be applied in conventional traction motor form, whilst new signalling, paved permanent way and high-speed overhead line developments now make 300km/h (186mph) a realistic objective for the development of existing rail applications.

British Rail have already introduced diesel-powered 200km/h (125mph) High Speed Trains (hst) on a number of routes, relying on the development of existing track and signalling technology, and the 248km/h (155mph) 25,000V electric Advanced Passenger Trains (apt), the first of which are due to enter service soon, will operate under similar conditions.

Beyond 300km/h the problems associated with physical contact between wheel and rail make contactless operation more attractive, in the form of tracked air cushion or magnetic levitation vehicles. The British tracked hovercraft 'Hovertrain' prototype had topped 160km/h (100mph) under test before development was cancelled in favour of existing technologies and magnetic levitation, while the Germans are still working on pre-prototypes of a 500km/h (310mph) maglev train proposal.

The prototype British Rail maglev vehicle is a 12-seat capacity car weighing 2.65 tonne and supported on a single rectangular concrete guide rail by a pair of lift magnets in each corner, with current collection from a side conductor. Guidance as well as lift is given by offsetting the suspension magnets slightly over the guide rail, while propulsion is by two single-sided linear induction motors. Preliminary calculations, allowing for a 12.7mm ($\frac{1}{2}$in) air gap while the vehicle is in 'flight' show that the operating costs are not unlike those of a

This experimental maglev vehicle (above), developed by a German aerospace company, employs magnetic principles for suspension, guidance and propulsion, using linear motor techniques.

similar but rubber-tyred vehicle.

In addition to electro-magnetic levitation, some researchers have been investigating electro-dynamic levitation, in which lift is provided by moving powerful, possibly cryogenic, super-conducting magnets over an aluminium track. The advantages of electro-dynamic levitation are that lift, guidance and propulsion are all derived from the one device, and size is not such a limiting factor because the hover height increases with speed. But, like the maglev proposals, no fail safe system has yet been perfected to deal

with the very real problem of sudden loss of levitation at high speed and the consequent 'crash landing'.

And, like the monorails and personalized rapid transit (prt) systems of yesteryear, these proposals require special vehicles and tracks and are in no way compatible with present railway systems and technology. Thus, just as supersonic air transport can only be justified economically on transcontinental routes, so ultra-high speed agt can only be justified over long continental distances.

For the foreseeable future most railway administrations will prefer to see the enormous cost of such a project, involving the construction of an entirely new line, ploughed instead into the more widespread development of their existing systems. With the best British, French, German, Italian and Japanese inter-city services already competing favourably, both financially and on a time basis, with subsonic aircraft for centre-to-centre trips, it seems likely that the more novel forms of agt, although practically demonstrated, may remain on the drawing board for some time.

The Americans and Japanese are continuing development of ultra-high speed tracked air cushion vehicles. This is an American jet-powered tacv prototype, (above) on its desert concrete test track.

Glossary

Banking:
Assisting a train by propelling at the rear. The propelling locomotive is known as a 'banker'.

Baseplate:
The support, usually of iron or steel, through which flat-bottom rail is spiked or screwed to the sleeper.

Block working:
The standard method of working trains using block telegraph instruments.

Bogie:
A short, usually four- or six-wheeled independent sub frame to carry one end of a locomotive or carriage.

Boiler:
The pressurised steel or copper assembly on a steam locomotive in which water is converted to steam.

Cab:
The control area of a steam, diesel or electric locomotive.

Catenary:
Collective term for the entire overhead structure on overhead electrification systems. The 'contact wire' is suspended from the main supporting 'catenary wire' by 'dropper wires'.

Chair:
A support, usually of cast iron, for bull head-type rails.

Chimney:
The orifice through which exhaust steam and gases from a steam engine are ejected to the atmosphere. Known as the 'stack' in America (but *NEVER* as the 'funnel').

Conductor:
The railway official in charge of a train and responsible for timekeeping, etc. In Britain often also known as a 'Guard'.

Conductor rail:
Special rail, usually of high-conductivity iron, which is mounted on insulators alongside the running rails to supply electric current on third rail systems of electrification.

Contact wire:
The overhead wire, usually of copper, which carries the current in overhead electrification schemes.

Crossing:
The flat intersection between a road and railway. Usually known as a 'level crossing' in Europe and a 'grade crossing' in America.

Crossover:
Two connected points or switches enabling trains to cross from one running line to another.

Cowcatcher:
A protective framework suspended from the front bufferbeam of locomotives used over unfenced, rural lines to brush aside any obstructions on the line, animal or otherwise. Known as a 'pilot' in America.

Fast or through line:
Not necessarily a high speed line but merely one normally used for non-stopping trains.

Firebox:
The enclosed area behind and below a boiler in which combustion takes place.

Fireman:
The second member of a steam locomotive crew, responsible for maintaining steam pressure and managing the fire. Also known as a 'stoker'.

Footplate:
Originally the raised platform above the driving wheels on a steam engine used to gain access to lubricators etc., but now used as a generic term for the driving/firing position on a steam locomotive.

Hump:
A raised section of track at the beginning of a marshalling yard over which wagons are propelled to gain momentum.

Marshalling yard:
A large group of sidings used to sort incoming freight trains into new trainloads for different destinations.

Pantograph:
Special insulated, spring loaded device mounted on the roof of electric locomotives and trains to collect current from overhead wires.

Piloting:
The practice of assisting a heavy train by attaching an additional locomotive, or 'pilot', to the front of a train.

Points, switches:
The system of moving blades and crossing rails which enables trains to be directed along a particular line at a junction. Also known as a 'turnout'.

Pony:
A two-wheeled bogie, usually at either the leading or trailing end of a locomotive.

Regulator (1):
The device usually worked from the cab by levers and rods, which controls the admission of steam to the cylinders on a steam engine, and thus the speed. In America known as the 'throttle'.

Regulator (2):
A railway official responsible for controlling the movement of trains over a wide area, including the provision of crews.

Running lines:
The tracks actually used for train services, as opposed to sidings.

Shoe:
Spring-loaded current collector, usually carried on an insulated 'shoe-beam', which is mounted on bogies of electric trains on conductor rail systems.

Sidings:
Tracks provided specifically for storing trains between trips, or when not in use.

Sleeper (1):
Transverse strip of wood, metal or concrete to which the running rails are secured, and which maintains the gauge. Known in America as a 'tie'.

Sleeper (2):
Special carriage equipped with bunks instead of beds for overnight travel.

Slip (1):
An arrangement for detaching portions of a train for various destinations while on the move, using special slip coaches equipped with slip couplings.

Slip (2):
To lose adhesion on a locomotive, either because of wet rails or a heavy load.

Slip (3):
A diamond crossing combined with one (single slip), or two (double slip) crossover connections.

Smokebox:
The enclosed area at the front of a steam locomotive boiler through which exhaust steam and gases are passed to the chimney.

Snow plough, or plow:
A device to keep running lines clear of snow. Can be any size from a small, bufferbeam-mounted 'patrol' plough to a purpose built, self-powered vehicle.

Superelevation:
The practice of raising the outer running rail on a curved section of track so as to tilt trains inward and thus enable them to negotiate the curve at a higher speed.

Transition curve:
A short length of track, of no fixed radius, leading from a straight to a curved section of line.

Tank engine:
A steam locomotive with its water tanks mounted either above (saddle or pannier tank), alongside (side tank) or below (well tank) the boiler.

Tender engine:
A steam engine with a separate 'tender' behind it for coal and water.

Track:
Collective term for the complete assembly of two running rails, sleepers, and fittings which form a single running line.

Truck:
A railway freight vehicle.

Index